An Encyclopaedia of Flying Saucers

A. Vernon Bowen

Edited by
Robert M. Wood, Ph.D.
and Ryan Wood

ISBN: 978-0-9772059-2-9 (Paperback)

Published by Wood Enterprises, Broomfield, CO.

First Printing 2007
Author: A. Vernon Bowen

TABLE OF CONTENTS

PREFACE

Robert M. Wood

On June 6, 1999, Timothy S. Cooper wrote on a package:

"Received 6/6/99
Timothy S. Cooper
No cover letter
No postage"

The package was a "Jiffy Padded 4 Mailers by Sealed Air" with a notation "contains over 60% recycled fibers/recycle after use" on the reverse side.

The size of the package is 9.375 inches x 14.25 inches, and contained about 330 pages of the Bowen manuscript, together with a couple of dozen pages of other UFO-related material. The Bowen manuscript pages were incomplete since they were missing any front matter that would identify the author at that time. Tim Cooper later received the missing few pages that included the title page that identified the author as Vernon Bowen.

The return address was a stamp, which read:

FREEDOM OF INFORMATION/PRIVACY OFFICE
US ARMY INTELLIGENCE AND SECURITY COMMAND
ATTN MCSF-F1
FORT MEADE, MARYLAND, MARYLAND 20755-5995

The address was typed on an Avery label (4 inches x 1 7/16), reading

```
Mr. Timothy S. Cooper
PO Box 1206
Big Bear Lake, CA 92315
```

Done in pica type with Courier type font.

Joint Examination of Contents

I (Bob Wood) had received a call from Tim Cooper saying that he had received some material in the mail that was pretty interesting. Arrangements were made to visit with Tim in Big Bear Lake, where Tim lives. Bob arrived about 10 AM, and then went to Denny's to have something to eat. In the restaurant, Tim presented the package to Bob, who carefully began to pull out the contents. This meeting took place in the summer of 1999.

The individual pages were old and a few pages were described as fragile. Most of the pages, however, appear to be old but in good condition. Most pages were numbered at the upper right in green or black in with a page number, with the lowest being 9 and the highest being 319. Significant was the fact that most of the pages were either marked "CONFIDENTIAL" or "TOP SECRET/MAJIC" stamped in red at the top and bottom, usually on top of the typing on the pages. The Top Secret markings began on page 221, the beginning of Chapter XII, titled, "The U.S. Air Force and Flying Saucers."

A large number of the pages had had typed pieces glued to them prior to being numbered, the pieces being short descriptions of individual references to flying saucer newspaper or magazine articles or books. These individual pieces of paper had been glued to the 8.5 x 11 inches pages, and the glue had deteriorated, and most of the pieces were falling off the pages. Some of the pages also had markings on the back, where a handwritten note had apparently been made to be used as an insert for the opposite page.

Many if not most of the pages had ink notations of an editorial nature. Most of these were clearly made by author Vernon Bowen as editorial corrections of his own work. There are, however, numerous passages that are underlined in ballpoint ink as if for emphasis, and there are several individual phrases added by various writers at various places. These will be discussed in detail in the next section of this front matter.

My Reaction to the Manuscript

I immediately read the manuscript from beginning to end after placing the pages in Avery protective envelopes to avoid further deterioration. The loose clippings that had come off were glued back approximately where they seemed to have fallen off, but since they were all dated and intended to be in chronological sequence, it made no difference. My reaction was that the author was a serious student of flying saucers, and that this book, if it had been published at the time of completion (circa 1960) it could easily have been a good seller, since the UFO/flying saucer market was quite hot at that time. I was impressed with the depth of knowledge historically and particularly the completeness with which Vernon had attacked the literature on the topic, apparently spending hours and hours in the New York City and other public libraries. It was clear that Vernon Bowen was a skillful writer, having a record of accomplishment of publications shown on the title page that follows.

It was obviously interesting to see if Vernon Bowen was still alive, and the front matter of his manuscript gave several clues to his location, including a paragraph that said,

At present, Vernon Bowen is a deacon in First Congregational Church of Greenwich, Old Greenwich Connecticut, Chairman of the church's Public Relations Committee, originator of the church's monthly illustrated newsletter, writer of the church's special book on fund-raising, and the writer of Marietta College's bluebook for fund-raising, which has been credited with the raising of a substantial number of dollars over the years.

This was a clue that permitted me to call the church, and the helpful church office immediately told me when he died, and that he was survived by a son, Patrick H. Bowen, and gave me his telephone number. A call to Pat immediately established that he was the right person. He said that his father's reference files that filled an entire file drawer were still available. Pat was extremely enthusiastic about the possibility that the manuscript would be published.

Preparation for Publication

In the middle of the year 2000, I initiated the transcription of the manuscript into an electronic format by a professional secretarial service in Newport Beach, California. This work was completed in November 2000. The typing was done chapter by chapter, using Courier font at 12-point size to replicate the originals as closely as possible. The secretarial work was then proofread by me and corrected electronically. The following criteria were used to type the manuscript:

- Paragraphing was retained.

- Spelling errors were corrected. There were relatively few.
- Original author's editorial corrections were included.
- Security caveats are omitted in this draft. There are three levels shown on the original pages: (1) no marking, (2) CONFIDENTIAL, AND (3) TOP SECRET/MAJIC.
- There was no attempt to retain line-for-line replication.

The product of the secretarial service came to me in diskettes with the text in Microsoft Word, which I then put in my computer. At this time, I made final corrections to the secretarial work, as follows:

I put myself in Vernon's place and made sure that his corrections were the ones that had been used, and not those of the Air Force reviewers.

I made sure that all underlines done by Vernon's typewriter were included and that none of the Air Force underlines were included.

If there were errors, I corrected them unless I thought they were intentional on the author's part and were a "judgement call."

I kept the files separate; chapter by chapter because there were a few fragments that did not seem to fit clearly.

I then amalgamated the individual chapters together into one 500K file.

FOREWORD

Patrick H. Bowen

It starts with a 1939 Underwood portable typewriter. That was the year that Dad got his first job that recognized his writing skills (copyright with the Ralph Burns Agency). Perhaps the typewriter was purchased for work at home, or perhaps for writing more than copy for advertisements.

From the files, it appears that Dad had written great many fiction works in the 1930s that were not accepted for publication. The Great American Novel eluded him.

Success came as copywriter for various agencies. Along the way, he wrote several books for children (with the age of the audience increasing as I aged) and two musical recordings. Among his unpublished nonfiction is "My War with the Birds and Bees" about the trials and tribulations of a suburban homeowner dealing with fauna. Squirrels were Number One on the hit list of pests. To me, the manuscript is hilarious, and I cannot understand why no one accepted it for publication.

But back to the 1939 Underwood. Virtually every word of this book was hammered out at home on the Underwood. Dad's typing system was Hunton Peck, and he was very fast at it. Mom was a schooled typist, but she never seemed to be involved in Dad's writings.

The book was written between 1967 and 1971, when I was in college in places hundreds of miles from home. An overflowing file drawer of reference materials on flying saucers had been moved for fifty years from place to place, knowing how much the book meant to Dad.

The end of the Underwood for Dad and the book was 1961, when the Underwood went with me to law school and the manuscript went to the USAF. The Underwood cranked out ten to twelve case summaries a day, resulting in carpal tunnel trouble on both wrists. Obviously, being a trained typist did not protect me from this condition. The Underwood still lives in my office, as a reminder of both the book and its subsequent adventures. I doubt that I would buy a ribbon for it today.

In retrospect, I wish Dad had talked more about the book. You know the questions, such as why did he pick that subject on which to write a major non-fiction work, and why he chose to send it to the USAF before trying to have someone publish it

Vernon Bowen

1947-1955
51 Keofferam Road
Old Greenwich, Conn.

1955-1959
120 Woodside Drive
Millbrook, Conn.

1959-present
26 Shore Acre Drive
Old Greenwich, Conn

AN ENCYCLOPAEDIA OF FLYING SAUCERS

VERNON BOWEN

Other writings by Vernon Bowen

Children's Books

THE LAZY BEAVER

THE WONDERFUL ADVENTURES OF TING LING

SNOW FOR CHRISTMAS

THE EMPEROR'S WHITE HORSES

(All published by David McKay Co.)

Records (Collaborations)

THE LITTLE TUNE THAT RAN AWAY (DECCA)

LITTLE TOMMY TINKLE (SIMON & SCHUSTER GIANT GOLDEN RECORD)

ABOUT THE AUTHOR

Vernon Bowen is an advertising copywriter and supervisor. At present writing, he is copy supervisor on Frigidaire, Division of General Motors, for Dancer-Fitzgerald — Sample, 347 Madison Avenue, New York City.

Formerly, for ten years, he was with the Geyer Agency, now Geyer, Morey, Maddern and Ballard. While there, he wrote and supervised copy on Kelvinator, Division of American Motors Corporation. And while there, he originated and wrote the Rambler cartoon campaign which has been credited, in part, with taking Rambler from a poor fourth into a strong position of contender with the "Big Three" — and in helping to raise American Motors stock from a low of 5 3/4 to a high of 99 1/2.

In his spare time, Vernon Bowen has also written free-lance material. All of his published writings are in books or phonograph records for children.

One of his children's books was a Junior Literary Guild selection. Three of them are now used to some extent for remedial reading in certain public schools.

His last book, *The Emperor's White Horses*, the story of what happened to the famous Lipizzaners of the Spanish Riding School, Vienna, was double-checked by those who participated in the saving of the horses: Colonel Alois Podhajsky, Director, The Spanish Riding School, Hoffburg, Vienna; Mr. Charles R. Codman, Col. ret., (deceased), who was the aide of the late General George S. Patton, Jr., U.S. Army, and who was present at the special performance given for General Patton and his spear-head armored division at Hostau; Mr. R.F. Perry, Col., ret., Alexandria, Va., who visited with members of the Spanish Riding School in Czechoslovakia; and Mr. Charles H. Reed, Col., ret., Richmond, Virginia, who really spearheaded the saving of the Spanish Riding School and its horses while on his mission of persuading the head of German Intelligence to turn over to the U.S. the many truckloads of documents buried on the Czech-Austrian border — documents which are still secret today.

Vernon Bowen is about as American as the Ohio dirt he came from. One of his ancestresses, by family tradition, was Pocahontas. Another ancestor, of this same strain, was John Perrot, later Parrot, who rode into Harrodsburg with Daniel Boone to colonize Kentucky. His paternal grandfather served with Fremont in Missouri.

Bowen went to the public school in his native village of Newtown, Ohio, to Eastern High School in Cincinnati, Ohio, and to Marietta College, Marietta, Ohio. He graduated from Marietta in 1927, Cum Laude, Phi Beta Kappa. He is a member of Alpha Sigma Phi college fraternity, as is his son, who is in Marietta now. He is also a member of his fraternity's honorary fraternity, Delta Beta Zi, the original name of the fraternity when it was founded at Yale.

At present, Vernon Bowen is a deacon in First Congregational Church of Greenwich, Old Greenwich Connecticut, Chairman of the church's Public Relations Committee, originator of the church's monthly illustrated newsletter, writer of the church's special book on fund-raising, and the writer of Marietta College's bluebook for fund-raising, which has been credited with the raising of a substantial number of dollars over the years.

Long interested in education in Boy Scouting, and in modern methods of teaching, Vernon Bowen lives with his wife in a house that looks out over Greenwich Cove and the striper grounds where he hopes to be out this summer, fishing.

Names of Friends, Neighbors and Associates

Elliot Detchon, Col., USMC, ret. present associate at Dancer-Fitzgerald-Sample, Inc., N.Y.

Arthur Jones, personal assistant to John D. Rockefeller, Jr. At times, in government service either for the government, or for the Rockefellers. Over the Andes by mule, not too many years ago. At one time, wanted me to consider working for Rockefeller Foundation on Education.

Eugene Corthesi, Chairman of the Board, Nestle's parent company, Vivay, Switzerland. Worked with him in Old Greenwich in Boy Scouting.

John Mueller, Col. ret. head, RCA Communications. His son and my son are good friends. They both want to go to Alaska this summer to work on this country's Early Radar Warning System — up with the polar bears.

Maurice Ayers, one of the executive vice presidents of Kennicott Copper Company. Former neighbor. Fellow stock market hobbyist. We all play bridge together about once a week.

Vernon Myers, publisher of *Look Magazine*. Fraternity brother. See him occasionally. *Look* gets some billing from the Frigidaire account.

Joyce Swann, publisher, Minneapolis Star-Journal. Fraternity brother. We've worked together occasionally on fraternity public relations matters.

Pat Geyer, Chairman of the Board, Geyer, Morey, Maddern & Ballard. Chief stockholder in agency I formerly worked for.

Sam Ballard, President, Geyer, Morey, Maddern & Ballard.

George Romney, President, American Motors Corporation.

Bernie Chapman, Sales Director, American Motors Corporation.

Walter Jeffrey, Head of Kelvinator, American Motors Corporation.

C. William Cleworth, President, Cleworth Publishing Co., 1 River Road, Cos Cob, Conn. (Look him up in Fortune).

W. Bay Irvine, President, Marietta College, Marietta, Ohio.

General George Bush, (Headed the Aleutian campaign, World War II.) Roommate in college. Haven't seen him in years. May be in Pentagon.

Dr. Lyndon O. Brown, Chairman, Executive Committee, present agency. My superior. National authority on research. Former college president. Author of several books.

Lyle Shepard, President, Carborundum Corporation. Fraternity brother.

Dr. Vincent Daniels, pastor, First Congregational Church of Greenwich, Old Greenwich, Conn.

Dorio Mutti, Student at Rutgers University. From Parma, Italy. Admitted because of the State Department. One of the boys who went on Harry Morgan's good-will trip around the United States in Rambler given to them by George Romney. (See *Reader's Digest*, February 1960, lead article). We took Dorio in because the kid had no place to stay after he returned from the good-will trip. He became our second son. Dorio was not a Commie when he came here, even though he came from Parma, a Commie town with a Commie Mayor. He was carefully screened before he was admitted – and picked because he was *not* a Commie. But he was bitter. Nobody had invited him into their hearts. We did. He became one of the family. Because he was homesick, my wife boned up on North

Italian cooking. She concocted dishes for this boy that you can't even get at “21.” He got the sixty-four dollar treatment. He went everywhere with us. He was one of us. Check Dorio's reports, which he wrote in our playroom, back to the Parma newspaper. Even Parma's Commie mayor has admitted that this brilliant “second son” of ours, has helped to enlighten Italy — and Europe, on the real “inner core” of Americans. That’s one for our side, against the Red Tide.

FOREWORD

A. Vernon Bowen

Before you start this book, let's get the record straight.

I have never seen a "flying saucer."

I don't *know* anything about "flying saucers."

I am not a "flying saucer" expert.

I am not a member of any "flying saucer" club. Furthermore, I do not care to be.

I have never gone to a "flying saucer fan" convention. I don't intend to.

I am not a "flying saucer" *fan.* I don't ever intend to be.

I have never lectured on "flying saucers." I don't ever intend to.

I have never seen any "little men."

I do not even know anyone who has seen a "flying saucer," or who has claimed to have seen one.

I am not a member of any civilian "flying saucer" investigating committees. I do not intend to be.

I am not connected with the U. S. Air Force

I am not an intelligence agent.

I am not a counter-intelligence agent.

If you expect to find any "secrets" here, go on to something else. I have no access to classified material. Furthermore, I don't want to have. This isn't that kind of a book. There is nothing here that has not been taken from public sources — newspapers, magazines, and books.

This is not a *revelation.* It is a *compilation.*

I started putting this mass of material together in 1947, the year the first alleged "sightings" of unidentified flying objects, technically called UFO's, common named "flying saucers" were reported.

I have assembled it, bit by bit, over the years, because I felt that sometime, long after the original sources might have become difficult or impossible to obtain, someone, and perhaps many, might want a fairly comprehensive bibliography and commentary on data published over these thirteen years. They have been most momentous years, as all of us know.

Vast strides forward have been made in our knowledge of the world we live in. How vast this has been, I do not know. I can only guess. Others, in the military, and elsewhere, will know better than I.

And speaking of the military, don't buy this book in the expectation that is an attack against the United States Air Force — and the fact that it won't, in the words of professional "flying saucer" agitators, *tell all.*

I sleep safely in my bed at night, and work safely in my office at day, because men of USAF are always upstairs protecting me. So are a lot of other dedicated men in subs and on ships and in lonely outposts like Thule.

Year after year, for 13 years, USAF has been badgered and bedeviled by all kinds of characters who have accused the Air Force of holding out on information that the public should know.

It has been accused, not only of concealing information, but of chivvying the most hysterical of "saucer" sighters, particularly those who have babbled about "landings," into insane asylums.

It has been accused of harboring "little men" neatly pickled in alcohol...and of heckling those "who knew too much" about "flying saucers" into silence.

If you'll look at the record, you'll find that the Air Force has charitably stood still under the most scathing attacks, many amounting to pure, vitriolic calumny. It has permitted the publication of the most nauseating tripe about "flying saucers," without batting an eye.

Furthermore, USAF permitted publication of an article in TRUE, the Magazine for Men, and a complete book, by Captain Edward J. Ruppelt, USAF, the officer in charge of Project Blue Book, the official USAF UFO investigative body. Mr. Ruppelt's writings appeared after he returned to civilian life. His book is excellent, authoritative, and sometimes revealing.

I haven't heard that the Air Force ever persecuted him for his writings...or, for that matter, anybody else.

The quarrel between the "saucerians" and USAF is that the Air Force will not come out categorically and state that many UFOs sighted have been extra-terrestrial, with irrefutable proof in the shape of pickled "little men," chunks of fallen "saucers," or whole "fallen saucers," authentic still photos and movies of "unknowns," etc., etc., etc.

USAF has never denied the *possibility* that some UFOs, as reported, could be extra-terrestrial. In fact, it was one of the first agencies to suggest such a possibility.

The only trouble is — it hasn't any definite *proof*.

It is quite true that you cannot obtain certain classified information on flying saucers. But these are terrestrial saucers, man-made, that we may all see some day soon.

There is no secret about the existence of these. They have long since been announced to the public. The Russians have announced that they have one. The English have reported a successful flight of their saucer over the waters of the

Channel. The United States has published in the press, a drawing of its proposed "vertical jet riser." And the Canadians, as reported in the *Financial Post*, Canada's weekly equivalent of *The Wall Street Journal*, are hopeful that the A.V. Roe saucer will be purchased in quantity by the U.S.A.

Everybody's got saucers. They'll be up in the air like pies in the sky before too long.

But this is where the security come in. For who's got the best one? Macy's isn't going to tell Gimbel's — until the sale starts. That's for sure.

But USAF you will find, if you follow the record carefully, as I have, through its own news releases, has kept all of us in this country pretty well informed on progress made in weapons of defense and offense — including a long list of releases on flying saucers (real) and on allied fields of investigation.

Further news on the real thing you will find — not in science fiction stories — but in the news columns and the financial pages of our newspapers, in scientific articles, in the advertisements of aircraft makers and other in the trade magazines, in the "Help Wanted" advertisements in the financial pages of *The New York Times* every Sunday and, not surprisingly, in the action of certain stocks in the stock market.

USAF, to the best of my knowledge, and in my opinion, has tried very carefully to keep us all informed of what is going on, without revealing anything which might give aid and comfort to a potential enemy.

Granted that USAF has been made to look red-faced at times because of conflicting press releases, or because it could not admit to having observed something when it did because of security reasons, you will find that it has issued a vast amount of pertinent information.

And, as for being red-faced, you will find in this heterogenous collection of materials words which will haunt the men who uttered them — and the publications that published them – for rest of their lives.

Maybe some of these utterances were made, and writing written, for security purposes. In all charity, I prefer to think so.

At any rate, let us let USAF and other branches of the services keep on guarding our secrets. I, for one, don't want to know any. (And since I devote a whole chapter in this book to USAF and its attitudes, I don't care to belabor the subject here. May I say, however, that, although I do not intend to cudgel USAF, I reserve the right, as a reporter, to.)

So — on with the reporting.

I cannot vouch for the authenticity of any of the alleged "sightings," "landings," "little men,", or any of the other oddities reported here. I wasn't present at any of them. I do not know whether they happened or not. I only report on what public record stated that people *claimed* they saw.

I can vouch for the fact that I found everything included here in the public record, that I read every newspaper article, magazine article, and book which I quote.

Remember, as you read this book, that it was started thirteen years ago. It reflects, in its beginnings, a certain amount of the incredulity that was reflected in all publications at the first "sightings."

Since then, a great deal has happened.

We are now conditioned to the idea that, before very long, as time goes, Man will be exploring outer space. There are still difficulties. But we take it for granted.

We have made tremendous advances in knowledge in the past thirteen years. And, as old knowledge and old concepts crumble, as Man stands poised to penetrate the innermost secrets of the Cosmos, the progress of the past will seem as nothing, compared to the age that lies ahead.

May you enjoy reading this book, as much as I have enjoyed putting it together. It is the work of a chronicler, not a fictioneer.

Vernon Bowen
Old Greenwich, Conn.
March, 1960

CHAPTER 1
THE QUESTION

What are flying saucers?

Are they a secret, terrifying weapon of the United States? Are they the weapon or photographic reconnaissance device of another power? Are they space craft of visitors from Venus, Mars, or from still other planets outside our solar system? Are they robots, operated by remote control from somewhere beyond our atmosphere? Are they "thought forms" given substance and projected by higher intellects than our own? Are they angelic forms from Heaven, come to warn the world of impending catastrophe?

Or are they hallucinations, mirages, rainbows, aurora borealis effects, optical illusions, apparitions, or other phenomena due to air lenses, ice crystals in the atmosphere, cloud layers, temperature inversions, or other quite natural and well-understood aerial manifestations?

Or are they one of the most colossal hoaxes ever foisted off on a gullible mankind?

All of these questions — and more — have been asked and answered, often quite vehemently, by a great many people during the past thirteen years. Practically everybody has gotten into the act of explaining, debunking, or wildly romanticizing the saucers. Newspaper and magazine writers, radio and television commentators and comics, sober scientists, crackpots, the Army, the Navy, the Air Force, the Marines, and even the Coast Guard have had their say about this "mystery."

Many have tried to peer behind the curtain of security that cloaks the real nature of the saucers. All kinds of theories have been advanced, most of the theories being of a contradictory nature.

For, from the beginning, the subject of the saucers has been a subject of controversy — and often quite acrimonious controversy. Magazines have taken different sides of the question, even magazines under the same publishing roof, like *Life* and *Time*. Several important publications have tried to debunk saucers. Others, just as reputable and authoritative, have advanced the theory that saucers are extraterrestrial. Another magazine claimed that it had irrefutable proof that the saucers are U.S. secret weapons.

Even scientists have violently disagreed.

Several noted astronomers have claimed that no saucers have ever been seen by telescope by well-known observatories, that none has ever been photographed, that none has ever been caught simultaneously by the human eye and by a radar "fix." All of these claims, advanced as gospel, are completely inaccurate. Saucers have been seen by astronomers just as noted, and more noted, than the astronomer-disclaimants. They have been photographed — and by the heads of acknowledged observatories — in at least one instance by Schmidt camera, one of the world's greatest precision instruments. They have been seen simultaneously by naked eye and the eye of the radar — this according to the man who was head of the U.S. Air Force's official investigation of flying saucers. In his own words, writing in a well-known national magazine, he stated that on at least one occasion a saucer was observed by theodolite, a kind of surveyor's instrument used to track rockets, on three theodolites simultaneously.

Even different branches of the U.S. Air Force have not always agreed on what saucers might be — or else have gotten their publicity releases badly mixed at times. For, occasionally, while one release saying one thing would be issued from the saucer-investigating project at Wright-Patterson Field, Dayton, Ohio, another release, controverting that one, would come from the Pentagon in Washington.

And, while a governmental spokesman in one branch of the services would advance a theory, some scientist who had occupied a high place in the Air Force's original investigation of saucers would advance another theory.

The attitudes and the actions of the U.S. Air Force, in charge of the defense of U.S. skies, have been curious but understandable in the light of 13 years of almost unbelievable progress. In 1948 the USAF set up an investigative project. Almost two years to date later, it said it was discontinuing the project. It said all saucer records would be made public and put on display in the Pentagon. They never were. Shortly after this, the saucer-investigating project was resumed, under a new name.

Every now and then, some spokesman for the Air Force or some other branch of the armed services would come out with an "explanation" for flying saucers.

One explanation was "Skyhook" balloons, announced as a great secret more than a year after *Look* Magazine had given complete coverage to "Operation Skyhook," and more than *three* years after *The Saturday Evening Post*, in its two articles of April 30 and May 7, 1949, had already given the public practically the same news.

Another explanation was that of the Army when it broke the news that Noel Scott had produced saucers in a bell-jar at Ft. Belvoir, Virginia. This explanation was given for the sightings of saucers over Washington in July of 1952.

Immediately after this release, a well-known scientist stated publicly that he knew of no atmospheric condition that could have produced the phenomena observed over Washington.

On February 11, 1953, there appeared in the newspapers an article that said that the Canadians were building a flying saucer that would fly at a speed of 1,500 mph. On June 28, 1953, rather complete details on this saucer were carried in the public press.

On July 15, 1953, the USAF announced that a powerful new magnesium flare used for night aerial photography, the "Hellroarer," had been responsible for some saucer sightings over the past few years.

On July 20, 1953, quite a welcoming party waited at a spot along the Brush Creek, California, for the return visit of a flying saucer flown by a "little man" dressed all in Lincoln green, reported by two miners as having landed on May 20 and June 20 of that year. (The "little men" didn't show.)

In the May 31, 1954 issue of *Life* magazine, there appeared theoretical working drawings of the Canadian flying saucer, a description of the principle by which it would fly, the name of the man who invented it, and the name of the company building it.

In the June 11, 1954 issue of *Collier's*, in an article by Charlotte Knight, appeared the most persuasive argument yet that saucers are "Skyhook" balloons.

And in November 1, 1954 issue of *Life* appeared a two-page illustrated article telling of the reputed landing – all during the fall of 1954 – in the fields and villages of France, of strange, unearthly vehicles, and of strange and unearthly "little men" stepping out of them.

Who's crazy here?

Which paper do you read? Which magazine do you read? Who are you going to believe – if anyone?

Who is the wise man, who is the fool in explaining the flying saucer mystery?

Your guess is as good as anyone's. You, too, can become a flying saucer "expert" in three easy lessons. Certainly your theory would be no better — nor any worse — than a lot of them that have been dished up to bewildered, befuddled and exasperated public.

Here are just a few of the theories, explanations and claims that have been advanced by opposing schools to dispel in mystery of the saucers:

1. They are U.S. secret weapons.
2. They are Russian secret weapons.
3. They are Russian remotely-controlled photography devices.
4. They are from Mars.
5. They are from Venus.
6. They are angels.
7. They are from outside the solar system.
8. They are from the "dark" side of the moon.
9. They are flown by strange beings like insects, perhaps some kind of a bee.
10. They are odd effects caused by atomic explosions.
11. They are sent by other world visitors to observe the effects of atomic explosions and see how advanced we are.
12. They are sent by other-world visitors who want to colonize the earth.
13. They are sent by other world visitors who colonized the earth tens of thousands of years ago, or even millions of years ago, who wish to watch our progress.
14. They are from the Fourth Dimension or some other dimension.
15. They are space travelers who fly on magnetic waves and simply use the earth as a power plant, bouncing off our magnetic field into outer space again.
16. They are rainbows, auroras, mirages, light refractions, reflections, apparitions, and other natural phenomena.

17. They are "space animals" that live in the upper reaches of space.
18. They are "thoughts forms" projected by master minds from a non-terrestrial powerhouse.
19. They are "Skyhook" balloons, or the successors to "Skyhook" balloons, now released by the U.S. Air Force.
20. They are radar "ghosts."
21. They are an Air Force flare for night photography.
22. They are target discs, towed by known aircraft.
23. They are a British secret device.
24. They are of Spanish-Nazi origin.
25. They are Yugoslavian.
26. They are spots in front of the eyes, *muscae volitantes*.
27. They are a new and unknown natural phenomena that are due to our earth's travels in space. We are now entering areas in space where we are seeing things never seen before.
28. They are a form of mass hallucination.
29. They are a complete, cruel and heartless hoax.
30. They are the craft of a "lost race" that lives in vast caverns on earth.

Now, all of these explanations cannot be true. Perhaps one or two, or even three or four of them are true — but which ones?

In order to even begin to understand what might be behind this mystery — and why it has remained a mystery — it is necessary to start at the very beginning, and completely review the whole thing.

So here goes:

CHAPTER 2
THE START OF IT ALL

On June 24, 1947, there went out over this country's news wires, with simultaneous broadcast by nationwide radio, a startling, a sensational story.

On this date, Kenneth Arnold, a businessman of Boise, Idaho, a salesman of fire-fighting equipment who flew his own private plane, reported something that left this country thunderstruck.

Mr. Arnold reported that, at 2:59 P.M. on the 24th, while flying at approximately 9,200 feet over mountains near Mineral, Washington, he had seen 9 disc-shaped, tail-less, silvery-colored objects or craft flipping and flashing along through the sky.

The craft — if such they were—"flew like a saucer would if you skipped it across the water." The craft emitted blue-white flashes from their surfaces. They flew formation, as if linked together, between Mt. Baker and Mt. Rainer in the Cascade Mountains. Mr. Arnold estimated their speed as in excess of 1,000 mph. This was at a time when no known earth plane could fly that fast. Later figuring by Mr. Arnold and other airmen corrected this estimate to a speed of approximately 1,350 mph.

On the same day there was another report of the sighting of disc-like objects by a Portland prospector named Fred Johnson. He is reported to have watched several discs above the same Cascade Mountains. He watched them through a small telescope which he used in his prospecting. He is reported to have said that he had observed the compass hand on a special watch that he wore weave excitedly from side to side, indicating some kind of magnetic disturbance from the flying objects. He also reported to have observed that when the discs swept low, trees bent, as they would in a violent storm, after their passing.

Here was really fantastic and unheard-of news. The mass of the public had never heard of anything like this before.

But was it true? Or was the nation being hoaxed?

The latter possibility was made a little dim by a flood of reports of "sightings" that began to pour in, once the Arnold sighting had been given national prominence.

For now people began reporting that they had seen things before Arnold — at Oklahoma City in May; over Weiser, Idaho, on June 12; at Spokane, Washington, on June 21.

On June 27, according to published reports, a formation of discs flashed past an Air Force pilot's plane near Lake Meade, Idaho.

On the 4th of July, hundreds of citizens of Portland, Oregon are reported to have watched dozens of discs flying very high and at very high speeds over their city.

On the afternoon of the 4th, Captain E.J. Smith, of United Airlines, his co-pilot Ralph Stevens, and stewardess Marty Morrow, flying an airliner over Emmett, Idaho, reported seeing nine discs, each bigger than the plane they were in, in the sky ahead of them. They watched the objects for several minutes.

On July 8, experts at Muroc Air Force Base watched six discs flashing in the sky.

On July 10, a well-known astronomer, his wife and daughter, on an automobile trip between Clovis and Clines Corners, New Mexico, observed an unknown craft or object in the sky for some time. It was estimated to be 100 feet in diameter, 250 feet long.

By this time, sightings had been reported, not only in the United States, but over Mexico, Turkey, Germany, Holland, Paraguay, the Scandinavian countries, and over ships at sea.

People everywhere were reporting unknown discs, or different-shaped unknown objects, flitting through the skies. One man on the west coast solemnly reported that such objects had been flying across his back yard for years. Hoaxers and pranksters got into the act, with one joker throwing a round piece of plywood, fitted with a burnt-out radio tube, off his rooftop to scare his neighbor.

Publications, scientists, commentators and crackpots entered the fray.

The sowing of practically complete chaos started at this time. And as time went on, this chaos, either by the very nature of the subject, or by deliberation, was compounded.

Here was one that could really attract the lunatic fringe.

And in the beginning, the whole thing seemed lunacy to a great many people. The subject was treated with a great deal of merriment by many publications.

The idea that saucers could exist, and that they could travel at such fantastic speeds, was ridiculous. It was an idea that was treated with amused contempt. So was the idea that the earth could be visited by other beings — either super intelligent or super-monstrous — from other worlds. Such an idea was the dream of science fiction writers. It does not fit the teachings of orthodoxy. And, for years, the vast majority of scientists, and all publications of a truly scientific nature, hewed to this choleric contempt — at least in all public expressions — for the extraterrestrial theory.

The scientists, for the most part, had categorically stated for years that Mars is unhabitable by humans or humanoids because of sparsity of atmosphere, Venus because its atmosphere consists largely of carbon monoxide, Mercury because it would be too hot so close to the sun, Jupiter because it would be too cold, Saturn, Neptune and the rest of them for the same reason; and that the nearest possible habitable spots for human-like life are light years away.

Ergo: craft from extraterrestrial places are impossible.

Furthermore, there were many other reasons, and very good ones, to prove that the objects being observed were either known natural aerial phenomena — or hallucinations.

One of these reasons was that in 1947, the United States, which all U.S. experts believed to be the most advanced in the field of aeronautics, was trying to create aircraft which could break the speed of sound, which is variable according to altitude and to temperature, but which is generally accepted as around 760 mph at sea level. This country actually had broken the speed of sound, with one experimental plane, in that year — but not at sea level. And this news, at the time, was top secret.

The unknown craft had speeds estimated at first at around 1,350 mph. Later observations upped this slowpoke speed to from 9,000 to 18,000 mph.

The new and strange craft often flew at high, impossible heights, 50 miles or more above the earth.

In 1947, the world's altitude record was still that made by Anderson and Stevens, of the United States, on November 11, 1935. The height they attained in a balloon was 22,066 meters, 72,395 feet, or something less than 14 miles. This height was still carried as the world's record by the 1954 *World Almanac,* although it had been secretly broken by one U.S. flyer. In August, 1954, the USAF released news that another U.S. flyer, Maj. Arthur Murray of the Air Force, had flown a plane to a height of 15 1/2 miles. Later news issued by the Air Force upped this figure to more than 17 miles.

This was far, far below heights reported for the unknown flying objects.

In addition to these things, the experts who knew something about the technical difficulties involved in supersonic flight and stratospheric heights knew that there were far more questions to be answered. The physicists, the aerodynamicists, the metallurgists and other scientists, working carefully with wind tunnels and pilot-testing planes that approached or surpassed the speed of sound, knew of many seeming impossibilities.

Take, for instance, the matter of metals. Aluminum, or Duraluminum, the metals that in 1947 were commonly used as "skins" for the aircraft, *creep* at sonic speeds. Furthermore, they melt completely. In addition, violent turbulence occurs when a plane of primitive design passes through the barrier at Mach 1, the speed of sound. It can go out of control. Its wings can fall off. It can disintegrate.

And additionally, there are problems of fuel, of the cooling of fuselages, of the heating of pilots, of oxygen supply, of tremendous hazards to the human body, not only in violent maneuvers, but in sudden changes in altitude. Human blood can boil; human bodies can explode if not fully protected when changing from a lower altitude to an infinitely higher one. The problems are comparable to those of a diver — in reverse.

American technology, possibly but not positively the most advanced at the time of the first sighting of the unknowns, had achieved miraculous advances in the 45 years since the Wrights first flew at Kittyhawk on December 17, 1903. But it had not advanced this far, certainly not according to published accounts of advances. This was the ultimate in mechanical conquest of the air.

For these craft, if craft they were, did things that were impossible in the light of all known data on existing aircraft.

They not only flew at impossible speeds and at impossible heights.

They performed impossible maneuvers. They could make right-angled turns at thousands of miles per hour, without slackening speed.

And, as more and more reports came in, and as it became evident that the ones to be taken seriously were not from crackpots or amateurs, but from trained technicians—airline pilots, astronomers, civil air field authorities, technicians in White Sands and other providing grounds — a composite of the "impossibilities" of the objects began to emerge.

And the impossibilities were not only a matter of speed and heights and maneuverability.

There was also the matter of shape.

The objects, as more reliable reports piled up, seemed to occur in a bewildering variety of shapes — disc shaped, sphere-shaped, torpedo-shaped, spindle-shaped, helmet-shaped, doughnut-shaped. They were observed to have a variety of colors — some appeared painted, as if with identification marks. Some glowed — blue, amber, reddish or reddish-orange. Some were reported as having windows or ports. Some made an exhaust noise. Others were silent. Some left smoke trails. Some left no wakes at all.

In some reports, observers spoke of a large, central object that released smaller objects, as if the unknown were a large "mother ship" releasing a brood of smaller craft in the skies. Some of the objects appeared to possess the ability to become invisible, "fading" into nothingness. Some exploded violently, leaving nothing.

All of them seemed to have common characteristics in high speeds, extremely high altitudes at times, incredible maneuverability.

One of the most baffling things about them was the uncanny silence of most of them. They made no more noise than a beam of sunlight. As we know today, and was lesser known in 1947, when a craft or object of conventional design passes through the sound barrier, there is a shattering concussion or explosion. An explosion so great it can rattle windows and break them, blow hangar doors off their hinges — a crash of thunder following a shock wave, so severe that it can be heard, felt, or sensed for miles.

But in the case of the unknown flying objects, swooping, skittering, rocketing across the skies, there was quite often no sound at all, even when they stopped, hung motionless, then took off at speeds again that must take them through the sound barrier. This was counter to all known laws.

Even more basic a paradox was the question of power, power that seemingly was unlimited, power that could drive objects at incredible speeds. The only known power on earth that could possibly drive craft at such speeds was atomic, and in 1947 atomic power, as far as is shown, was not at the stage where it could be controlled and shielded sufficiently to be used in driving even a submarine.

In many instances, the source of power in the unknowns did appear to be atomic, with a glaring blue light in the center of the craft, or a glowing blue halo surrounding it, or blue exhaust streaming from it.

It was the source of power that, coupled with flying objects that at times appeared to have no mass, which was most baffling of all.

There were other odd aspects to the unknowns. They seemed to be piloted, or controlled, by intelligence.

They approached airplanes, as if in curiosity. They "buzzed" them. They fled when approached. At times, they flew circles around aircraft. In one case, reportedly, they outsped a

3,000 mph rocket. In many ways, the things appeared more like skittery animals than human intelligences. They were very shy. They acted as if they did not care to be too closely observed.

They were other curious things about them. Many seemed to have an affinity for the ocean, sometimes disappearing toward the sea, or even falling into the sea.

Others, when alarmed, disappeared straight up. They vanished as if shot out of a cannon — but much faster. Their rocketing upward was something like that of a cork, which held under water and released, shoots to the surface, buoyed up by its lighter-than-water characteristic.

As several writers were quick to point out, it appeared as if the unknowns were propelled by some kind of magnetic, or anti-gravitational force.

None of the strange characteristics of the unknown objects fitted known patterns.

So they became hallucinations and impossibilities to many.

Among others, the many scientists connected with flying, here was something for which they could advance no reasonable explanation whatever. The objects, quite possibly, didn't exist.

Yet overwhelming masses of evidence said they did.

Somewhere, in the period between June 24, 1947, and the end of the year, the name for the objects — of all descriptions, sizes, shapes and mannerisms — came to be *flying saucer.* To the U.S. Air Force, the name was unidentified flying object, or UFO. But to the public, saucer it was — and is.

During this same period, there were reports and denials, claims and counterclaims, theory and counter theory. But a great deal of the initial furor had died down.

Then there occurred a tragic event that focused intense interest on the mystery again.

On January 7, 1948, a man met his death while pursuing a “flying saucer.”

It happened a few miles south of Ft. Knox, Kentucky. A strange object had been seen high over the field. It had also been observed at Madisonville, Kentucky, 90 miles away. It appeared to be a huge gleaming, or glowing sphere.

Captain Thomas Mantell, an Air National Guardsman who was in the air at the time, with two other Guard planes, was asked to investigate.

Mantell's last report was from 20,000 feet. Some minutes later, his plane violently disintegrated. The wreckage of it, when it hit the earth, was scattered over thousands of feet of area.

Officially, Captain Mantell's death was ascribed to anorexia, or blackout due to lack of oxygen. The object he was chasing was said to be have been the planet Venus. This official explanation was scoffed at in many quarters. There were wild stories of mysterious markings on parts of the exploded plane, as if it had been subjected to unknown forces or rays. You will find a great deal of this in various books on flying saucers that go into minute detail — little or none of it confirmable — on the manner of Captain Mantell's death.

On July 24, 1948, at 2:45 A.M., Eastern Airlines pilots, Clarence S. Chiles and John B. Whitted, flying at 5,000 feet, saw, some 20 miles west of Montgomery, Alabama, a giant, torpedo-shaped object with an intense, blue-white glowing interior. It passed their plane at extremely high speed, leaving a violent prop-wash, jet-wash, or similar turbulence in its wake as it passed them.

On October 1, 1948, National Guardsman George F. Gorman reported that he had had a "dogfight" with a brilliant light that maneuvered, over Fargo, North Dakota.

On April 24, 1949, a group of highly-skilled technicians near Arrey, New Mexico, tracked through theodolite an object high above the earth. Estimated height: 56 miles. Estimated speed: 7 miles per second. It made a right-angled turn at this same high speed.

These were the kind of sightings that gave substance to the evidence there were unknown aerial objects in the skies.

And month after month, and year after year, they continued to come in.

The oddest fact of all about the appearance of the unknowns was that they were not something completely new, as the great mass of the public supposed. Identical manifestations had been seen on earth — or in the skies above earth — before.

Because this is the very heart of the mystery — or the very heart of the hoax, if it is such — it deserves a chapter by itself. So here it is:

CHAPTER 3
THE HEART OF THE MYSTERY

Flying saucers, or unknown flying objects such as people started reporting from 1947 onwards (actually since 1938, although few people even knew this) were not new.

In fact, they were not new by a couple of thousand years of recorded history. As far back as 222 B.C., or thereabouts, such phenomena had been observed and reported, by scientists, by the clergy, by writer-chroniclers of those early days.

These ancient, medieval and modern reports told of the sighting of exactly the same kind of aerial phenomena — balls of fire, changing color, winking in and out; discs; cones, spindles, cigar or torpedo-shaped objects. They also told the same story of objects that flew at amazing speeds; objects that flew with a sound of machinery; objects that flew noiselessly; objects that left a smoke-trail or jet-trail behind them; objects which left no traces at all. Among the reports were those which told of meteors, or meteor-like objects which flew formation and could halt or maneuver.

In addition to these, there were numerous reports from the immediate past, particularly in the 19th Century, by reputable, world-famous astronomers, not laymen, of such odd things as lights as seen on the moon and Mars, particularly lights in geometrical pattern; objects seen crossing the face of the sun or the moon; huge discs seen moving at high speeds in outer space, in explanation of which no reasonable scientific theory could be advanced.

In addition to these reports, there were reports in medieval annals of landings, or near-landings of flying craft. In the old Irish annals, as reported by modern flying saucer writer,

Harold T. Wilkins, there is a report of a craft that came down close to earth near a church one Sunday. It dropped an anchor, which hooked onto the arch of the church door. A man jumped overboard and "swam" down through the air to release the anchor. The churchgoers wanted to seize the man, but the bishop forbade this, and the air traveler swam back up to his ship.

Another account, in the ancient Irish annals, states that a man in a "demon ship" hurled a dart at a salmon in a stream below. When the dart fell short, the man "swam" down from the ship to retrieve it. He was seized by an Irishman on the ground. Whereupon the man from the ship said that he was "drowning" and was released to swim back to his ship.

There are many old reports that, read one way, indicate that the earth has been visited by intelligence, humans, or humanoid beings from some place other than earth — or from some unknown place on earth — for thousands of years.

In addition to this evidence, there is considerable other evidence — again, depending on how you look at it — to indicate that there has been considerable odd activity in the skies over the earth for many, many centuries. For, from time to time, if the reports have been accurate, there have fallen to earth strange substances from the skies — shaped pieces of metal; shaped stones. Flesh. Blood. Slag. Hair. All these and more, in addition to the rains of toads, frogs, fishes and other animal life that can be explained away in terms of water spouts, cyclones and other natural phenomena, though why a water spout should pick up only toads or fishes of just one species has never been adequately explained.

In addition to this, there is some evidence to indicate that, at different times and in different ages, people have been "kidnapped" by something in the sky. There have been instances of whole ship's crews disappearing mysteriously at sea, and aircraft flying into clouds, never to be seen again. There was at least one famous instance where a man in an open field disappeared at night, with those on the ground hearing his voice growing fainter and fainter up in the sky.

There is still other evidence to indicate that strange things may have gone on in the past in or skies. Consider the odd "tracks" in the snow, all over England one night. They were regularly spaced marks that not only covered vast amounts of mileage in one night's time, but that went up straight walls and over the roofs of houses in a bee-line, tracks that could have been made only by something in the air.

Since a strange, hermit-like man made a life's study of odd things that science could never explain, and since much of his studies indicated visitors from other worlds, there is no necessity for going into great detail on these things here.

But because his name and his writings weave in and out of the flying saucer enigma like the leit motif of a symphony, it is apropos to include something about him and his works in this book.

Any volume on saucers would be incomplete without the ghost of this strange man flitting gleefully in and out of its pages with a sardonic "I told you so!"

For he was the herald, the prophet — and conceivably the father — of the belief that flying saucers are a manifestation from outer space.

He probably has given the material for more plots by science fiction writers than any other writer who has ever lived, with the possible exception of the grandfather of science fiction, Jules Verne.

This man's name was Charles Fort.

He deserves a chapter by himself.

So here it is:

CHAPTER 4
CHARLES FORT

Charles Hoy Fort was born August 9, 1874, in Albany, New York. He died May 3, 1932, in the Bronx, New York. He was a recluse. He had, according to his biographer, Tiffany Thayer, neither friends nor acquaintances. The only person he ever welcomed to the home he shared with his wife, besides Thayer, was Theodore Dreiser.

For over 26 years, Fort assembled data for which science had no explanation — sightings of "space ships," falls of strange materials from the skies. Strange disappearances and equally strange appearances of human beings. Occurrences that looked like levitation and tele-transportation of objects, including human beings. Reports of apports and transports and things seen in the skies and heard in the skies, including the seeming sounds of great battles fought above the clouds.

Many of the reports that Fort assembled — and from leading scientific publications of their day — were of strange occurrences on the moon or on nearby planets — a parade, a vast procession of lights on the moon; strange bodies crossing the surface of the moon or sun; strange lights, like searchlights, projecting from the rim of Mars.

And always, always, always, reports of strange, unknown craft, unknown lights, even of beings and voices appearing and being heard in the skies.

Many of the theories put forth by current writers, in fact, practically all of them, were advanced by Fort as early as 1919. Space ships. Space animals that live in the "sea" above us. Callers from Venus or Mars. Unknown lands close to our planet. All of his researching among museums, libraries, scientific journals and newspapers indicated to him that there is something wrong about our sometimes smug beliefs about the nature of our universe and a well-ordered, inexorably-patterned, completely predictable world. His chief belief was that knowledge, like time-space, is relative. And that beliefs change from one era to another.

Fort did most of his collecting in the British museum and in the New York Public Library. He worked among old issues of scientific publications and among old issues of newspapers.

Out of his prodigious note-taking and classifying, he wrote four books:

THE BOOK OF THE DAMNED
Copyright, 1919, by Boni and Liveright, Inc.
Copyright, 1940, by Tiffany Thayer

NEW LANDS
Copyright, 1923, by Boni and Liveright, Inc.
Copyright, 1940, by Tiffany Thayer

LO!
Copyright, 1931, by Claude Kendall

WILD TALENTS
Copyright, 1932, by Charles Fort

After Fort's death, Tiffany Thayer, advertising man and author, established the Fortean Society with the object of carrying on Fort's work. Since 1931, Mr. Thayer stated in the one-volume reprint of all of Mr. Fort's works, he paid the society's bills. Mr. Thayer was secretary of the society. Mr. Thayer, whom I met twice in my lifetime, the last time shortly before his death, died on ________(date).

All of the books of Charles Fort were published in one volume in 1941, by the Fortean Society, with an introduction by Mr. Thayer, by Henry Holt and Company.

(As a note to be interjected here, it may be observed that Henry Holt and Company also published the book on flying saucers by Frank Scully and one of the flying saucers books by Major Donald E. Keyhoe, whose books you will find mentioned later.)

To Charles Fort must be given the credit for first advancing the belief or theory that space ships with beings from other worlds have been visiting our earth for years — if not centuries.

And to him also must be given the credit for stubbornly writing book after book to justify his beliefs, even though in most quarters his books were only jeered at.

Yet, no less eminent an author than Booth Tarkington wrote the introduction to one of his books, a distinguished Chief Justice of the United States Supreme Court was one of the members of the Fortean Society, and thousands of people were given a lasting sense of wonderment by Charles Fort's writings.

This author read them years ago, when they were first published. He has read them since. He has re-read them now, in putting together this book. Many of the early "sightings" set down in this volume are taken from the data Mr. Fort assembled.

He set down some profoundly disturbing stuff.

He will sow in your mind some doubts that will always linger with you.

Perhaps time will prove Charles Fort right as rain. Who knows?

CHAPTER 5
THE EVIDENCE OF LEGEND

In addition to the material gathered by Charles Fort — and by several other writers who put together somewhat similar material — there is evidence in the legends of various races that "flying saucers" are no new phenomena.

The folk tales of the world, passed from generation to generation, abound in references to unknown aerial objects, to visitors whom they called the "gods," from unearthly lands, and to lands much nearer or much more accessible to earth than we "moderns" are willing to concede.

The Hawaiians in their legends say that they saw flying saucers as long as 2,000 years ago. Their name for them: *akualele,* or "flying spirits." Shapes: Balls of fire, cones, discs of various colors.

The Paiutes have a legend dating back centuries that the flying saucers are piloted by a "lost race" that lives in the interior of the Panamint Mountains.

The Indians of the Canadian North claim that, in the ancient days, the "gods" used to arrive in "flying machines" to give them aid and counsel.

The Navahos have a legend that their ancestors came to earth on a "meteor."

The ancient Sanscrit writings, particularly the *Mahabarata* of the Hindus, is full of references to a civilization as far advanced as that of ours today. The writings speak of bombs of fantastic power, aircraft, submarines, frightful wars, battles of races, and the destruction of great cites and even whole civilizations. You can read their writings for yourself in existing translations. But you may have to visit the Oriental Room of the New York Public Library, at the corner of 42nd Street and Fifth Avenue, New York City to find them, or to some other great metropolitan library. I read certain parts of the *Mahabarata* over 25 years ago, long before I ever heard the word "flying saucer." I was amazed at what I read then. I still am.

The ancient Greek writer, Herodotus, father of history, wrote of the legendary race of the "Hyperboreans," whose home was placed in a paradise "beyond the North Wind." Their life span was said to be 1,000 years.

The ancient Greek dramatists, when they got their stage characters into inextricable situations, resorted to the device of the deux ex machina, the "god from the machine," arriving to solve the situation. Not a god appearing by magic, but in a celestial vehicle, a machine.

Irish legends are laden with references to the use of cosmic forces and of aircraft.

"Bellerophon, in Greek legend, flew a mechanical "horse."

Solomon, in Arabic legend, had a flying machine. And Arabic literature, of course, abounds in references to "flying carpets."

The Bible contains cryptic references: Genesis, Chapter 6, verses 1, and 2. "And it came to pass, when men began to multiply on earth, and daughters were born unto them, that the sons of God saw the daughters of men that they were fair; and they took them wives of which they all chose."

Now this passage in the Bible has long been one for theological dispute. Even early church fathers disagreed as to its believability. Tertullian, one of these early fathers, believed it. Augustine, an equally eminent founder of the church, rejected this idea that "fallen angels" could come down from heaven and mate with the daughters of men.

According to Dr. Charles Francis Potter, M.A., B.D., S.T.M., Litt. D, writing in his book, “The Lost Years of Jesus Revealed, Newest Revelations of the Dead Sea Scrolls,” a paper-back Gold Medal Original published by Fawcett Publications, Inc., Greenwich, Conn., this story was a favorite with the Essenes, at Qumran. Dr. Potter also writes that the story was expanded upon at great length, in the community of Essenes at Qumran, in the early books: *The Book of Enoch, Jubilees, The Testament of Reuben*, and *The Testament of Naphtali.* I have not read these apocalyptic books. I intend to as soon as new translations from the newly-found library of the Essenes at Qumran are made available.

If the story reported by the ancients is true, then one conclusion seems inescapable: the “Sons of God” were beings of flesh and flood, of the same chemical composition of the “daughters of men,” subject to the same ills of the flesh that we are all heirs to, subject to the same joys and pangs of domesticity, and, in the end, subject to death.

If they were not — I agree with St. Augustine. The whole thing, in that case, must have been a colossal fabrication.

Who were these “Sons of God,” and where did they come from? Evidently, they had no women with them. The Bible is very specific in its writing. It says “of which they all chose.”

In Genesis 6, Verse 4: There were giants in the earth; and also, after that, when the sons of God came in unto the daughters of men, and they bore children to them, the same became mighty men which were of old, men of renown.”

This admixture of Man and superior beings, if such it was, was unfortunate. Here is verse 5: “And God saw that the wickedness of man was very great in the earth, and that every imagination of the thoughts of his heart was only evil continually.”

Retribution: The Flood

Centuries later, as the wickedness of man persisted, Genesis, Chapters 18 and 19, another portion of humanity was wiped out. Three angels visited Lot and told him that Sodom and Gomorrah, the cities of the plain, would be destroyed from the skies. Reasons: homosexuality.

I cite the reason because it has an exact parallel, in legend, or tradition, from the Western Hemisphere of the world. I'll come to that in a moment. But before doing so:

On February 9, 1960, a Soviet scientist, physico-mathematician, M. Agrest, as reported in a dispatch from *The Associated Press* in Moscow, suggested that Sodom and Gomorrah were blown to bits by a nuclear blast set off by invaders from outer space.

His theory, presented in a *Literary Gazette* article, according to AP, was "transmitted seriously and in detail by the Soviet news agency, Tass."

This scientist also suggested that "possibly a gigantic space ship approached the earth at a speed close to that of light and then braked for a landing."

"The landing may have been in the area of the Baalbek Terrace, a platform of huge stone slabs in the Anti-Lebanon Mountains of Syria, or the slabs may have been constructed as a launching platform by the space travelers. "Nobody," said the author, "has satisfactorily explained the existence of the Baalbek terrace."

"This area, relatively speaking, is not far from the Libyan Desert, where glassy bodies called tektites, containing radioactive isotopes of aluminum and beryllium, have been found. The scientist said these particles are at least a million years old and products of extremely high temperatures, and may be the traces of the spacemen's atomic missiles."

Now — for the parallel to the Biblical story — from the Western World:

The Peruvian Indians have a legend that giants once came to Peru out of the sky, built the cyclopean structures that are to be found in that country, and then were destroyed by the gods because of homosexual practices which they indulged in because they had not brought any women of their race with them. Since Peruvians, under the Inca, had no written language, but only the *quipu*, the knotted cord, which was used as a "memory" device for Inca bookkeeping, we have nothing but oral tradition to go on.

Now, this might be the fairytale explanation of a race of primitive culture in trying to account for structures built by an advanced race which preceded them. But, wherever cyclopean stonework is found throughout the world, there are legends of giants as the master builders. And, although the flood, which is a world-wide tradition, was supposed to have wiped out the race of giants, the genes and chromosomes of the race evidently persisted in the blood of Noah and his descendants. For this, we again have as authority, the Bible.

In Numbers, Chapters 13 and 14, it states that a race of giants, named Nephilim, was still surviving in Canaan when the Israelites left Egypt. As the story goes, Moses sent out twelve spies, one each from the Twelve Tribes, each one the head of a tribe. (For the Irish trade: one of them was named Oshea, but Moses called him Jehoshua).

These twelve key intelligence officers went to spy out the land. When they came to Hebron, beside the brook of Eshcol, as reported by the chronicler, they cut one bunch of grapes from a grapevine. The one cluster of grapes was so huge that "they bare it between two upon a staff." This is an interestingly historical and botanical note indeed, when one puts it beside the report of the spies that follows: "And they brought up an evil report of the land which they had searched unto the children of Israel, saying, 'The land, through which we have gone to search it, is a land that eateth up the inhabitants thereof; and all the people that we saw on it are men of great stature. And there we saw the giants, the sons of Anak, which come of the giants: and we were in our own sights as *grasshoppers*, and so were we in their sights.'" (The italicization is mine.)

The Israelites did not attack, because of their fear of the giants, and for this reason, because of their lack of faith, by the word of the Lord to Moses, the tribes were turned away from the land of the Amalekites and the Canaanites and made to wander for 40 years in the wilderness.

Again, the Bible, in Joshua 12:4, mentions a race of giants in recording the kings and lands that the Children of Israel smote: "And the coast of Og, king of Bashan, which was the remnant of the giants that dwelt as Ashtaroth and at Edrei."

Again, in Deuteronomy 2:11: "The Emims dwelt there in times past, a people great, and many, and tall, as the Anakims; which also were accounted giants, as the Anakims, but the Mcabites call them Emims." And of the land of Ammon, Deuteronomy 2:20: "That also was accounted a land of giants; giants dwelt therein, in old time; and the Ammonites called them Zamzummims. A people great, and many, and tall as the Anakims; but the Lord destroyed them before them; and they succeeded them, and dwelt in their stead."

The Children of Israel, according to the chroniclers, destroyed every city, every last inhabitant of the kingdom of Og, and all the other cities of the giants, killing every man, woman and child, right down to the last babe in arms.

Evidently, all of them — or their genes and chromosomes, were not extirpated, however, for later on in the Biblical history, David the shepherd slew the giant Goliath at the Battle of Elah. Goliath's height was given as 6 cubits and a span. Since the Hebraic cubit was something over 18.20

inches, and the span the width of the hand with fingers and thumb outstretched, Goliath measured nearly ten feet tall. Quite a broth of a boy.

In Cornwall, according to the old, old folktale of *Jack the Giant Killer*, a character named Jack merrily killed the last of the race there. Judging from this story and others, the giants did not seem to have the same stature of brainpower as they had in brawn. In fact, they appear somewhat stupid. But the story is pretty explicit in stating who they were, what their names were, where they lived.

In Greece, or in one of the isles of the Mediterranean, Ulysses killed one of a race or tribe of giants, in one-eye Cyclops. Judging from the Greek tale, and from many, many fairy tales, including the ancient story of Jack and the Beanstalk, the giants were cannibalistic.

As if to support all these old tales of giants in the earth, giant skeletons have sometimes been found, chiefly in Europe, particularly in Russia.

But giants are not the only deviation from the normal height of man that are recorded in legend. In the folk tales of the world there are many stories of a race of "Little People" that once lived on earth. Irish literature is full of references to the "Little People." The Irish peasantry was — and still is — afraid of them. Irish country folk believed — and still believe — that the "Little People" lived in the earth. Irish tales speak of them appearing from — and disappearing into — mound-like structures, the cromlechs or burial mounds of the ancient Irish. These "Little People," as reported in the tales, are shy and suspicious of men. They sometimes have magical properties, including the ability to make themselves invisible. They know where treasures are buried, and are guardians of treasure. They are sometimes mischievous and, at times, malicious.

Cornish miners, "Cousin Jacks," told tales of "Little Men" that they sometimes saw, and often heard, in mines far underground.

German miners told tales of cobolds, dwarf-like creatures found in mines. "Little men." Often bearded. Often carrying lanterns to light their way. (Science fiction writers would have you believe that these were extra-terrestrial creatures, looking for such minerals as uranium.)

The Cherokee Indians, like the Irish, told in their legends of a race of "Little People" — a whole nation of them, that lived in the United States. The homeland of this pigmy folk was in the state of Tennessee. The Cherokees regarded the "Little People," with superstitious awe, just like the Irish — and for the same reasons as the Irish.

In the North, the Ojibway tell of the "Little People" who instructed them in arts and crafts.

"Dwarfs" figure in other folk tales; seven of them in the story of Snow White; just one of them, named Rumpelstiltskin, in the story of the maiden who had to spin gold from straw. The race stories of Europe, collected by the Grimm brothers as fairy tales, are filled with such references. The tale of *Karl Katz*, which Washington Irving "borrowed," practically word for word, and retitled as *Rip Van Winkle*, with a setting in the Catskills, centers around dwarfish, bearded men playing at ninepins in the Harz mountains.

In Hawaii, the present-day Hawaiians say, the Polynesians on the Island of Kauai were preceded by a race of dwarfs, the Menehunes, the builders of hewn-stone ditches on Kauai. They were of a superior culture, as the Hawaiians who followed them did not know how to work stone.

All of these race tales of gnomes, dwarves, cobolds, leprechauns and such "Little People" agree in most details.

They are "little men," not monsters. They are shy. Many are miners. Many are described as bearded.

(Refer to what certain Frenchmen thought they saw climb out of landed flying saucers in fall of 1954 throughout France.)

As if in corroboration of some of this — at least that there once lived on earth a pigmy race much smaller than the pigmy tribes we know today — there have been found from time to time skeletons of a tiny race of people, notably around Palestine. The skeletons are generally found in burial vaults connected with long passages cut through solid rock, as if the little people had had to go underground to survive the onslaughts of bigger and more rapacious men.

Before we leave these folk tales, there is another very curious thing to record: the fairy tales of many lands, particularly the Oriental, tell of men who were enticed to an enchanted land somewhere to stay "months," only to return to earth and find that centuries had elapsed. This is a story of the relativity of time-space.

Actually it is the theory of time-dilation, a part of Einstein's *Special Theory of Relativity* which deals in part with speeds approaching the velocity of light. Some of Dr. Einstein's theories on things that happen when velocities approach the speed of light has been demonstrated.

The idea of time-dilation is this: If you can travel away from earth at the speed of light and keep going in one direction, you will grow no older, or very little older. To give you an extreme case: Dr. Eugen Sanger, once in charge of the German Air Force's rocket research plant at Trauen, and one of the world's experts on hypersonic flight, once made some interesting calculations. He computed that a theoretical spaceship, circumnavigating the Cosmos, assuming a distance of 10,000,000,000 (10 billion) light years, achieving

99.999,999,999,999,999,996 per cent of the velocity of light (which is 186,000 miles a second), would give the crew the impression that they had traveled only 33 years. Yet their elapsed time would be 10,000,000,000 (10 billion) years.

This feat, however, according to Dr. Sanger's calculations, would require the total conversion into energy of a mass about the size of the moon — which is hardly likely to ever occur.

But it's interesting to note that the ancients should have known a few things — or suspected a few things — about time and space that we are just beginning to know.

Now — does this setting down a little bit of the folk lore and legendry and the mysticism of mankind indicate clearly that the earth has been visited from other worlds, or colonized from other worlds, and that we have been blind to these facts for years and years?

It does nothing of the sort.

But it is the kind of material which one can be used — and has been used — in the advancement of the theory that saucers — whatever they are — originate in outer space, in lands unknown.

Now that we have touched upon this, let us depart to another subject, or series of subjects, perhaps allied to the phenomenon of flying saucers. A great deal has been written about these subjects. There may not be any connection whatsoever between them and saucers, but they have been linked in articles, books, and in the public press. They belong in the record. So here they are:

CHAPTER 6
SIMILAR AERIAL PHENOMENA

In addition to flying saucers of different shapes and sizes, in addition to things that maneuver, things that land, things that appear to have substance, other things of a somewhat similar nature have been reported. Some of these things have been reported, like saucers, for millennia. Others are fairly recent. Some of the recent ones have been very interesting.

All of these things are lights. A brief description of each follows:

Will-O-The-Wisps

From time immemorial there have been seen on this earth luminous balls or globes of light that hover and flit just above the ground. Superstition has always gathered thickly around these lights. The technical name given to them is ignis fatuus, or false fire. Another name is fox fire, which is probably a corruption of the first. The common name is will-o-the-wisp.

The accepted explanation of the will-o-the-wisp is that it is methane, or marsh gas which has become ignited. But these lights have been seen miles from swamps. They have been observed flitting down roads, across hills, across barren desert country. When chased, they outdistance the pursuer. They twist and turn, as if motivated by intelligence.

No one, so far as is known, has ever caught a will-o-the-wisp, scrutinized it, dissected it, measured its light and heat, put it under a microscope. They don't stay around to be measured. This writer will hazard a guess that when someone really studies the will-o-the-wisp, he will find it to be a highly-charged, highly-ionized ball of electricity of some kind — electricity so charged that when a human body gets near it, the mass of ionized particles is repelled, and appears to flee.

In Australia, there is a similar phenomenon known as the Min-Min light, a large sphere of light, associated with omens of bad luck to the superstitious.

In the state of Nevada, a similar phenomenon has often been observed by sheepherders in lonely stretches of country. They were described in an early issue of FATE Magazine, by Kenneth Arnold, the original reporter of flying saucers.

The Brown Mountain Lights

In northwestern North Carolina, in Avery County, on the fringes of the Great Smokies, is Brown Mountain. From the top of this mountain, as reported by competent observers, balls of light, of an orange or greenish-white color, rise into the sky. Some rise slowly. Others rise swiftly. Some are fuzzy in outline. Others quite sharp and clear. They cannot be due to marsh gas. There are no marshes on the side of the mountain. They could be natural gas, which somehow ignited on contact with the air. But lighted gas generally does not hold its shape as a sphere of flame.

The Brown Mountain lights have never been satisfactorily explained. But this writer will hazard another guess that if they are ever really studied, and their secret learned, they will be found to be charges of electricity. As we are beginning to understand, the earth is a gigantic vacuum tube. In the relationship between the earth, the sun, the moon, the other planets and the rest of cosmos, with violent forms of electric rays passing from one to the other, there must be many mysteries which we do not understand today. Many of these, without a doubt, would fit into a range of the spectrum which would be visible. It is within the range of possibility that visible charges of electricity, held together by some kind of cohesion between agitated, ionized atoms, could enter the atmosphere of the earth, or depart from the atmosphere of the earth — in the form of *lights*.

The Foo Fighters

During the latter part of World War II, Allied flyers were mystified by red, green, blue, orange or yellow balls of luminous light that often appeared from nowhere, flew formation with aircraft for a while, and then disappeared, often at terrific speeds.

According to author Harold T. Wilkins, writing in FATE Magazine, U.S. Navy flyers in the Pacific zone of operations were briefed by Intelligence to expect the appearance of such phenomena.

When the "Foo Fighters," "Foo Balls," or "Kraut Balls," as they were also called, first appeared, over Germany, it was thought that they were a new Nazi secret weapon. But the balls seemed harmless. They made no hostile moves. But they did appear at times to be guided or remotely controlled by an intelligence.

They were seen by Japanese airmen, as well as by Allied flyers. The Japanese, as reported by Mr. Wilkins, were said to have believed that the spheres of light were an American secret device.

A great many flying saucer sightings fit into the "Foo Fighter" pattern of characteristics. The light with which Lieutenant Gorman engaged in a "dogfight" over Fargo, North Dakota, fits the "Foo Ball" pattern. So do lights reported over Korea and Japan by American flyers who flew in the Korean War.

For more about these odd lights, read Mr. Wilkins' article in FATE, August — September 1951, or read his book on flying saucers.

The Fireballs of the Southwest

As early as 1943, observers in Arizona, New Mexico, Oklahoma, Texas, Colorado, Utah and Nevada reported seeing meteor-like fireballs of exceptional size flashing through the skies over a seven-state area. The fireballs did not behave like meteors. Greenish-yellow in color, they vanished in a blinding flash. But there was never any noise, nor were there any fragments from the explosion. In one instance, two flew side by side and crashed near Cloverdale, New Mexico, sending up a double mushroom of smoke, with no noise, or recoverable fragments.

The world's best authority on the subject of these green fireballs is Dr. Lincoln La Paz, Director of the Institute of Meteoritics at the University of New Mexico.

Some astronomers have claimed that the fireballs were just meteors, nothing else.

But Dr. La Paz has pointed out that they could not be meteors, for some very good reasons:

1. The fireballs were not the same green as meteors. Their color was too green.

2. They were noiseless. Meteors make just as much noise as a jet, or far more, when they crash through the sound barrier.

3. They did not follow the curve of the earth in flight, as meteors do. The fireballs flew in straight, level flight.

4.The fireballs left no fragments when they exploded.

Put all of these phenomena together and perhaps you have something of little-understood, electrical nature, and perhaps you have something that will help to explain flying saucers. Or perhaps you have nothing at all — simply some unrelated phenomena — that only deepen the misunderstanding.

But all of these elements have been thrown into the flying saucer picture.

Now that we have those behind us, perhaps we'd better go on to flying saucer sightings, a list of things that people reported seeing over the years. No book on flying saucers could possibly be complete without a goodly selection of these. So here they are:

CHAPTER 7
THE SIGHTINGS

Over the years, over the centuries, there have been thousands of reports of sightings of "flying saucers" and other unknown aerial objects in the sky, with many such objects seeming to have the property of maneuverability.

The U.S. Air Force, which stated on April 14, 1953, that 20% of all current sightings remained classified as "unknown," cut this high percentage down to 10% in a December, 1954, report on sightings.

No attempt has been made here to list all sightings. This would require several books alone. The sightings listed are those picked up from various sources, with enough early sightings listed to show the similarity between those of the 19th Century and the 20th.

No attempt has been made to check any of these sightings. Since this writer works from 9:00 to 5:00 in a New York advertising agency five days a week, he has no time for travel from coast to coast, questioning people on what they reported seeing. Such a check would be useless, anyway. The U.S. Air Force, from the beginning, has checked constantly — and is still checking today. It reports that there is no tangible evidence, of any sort whatsoever, to prove the existence of flying saucers. And how can you check, anyway? Someone reports seeing a "flying saucer." It is seen only a few seconds, or a few minutes, and then is gone. It leaves no traces of its passing. If it explodes, it leaves no fragments. It is as evanescent as a moonbeam. How are you doing to prove what you saw?

I have to take for granted in the case of sightings that what people reported seeing, they saw — or they thought they saw. I'm taking for granted that most of these people were sober, decent, conscientious, respectable citizens who tried to do their duty in reporting something, even at the risk of winning only ridicule from their friends.

Perhaps some of them didn't see what they thought they saw. Perhaps some of the sightings listed here are pure hoax, or pure fabrications out of the minds of some misguided individuals who willed themselves into seeing something that just wasn't there. Maybe a lot of people saw something done with mirrors. But all of them certainly believed that they saw something when they saw it. They were there. The critics are skeptics weren't. So I am setting down, as reported in many sources, what they thought they saw.

And it's amazing how few people, really, amidst all the "scare" of flying saucers, have reported seeing them. All you have to do to get yourself some publicity — and there are tens of thousands of our citizens who would not be loath to receive some — is to report sighting a flying saucer. You can get yourself written up in newspapers, interviewed by Air Force Intelligence, win national prominence, have your name mentioned in flying saucer books. But evidently people — even the most avid for publicity — do not care for this method of publicizing themselves. In the first nine months of 1954, only 259 sightings were reported. Figuring that 90% of these were explainable, that leaves only 26 reports of genuine "unknowns." This from a possible hysterical earth-population of several billions. (Check USAF reports from '55 through '59.)

So let's set down the sightings reported as rarities, not commonplace, things so unusual that observers were willing to brave ridicule to report what they had seen.

Here are some of the most significant ones from the thousands.

May 16, 1808. Skeninge, Sweden. About 4:00 P.M. Numerous round bodies appeared against face of sun. Dark brown, seemingly size of hat crown. Procession lasted two hours. Some fell to ground, left only a film, which soon dried and vanished. Things were often seen linked together in chains. Seemed to have tails eighteen to twenty feet long. Transactions of the Swedish Academy of Sciences, 1808-215, translated for the *North American Review*, 3-319. (Charles Fort).

November 13, 1833. Niagara Falls. Large luminous body, shaped like a square table, almost stationary for a time. *American Jrnl. Sci.*, 1-25-391 (Charles Fort)

About 1838. India. Disc from which projected a hook-like form. Diagram given. Disc looked about size of moon, but brighter. Visible about 20 minutes. By G. Pettit, in Professor Baden-Powell's Catalogue (*Rept. Brit. Assoc.*, 1849). (Charles Fort)

June 18, 1845. 900 miles east of Adalia, Asia Minor. Brig *Victoria*. Three luminous bodies were seen to issue from the sea, at about a half mile from the vessel. Visible 10 minutes. Reported from the *British Association*, 1861-30 (Charles Fort) (Note: At about time of observation reported by captain of Victoria, Rev. F. Hawlett, F.R.A.S., was in Adalia, 900 miles away. He, too, saw the spectacle. In his view, it was a body that appeared, and then broke up. He observed it for a time he estimated to be between twenty minutes and a half hour. (It must have been huge to have been observed at a distance of

900 miles.) The phenomenon was also reported from Syria and Malta as two very large bodies "nearly joined."

Nov. 19, 1847. Oxford. Listed by Lowe. Large aerial object. Stationary twice in 7 minutes. *Rec. Sci.*. 1-136. (Charles Fort)

Oct. 10, 1864. M. e, France. Long, luminous body, tapering at both ends. Observed by 3 witnesses. L'Anne Scientifique, 1864-54. (Charles Fort)

Summer, 1868. Copiapo. Chile. Object in sky. Carried lights. Propelled by noisy motor. Covered with scales which clashed together with metallic sound. *Zoologist*, July 1868 (Charles Fort)

March 22, 1870. Barque *Lady of the Lake.* Lat. 5° 47'N., Long. 27° 52' W. Circular cloud. Included semicircle divided into 4 parts with a long tail. Greyish in color. Traveled *against* the wind. "Came up obliquely against the wind, and finally settled down right in the wind's eye." Observed for 1/2 hour. Lost to sight in evening's darkness. *Journal of the Royal Meteorological Society*, 1-157. (Charles Fort)

August 1, 1871. Marseilles. Reported by Coggia. Large body, colored red, moving slowly, visible 15 minutes.
Chem. News, 24-193. (Charles Fort)

April 24, 1874, Prague. Professor Schafarik. Saw dazzling white object slowly traversing disc of moon. *Astronomical Register*, 23-205 (Charles Fort)

July 6, 1874. Oaxaca, Mexico. Something like gigantic trumpet, suspended, vertical, oscillating gently. Estimated length, 425 feet. Observed five or six minutes. (Note: compare with 1950 Mexican sightings listed in this book.) *Sci. Am. Sup.*, 6-2365. (Charles Fort)

May 15, 1879. Persian Gulf. Commander J.E. Pringle, H.M.S. *Vulture*. Waves of light passing under *Vulture*. "...appearance was that of revolving wheel...whose spokes were illuminated." Shafts estimated 25 feet broad, velocity 84 mph. Duration about 35 minutes. *Nature*, 20-291 (Charles Fort)

June 5, 1880. Off coast of Malabar. R.E. Harris, Commander of the A.H.N. Co's steamship *Shajehan*. 10:00 P.M. Waves of brilliant light with spaces between. Nature, 21-410 (Charles Fort)

August 20, 1880. M.A. Trecul, French Academy. Reported by Flammarion. Brilliant yellowish-white body, apparently 35 to 40 centimeters long, about 25 centimeters wide. Torpedo-shaped. Or cylindrical body. Dropped something and disappeared in clouds. Whatever dropped, dropped vertically, like heavy object, left luminous train. No sound heard. *Thunder and Lighting*, p. 87. Flammarion. *Comptes Rendus*, 103-849. (Charles Fort)

November 7, 1882. Royal Observatory, Greenwich, England. E. Walter Maunder, astronomer. Sighting followed violent electrical storm. It was a great circular disc of greenish light that appeared in the East-Northeast. Moved from horizon to horizon in two minutes. As it passed above moon, shape was observed as almost that of elongated ellipse. Other observers called it cigar-shaped, or like a torpedo, or spindle or shuttle. It was widely observed by many others than Astronomer Maunder. Estimated height: 133 miles above earth. Estimated speed: 10 miles per second. Maunder himself wrote up this sighting, and many years later he felt that it was a natural phenomenon of some kind, but the most extraordinary he had ever observed. It sounds quite like many modern "saucer" sightings.

February 24, 1885. Somewhere between Yokohama and Victoria. Lat. 37° N., Long. 170° E. Captain of barque Innerwich was roused by mate. Mate had been watching something unusual in sky. Captain went on deck, saw sky turning fiery red. "All at once, a large mass of fire appeared over vessel, completely blinding spectators." Then the fiery mass fell into the sea. The water it cast up rushed towards the vessel with a noise that was deafening. The barque was struck flat aback. The master declared that the awfulness of the sight was beyond description. *Science*, 5-242 (Charles Fort)

November 1, 1885. Near Adrianople. Object that appeared four or five times size of moon, moving slowly across the sky. *L'Astronomie*, 1886-309 (Charles Fort)

November 3, 1886. Hamar, Norway. Bright, white cloud. Emitted brilliant rays of light; drifted across sky; retained throughout its original form. *Nature*, Dec. 16, 1886-158. (Charles Fort)

1887. Enormous ball of fire seen to rise from ocean, near Cape Race. Rose to height of fifty feet, advanced toward ship, then moved away. Visible 5 minutes. *Nature*, 37-187. *L'Astronomie* 1887-76. Flammarion, *Thunder and Lighting.*

May 4, 1888, New Zealand. Object with oval nucleus and streamers with dark bands and lines suggestive of solid structure. *Nature*, 42-402. (Charles Fort)

August 5, 1889. East Twickenham, England. During violent storm. Object that appeared to be about 15 inches long and 5 inches wide, fell rather slowly. It exploded. No substance from it was ever found. *Nature*, 40-415. (Charles Fort)

Sept. 5, 1891. Crawfordsville, Ill. 2:00 A.M. Two icemen. Construction about 20 feet long, 8 feet wide, in sky, seemingly propelled by fin-like attachments. Moved towards icemen. Icemen moved. Object sailed away, making such a noise that Rev. G.W. Switzer, pastor of Methodist Church, was awakened, looked out window, and saw object circling in sky. Brooklyn Eagle, Sept. 10, 1891 (Charles Fort). Fort later wrote the Reverend Dr. Switzer to get his account of what had happened, and while the minister promised Fort that he would write him, Fort never got him to send the promised account.

October 1891. China Sea. Shafts of light that had appearance of rays of searchlight, under sea. *L'Astronomie*, 1891-312 (Charles Fort)

December 20, 1893. Virginia, North Carolina, South Carolina. Many observers. Disc-like, brilliant white luminous body passed overhead, from west to east. Seemed size of a table. The noise of its passage through the air was heard. It appeared to stand still for fifteen or twenty minutes. Either disappeared or exploded without sound. (Charles Fort)

August 26, 1894. North Wales. A disc, from which projected an orange-colored body that looked like an elongated flatfish. *Nature*, 50-524. (Charles Fort)

Sept. 20, 21, 1896. California. Prof. Swift. Two luminous objects in sky. *Astro. Jour.* 17-8, 103 (Charles Fort)

November 26, 1896. People on streetcar in Alameda, California. Observed huge, bird-shaped object. Brilliant light in nose. Shot across sky, turned and moved at terrific speed in direction of Hayward. From D.H. Menzel's book.

April 1897. Chicago and other points in the Midwest. This is a hotly-debated "sighting," or series of "sightings." In April, newspapers all across the country gave it front-page space. What it appeared to be to many observers was a cigar-shaped object, no observable motive power. It was first reported near Sacramento. Then people in Denver saw it. The New York *Herald* reported it on March 29 as over Omaha. There it was reported as a bright light, too big for a balloon. In Kansas City, it was reported as having a light greater than that produced by twenty stars. Reports in the *Chicago Tribune* said that people had said that it was a gigantic airship — an immense bird of polished silver. In Milwaukee it stopped for a quarter of an hour over City Hall. Some witnesses said that the bright light was suspended from a dark, oval-shaped body. Professor Menzel, in his book, said that this one had been called a hoax.

July 29, 1897. St. Mary's, Ohio. During eclipse of sun. Looked like knotted lightning. Photographed by L.E. Martindale. *Photography*, May 26, 1898 (Charles Fort)

Jan. 22, 1898. Viziadrug, India. Sir Norman Lockyer. During total eclipse of sun. Observed unknown body between Venus and Mars. *Jour. Leeds Astro. Soc.*, 1906-23. (Charles Fort)

Sept. 4, 1898. Lille, France. Red object in sky. Rectangular. Violet-colored band on one side, rest striped with black and red. Observed for ten minutes through telescope. It cast out sparks and disappeared. *Cosmos*, n.s., 39-356. (Charles Fort)

March 2, 1899. El Paso, Texas. Unknown luminous object in sky. *The Observatory*, 22-247 (Charles Fort)

March 8, 1899. Prescott, Ariz. Dr. Warren E. Day. Luminous object. Travelled with moon all day, until 2:00 P.M. Day before this, object was seen close to moon by G.O. Scott, at Tonto, Ariz. *U.S. Weather Bureau Report* (Ariz. Sec., March, 1899) Charles Fort

Oct. 28, 1899. Luzaroches, France. M.A. Garrie. Round, luminous object rose above horizon at 4:50 P.M. Looked about size of moon. Moved away, diminishing to a point. *La Nature* (Sup.) Nov. 11, 1899 (Charles Fort)

Dec. 7, 1900. Fountain of light on planet Mars. Observed by Dr. Lowell at Flagstaff Observatory. Observed by Prof. Pickering. Dr. Lowell tried to interpret it as code flashings of some kind. *Popular Astronomy*, 10-187, Lowell (Charles Fort)

April 4, 1901. Persian Gulf. About 8:30 P.M. (?). Capt. Hoseason, steamship *Kilwa*. Saw vast shafts of light. Shaft after shaft, revolving around a central hub at about 60 mph. Faint light. Lasted about fifteen minutes. No phosphorescence in sea that night. *Journal of the Royal Meteorological Society*,

28-29 (Charles Fort)(Note: notice similarity to this and story told by Commander J.R. Bodler, FATE, Sept. 1952, of wheel of light seen by him in Strait of Hormuz, Persian Gulf, off Iran, Nov. 14, 1949.)

May 10, 1902. South Devon, England. Great number of highly colored objects like little suns or toy balloons. *English Mechanic*, 75-417 (Charles Fort)

Oct. 28, 1902. Lat. 5°, 31' S., and Long. 4°, 42' W. 3:05 A.M. A.H. Raymer, second officer, steamship *Fort Salisbury*, and sailor on lookout. Saw huge, dark object bearing lights, in sea. It was slowly sinking. Two lights seen. Object had estimated length of five hundred to six hundred feet. Mechanism of some kind. Appeared like fins to observers. Making commotion in water. A "scaled back" was slowly submerging. *Zoologist*, 4-7-38 (Charles Fort) (See later press release on flying submarine)

Aug. 9, 1903. Argenteuil, France. M. Desmoulins. 11:00 P.M. Luminous object, moving from north to south. Red. Observed by five people for twenty minutes. Great luminosity in nucleus. Object ad also been seen on July 19th and 26th about five miles from Argenteuil. *Cosmos*, n.s., 49-259 (Charles Fort)

February 28, 1904. *U.S.S. Supply*. At sea. Lt. Frank Schofield. 6:10 A.M. Observed three meteors. Leading meteor egg-shaped, with an area of 6 suns. Smaller two objects seemed round. Appeared to be traveling in echelon. Made near approach to water's surface, then away from it. Appeared most remarkable. J.R. Aswell, *Readers Digest*, July 1952

Sometime in 1906. Douglas Carnegie, Blackheath, England. Reports that, in the Gulf of Oman at the entrance to the Persian Gulf, he saw shafts of brilliant light come sweeping across the ship's bows at speed between 60 and 200 mph. "Shafts of light came up from somewhere between surface. Intervening ship had no effect on light beams; they started away from lee side of ship, just as if they had traveled right through it." *Jour. Roy. Met. Soc.*, 32-280 (Charles Fort)

March 14, 1907. Malacca Strait. S.C. Patterson, second officer, P. and O. steamship *Delta*. "shafts which seemed to move around a center-like the spokes of a wheel — and appeared to be about 300 years long." Phenomenon lasted about half hour, during which time ship had traveled six or seven miles. Stopped suddenly. *Jour. Roy. Met Soc.*, 33-294 (Charles Fort)

Jan. 27, 1908. Employees of the Norwich Transportation Company, Mousehead. Saw a dark, globular object with structure of some kind on side of it traveling at great speed. Bright, moonlight night. Traveling against wind. *Eastern Daily Express*, Jan. 18, 1908 (Charles Fort)

Sept. 14, 1908. Northfield, Worcestershire, England. David Packer. Saw luminous appearance. Photographed it. Photograph showed light came from large, moon-like object. *English Mechanic*, 88-211 (Charles Fort)

March 23, 1909. Peterborough, England. Two constables. 5:10 A.M. Object, somewhat oblong and narrow in shape, carrying a light, moving over city, with sounds like sounds of motor. *Peterborough Advertiser*, March 27, 1909 (Charles Fort)

May 18, 1909. 11:00 P.M. Near road, near Caerphilly Mountains, Wales. A man named Lithbridge of 4 Roland Street, Cardiff, Wales. He saw, on the grass, at the side of the road, a large, tube-shaped construction. In it were two men, in heavy fur overcoats. When they saw Mr. Lithbridge, they spoke excitedly to each other in a foreign language and sailed away into the air. Newspaper men visited the place, found the grass trampled, and found a scattering of torn newspapers and other debris. *London Daily Mail*, May 20, 1909 (Charles Fort)

June 10, 1909. Capt. Gabe. Danish East Asiatic Co's. steamship *Bintang*. 3:00 A.M. Straits of Malacca. Vast, revolving wheel of light, flat upon the water, so vast center was near horizon. Display lasted fifteen minutes. Wheel moved forward, decreased in brilliancy and also in speed of rotation, as if meeting more and more resistance in water. *Scientific American*, 106-51 (Charles Fort)

Sept. 8, 1909. New England. Luminous body sailing overhead. Sounds from it, like the sounds of a motor. (Charles Fort)

Dec. 24, 1909. Willimantic, Conn. Object that was supposed to have been an "airship" hovered over town. Had several red lights and a searchlight. It was seen all over New England during the latter part of December 1909. (Charles Fort)

Early July 1910. Of coast of Normandy. Crew of French fishing smack, *Jeune Frederic*. Saw huge, black, bird-like object in sky. Suddenly it fell into sea, bounded back, then fell again, leaving no findable traces. *London Weekly Dispatch*, July 10, 1910 (Charles Fort)

Jan. 12, 1910. Chattanooga, Tenn. Thousands of people. Early morning. A mysterious white aircraft. Came out of the north on Wednesday. Traveled southeast. Returned north on Thursday. People reported hearing the "chug" of its engine. New York Tribune, Jan. 13, 1910. (Charles Fort)

August 12, 1910. Dutch steamer, Valentijn. Capt. Breyer. South China Sea. Midnight. Appearance above water of a horizontal wheel, turning rapidly, emitting a rotation of flashes. *Danish Meteorological Institute* (Charles Fort)

August 17, 1910. Forest, east of Dessau, Germany. Laborers. Saw object in sky that looked like balloon. It burst into flames and something the laborers thought was its car fell into forest. They searched for it, found nothing. London Times, August 19, 1910 (Charles Fort)

Jan., 1913. Unknown aircraft, carrying searchlight of power of sunlight. Seen over many parts of England during January and February of that year. No known English aircraft up. No known German aircraft.

Feb. 9, 1913. The most extraordinary procession of "meteors" ever seen. Passed over Toronto in one straight line, taking from three to five minutes for the passage. "Like an express train, lighted at night." — "the lights were at different points, one in front, and a rear light, then a succession of lights in the tail." The next day, dark objects were seen over Toronto. They passed from west to east, in three groups, and then returned west in more scattered formation, about seven or eight in all." *Journal of the Royal Astronomical Society of Canada*, 7-148. Professor Chant. (Charles Fort) (Note: these lights or bodies were seen from Toronto to Bermuda, flying in a straight line at an estimated height of 30 miles above the earth. They closely resemble the Lubbock lights, particularly with regard to the large, lighted bodies as parts of the squadrons. Both the 1913 lights and the Lubbock Lights have been explained as meteors.)

Oct. 10, 1914. Manchester, England. Black, spindle-shaped object seen in sky. Albert Buss. Clear-cut outline was surrounded by a kind of halo, giving impression of a ship plowing through sea, throwing up waves with prow. *Eng. Mec.*, 100-236 (Charles Fort)

Oct. 1914. In the Arctic. Mikkelsen. Reported on empty petroleum cask at advanced base. Cask riddled with holes as from blast of shot. No footprints about. No clues as to what happened. *Lost in the Arctic.* Mikkelsen. p. 345

July 16, 1916. Huntington, West Va. A formation having the shape of a dirigible. Luminous. Observed about 11 P.M. Observed through field glasses. It was seen to dim, disappear, then reappeared. Faded out of sight. Faint stars were seen behind it, ruling out possibility of solid body, like dirigible. (Note: Waxing and waning of object, like current sightings.) *Sci. American* 115-241. (Charles Fort)(Following this report, Charles Fort says this: "We now have several observations upon cylindrical-shaped bodies that have appeared in this earth's atmosphere: cylindrical, but joined at both ends, or torpedo-shaped. Some of the accounts are not very detailed, but out of the bits of description my own acceptance is that super-geographical routes are traveled by torpedo-shaped super-constructions that have occasionally visited, or that have occasionally been driven into this earth's atmosphere. From data, the acceptance is that upon entering this earth's atmosphere the vessels have been so racked that had they not sailed away, disintegration would have occurred: that, before leaving this earth, they have, whether in a tempted communication or not, in mere wantonness or not, dropped objects, which did almost immediately violently disintegrate or explode." Compare with recent sightings.)

August 1929. 400 miles off coast of Virginia. Traveling light in sky. Reported by Thomas Stuart, third mate of the steamship *Coldwater,* South Atlantic Steamship Line. "There was something that gave the impression it was a large passenger craft." Investigation failed to reveal any Translantic or Bermuda flight. *New York Herald Tribune,* Aug. 29, 1929 (Charles Fort)

1945. Over the Hump between China and India. Captain Charles Lane and co-pilot. Saw white object rushing up behind their plane at great speed. Instrument board of plane went haywire. The plane stopped in mid-air. Then disc rocketed into sky. Pilot switched on his plane's motors and plane resumed flight. (See similar story told by John H. Janssen, Morristown, New Jersey. *Daily Record* in New York Newspaper.

Later part of May 1947. Oklahoma City, Oklahoma. Private pilot. Huge, round object in sky. Object estimated to be flying three times faster than jet planes of that year. July 10, 1947 and in FATE Magazine, Sept 1949

June 12, 1947. Weiser, Idaho. People of Weiser. Two strange, fast-moving objects. July 10, 1947 and in FATE Magazine, Sept 1949

June 21, 1947. Spokane, Washington. Several mysterious objects at great height, flying at high speed. July 10, 1947 and in FATE Magazine, Sept 1949

Summer, 1947. A former Air Force pilot and his passenger. Jackson, Mississippi. Rocket-shaped craft. Estimated speed: 500 MPH.

June 24, 1947. Cascade Mountains. Fred Johnson, Portland prospector. Five or six disc-like objects banking in sky. Watched them through telescope. Noted agitation on compass hand of watch.

June 28, 1947. Air Force pilot. Near Lake Meade, Nevada. Six circular objects. Flashed past plane.

June 24, 1947. 2:39 P.M. Kenneth Arnold, Boise, Idaho, piloting his own 3-place cabin plane in state of Washington, between Chehalis and Yakima. Reported seeing 9 shiny discs flipping along over Mt. Rainer.

July 4, 1947. Portland, Oregon. Patrolman Kenneth A. McDowell. Reported 5 large objects, disc-shaped. Flew with dipping motion at great speed and disappeared. July 10, 1947 and in FATE Magazine, Sept 1949

July 4, 1947. Portland, Oregon. Patrolmen W.A. Lissy and D.W. Ellis. Reported seeing three round, flat discs, flying at terrific speed. Last disc fluttering in sideways arc. No smoke. No vapor trails. No sound. Estimated height 40,000 feet. July 10, 1947 and in FATE Magazine, Sept 1949

July 4, 1947. Portland, Oregon. Patrolman Earl E. Patterson, former Air Force pilot. Reported one disc. July 10, 1947 and in FATE Magazine, Sept 1949

July 4, 1947. Vancouver, Washington. Crew of deputy sheriffs. Heard Portland police broadcast, looked at sky over Portland and saw twenty to thirty objects like a flight of geese, reported a low humming sound. On July 10, 1947 and in FATE Magazine, Sept. 1949

July 4, 1947. Portland, Oregon. The Maury Island sighting. Two harbor patrolmen, Harold A. Dahl and Fred L. Chrisman, claimed that, on this day, they had been out in a boat and saw, over Portland, a number of doughnut-shaped craft in the air come to the aid of another such craft in distress. They said that the one in distress had jettisoned hot slag that had fallen on their boat, burning them and killing their dog. This was the sighting that Ray Palmer of FATE paid Kenneth Arnold to investigate. It was one of the incidents that led Palmer and Arnold to claim a cover-up by the USAF. Palmer also claimed that the samples of the slag he had obtained did not show the same analysis as samples U.S. Intelligence agents claimed were the only ones taken at the site. Both Dahl and Chrisman were said to have disappeared later. The first Project Saucer report said they had confessed that the whole thing was a hoax. Mr. Chrisman bitterly denied this in a letter to FATE, published in FATE, January 1950. To read the whole story, see FATE, Volume I, No. 1, Spring, 1948, or refer to the Arnold-Palmer book, *The Coming of the Saucers*, privately published by the authors.

July 8, 1947. Muroc Air Force Base. Pilots and ground officers. Six fast-moving, silvery-white objects.

July 8, 1947. Muroc Air Field, California. Lt. Joseph C. McHenry, billeting officer, reported seeing at 9:30 A.M. two silvery objects, either spherical or disc-like, moving 300 mph at 8,000 feet. The two objects disappeared. Then another appeared. Five witnesses out of seven saw it. Air Force maintained it was not experimental air craft.

July 8, 1947. Muroc Air Field. Noon. Colonel Gilkey, Maj. Richard R. Shoop. Thin, metallic object diving over field. A test pilot reported seeing strange object falling from great height at same time.

July 10, 1947. 4:47 P.M. Well-known astronomer. Between Clovis and Clines Corners, New Mexico. Bright, motionless object among clouds. Astronomer made calculations. So did wife and daughter who were in car with him. Object had hard, sharp, disc-like outline. Luminous. Had wobbling motion. Rose rapidly. Moved slowly across clouds. Disappeared behind cloud bank. Object estimated 250 feet long, 100 feet thick. No sound. No exhaust. No vapor trail. Object conformed to no known optical or celestial phenomena.

July 10, 1947. Over New Jersey. Aviation Editor. John H. Janssen, of Morristown, New Jersey, *Daily Record.* Took photo of four discs in flight. Two weeks later, according to his published account, two discs approached a plane he was flying, poised above him, stopped his engine, but kept the plane suspended in the air.

Flying discs break out over the U.S. il Life 23:14-16 July 21, 1947. This is a humorous report on the rash of saucer sightings from June on. Life is highly skeptical of the whole thing.

August 1947. George Adamski. Palomar Gardens, Mt. Palomar, California. Flight of strange lights overhead. Counted 184 of them. Moved at high speed. Stopped. Reversed high speed. (Fate, July 1951)(Read more of Mr. Adamski later in this book.)
August 1947. Two pilots on commercial run. Huge, black, wingless craft. No motor. High speed.

Jan. 7, 1948. Day of Mantell's death. Two hours later. Observers at Lockbourne Air Force Base, Columbus, Ohio. Watched large metallic disc for more than 20 minutes. Estimated speed: 500 mph. Glowed from white to amber, left amber exhaust trail.

1947. Elizabethville, Belgian Congo. Sighting made by dozens of people. Two discs appeared over uranium pits, suddenly shot off, zig-zagging. Authorities sent up Spitfire plane in pursuit. Pilot reported he got in so close he could see whirling rim. Estimated size of discs: 36 feet across. Gerald Heard

January 7, 1948. Godman Field, air base at Ft. Knox, Kentucky. Between 1:45 and 1:50 P.M. T/Sgt. Quinton A. Blackwell, chief operator in control tower. Saw strange object appear over field. Had been alerted earlier by military police and state police that a large circular object from 250 to 300 feet in diameter had been seen over Madisonville, Kentucky. As the whole personnel on the field watched the object and tried to puzzle it out, a flight of four P-51 fighters came over the field and were requested to chase the object. Two flyers broke off the chase somewhere between 18,000 and 20,000 feet. Capt. Thomas F. Mantell, Jr., pilot of the third plane kept going. He had no oxygen equipment. Somewhere in the sky Capt. Mantell probably blacked out from lack of oxygen. His plane evidently went into a dive and disintegrated. Pieces of it were found scattered over a wide area. (As to what lured Capt. Mantell to his death, most military authorities agreed that it was the planet Venus, or one of the Navy's giant plastic cosmic ray balloons, known to be loose in the Godman field area on the day of the tragedy.)

February 19, 1948. 7:20 A.M. East African Airlines plane, *The Lodestar.* Captain Bickness, pilot, his radio operator, and nine passengers, approaching Mt. Kilimanjaro, Africa's highest mountain peak. Observed aerial object, estimated 200 feet long, a giant tube with a hind fin. Three bands of rings around object. No windows. Hovered motionless, then shot away at estimated speed of 1,200 mph. No vapor trail. No exhaust. Estimated height: 30,000 feet or higher. Observed for 17 minutes. Movie film of object said to have been taken by Ray Overstreet, radio operator of *U.S.S. Robin Mowbray. Natal Mercury,* published in Durban said film was shown in Durban. Gerald Heard

March 22, 1948. Idyllwild, Ca. About 200 people. Saw huge disc, estimated at 40,000 feet. Disc had rear fin that seemed to whirl.

May 30, 1948. Capt. William Sperry of American Airlines. 7 miles west of Mt. Vernon, Va., while flying DC-6 at 300 mph at 7,500 feet. Was circled twice by "submarine with lights."

Summer, 1948. Clyde Tombaugh, discoverer planet Pluto. Las Cruces, New Mexico. About 11:00 P.M. Tombaugh, wife and mother-in-law sighted solid "ship," oval in shape, traveling at great speed from south to north. Blue-green glow. "Windows" on side. Glared blue-green with touch of yellow.

Last week of July 1948. Alice, Texas. Five citizens. Observed spherical object over town for two days. When planes were sent up to investigate, object disappeared.

July 24, 1948. 20 miles west of Montgomery, Alabama. Early morning. 2:45 .A.M. Eastern Airlines pilots Clarence Shipe Chiles and John B. Whitted. Both wartime pilots, one with 8,500 hours in the air with a log of more than 1,000,000 miles. flying at 5,000 feet, saw strange, torpedo-like object, approximately 100 feet long. No wings. Two rows of "windows" along fuselage, with intense, white light streaming from them. Wavering blue flame along belly of craft. Red orange exhaust flames fifty feet long. Left violent prop-wash.

July 25, 1948. Yakima, Washington. 2:00 P.M. — 4:30 P.M. Seen by hundreds of people. Silvery, "moon-sized" flying "blob" wheeling across sky above city. Had flashing lights, something like an air liner's fog lights.

October 1, 1948. Fargo, North Dakota. George F. Gorman, second lieutenant, North Dakota National Air Guard. Flying fast P-51 fighter. 9:00 P.M. Flew over local stadium to watch a night football game. Had a 27 minute "dogfight" with a brilliant light about eight inches in diameter, which constantly outmaneuvered him, outflew him by 160 mph, finally streaked up to 14,000 feet. Story partially corroborated by other observers.

October 29, 1948. Labrador. Goose Bay Air Force Base. About 3:00 A.M. Unidentified object in slow, level flight. Tracked by radar. Tracked again two nights later. On third night, tracked for 4 minutes. Speed: 600 mph.

November 6, 1948. Japan. Air Force operators tracked two strange objects, acting as if they were in dogfight. No fighter planes in area.

November 23, 1948. Near Furstenfeldbruck, Germany. Pilot flying F-80. Red circling light. Also picked up by radar. Flying at 27,000 feet. Estimated speed: somewhere between 200 and 500 mph. Went up to 40,000 feet.

November 18, 1948. Andrews Field, Washington, D.C. 9:45 P.M. Henry G. Combs, second lieutenant, Air Force reserve. Reported seeing dull, grey globe, six feet thick, twelve to fifteen feet across. Gave off frosty light. Rough edges. No blinking. No exhaust. Combs gave chase. The object, he reported, hit speeds as high as 600 mph. In the back seat of trainer plane was 2nd Lt. Kenwood W. Jackson, whose description of what happened differed from that of Combs.

April 24, 1949. Near Arrey, New Mexico. Five technicians of Office of Naval Research. Officer in charge, J. Gordon Vaeth, aeronautical engineer, Charles B. Moore, aerologist, General Mills, Inc. 10:30 P.M. Moore observed with naked eye, and through theodolite, whitish elliptical object, approximately fifty miles above Earth, 100 feet long, traveling at estimated speed of 7 miles per second. No noise, no vapor trail.

Late May 1949. Morning. White Sands Proving Ground. Commander Robert B. McLoughlin, U.S. Navy rocket expert.

White object, proceeding slowly westward. Suddenly took off at terrific speed. Disappeared over Organ Mountains.

Early June 1949. White Sands Proving Ground, during firing of Navy upper-atmosphere missile. Two small discs appeared from nowhere, joined the missile in flight at 2,000 feet per second, changed sides with each other, then shot ahead of the rocket and sailed upwards and eastwards. Seen independently by five different observers, all at different points of the compass. Commander McLaughlin, *True*, 1950

February 1, 1950. Dusk. Tucson, Arizona. 10,000 citizens of the city. Fiery object shot westward at approximately 30,000 feet. Smoke. Object appeared to slow over city, then speeded up and shot on.

February 22, 1950. Boca Chica Naval Station, Key West, Florida. Two glowing objects at great height. Radar indicated 50 miles up. Traveled at great speed.

February 23, 1950. Antarctica. Night. Commander Augusto Orrego, Chilean Naval officer. Two discs, one above the other, turning in circles at tremendous speed. The Commander took photographs as proof.

February 27, 1950. Reported in *Excelsior*, Mexico City newspaper. Villagers of Paso Hondo, near Guatemala border. Took fright at flight of cone-shaped objects, racing south over village, throwing out yellow-red sparks, trails of white smoke, and sounding like the boiling of a teakettle.

August 27, 1949. Noon. Pilot Francisco Lopez Urrutia, crew and passengers of Aerovias Reforma commercial plane. Over

Mexican state of Sonora. Disc-shaped object, estimated 16 feet in diameter. Appeared made of gleaming metal. Tail of fire 100 feet long.

Fall 1949. At an atomic installation. High-ranking Air Force officer. Daylight. Watching a radarscope. Detected five objects, apparently metal, flying south at great height, tremendous speed. Objects flying formation. Crossed 300 mile scope in less than four minutes.

March 2, 1950. Tonantzitlan, largest astrophysical observatory in Mexico, 80 miles east of Mexico City. Midnight. Strange, luminous object crossed sky. Photographed with Schmidt telescope. Object unidentified.

March 8, 1950. Vandalia Airport, Dayton, Ohio. Three TWA pilots, many other observers. Early in the day. Gleaming object in sky at high altitude. Four fighter planes from Wright Field went up to give chase. The object shot straight up at extremely high speed, hovered for a while miles above the earth, then disappeared.

March 8, 1950. Durango, Mexico. Whole city's population. Watched an unknown object in sky at great height from 11:00 A.M. until 12:00 noon. *True* magazine.

March 9, 1950. Durango, Mexico. Object appeared at noon again. Studied by E. Nuncio, professor of astronomy at Durango technical school. Object maintained 40,000 feet altitude. Shaped like top with red, pointed bottom. Remained motionless for a while, then swiftly moved east, not west, the way planets move. *True* magazine.

March 9, 1950. Mazatlan, Sinaloa, Mexico. 10:00 A.M. to 2:00 P.M. Manuel Maliachi, Mexico naval commander. Observed disc-shaped object through spyglass. Object hovered for hours, then disappeared toward northwest. *True* magazine.

March 10, 1950. Pachuca, Hidalgo, Mexico. 1:00 P.M. Observed by hundreds of Pachucans. White sphere-like object. Rotated on axis. Moved slowly across sky. Disappeared in bank of clouds. *True* magazine.

March 10, 1950. Mazatlan. Object that looked like automobile hub cap in sky. Hovered over Irapuato at 11:45 A.M. *True* magazine.

March 11, 1950. Crew of Compania Transporte cargo plane, flying at 11,000 feet, between Guerrero and Puebla. Reddish disc, about 6 1/2 feet in diameter. Passed 2,000 feet overhead at approximated speed of 400 mph, headed south.

March 11, 1950. Astronomical observatory, Culican, Mexico. Disc-like object watched through telescope. *True* magazine

March 11, 1950. Amateur Mexican astronomer. 9:00 P.M. Object in vicinity of Great Bear constellation. Moved southeast at great speed. *True* magazine

March 11, 1950. Monterrey, Mexico. Afternoon. Hundreds of observers. Object shaped like tennis racquet without handle. Sometimes stationary. Sometimes darted about. *True* magazine

March 11, 1950. Monterrey, Mexico. American Airlines group. Disc-like object in sky observed through theodolite and also by naked eye by forty passengers and crew of plane. *True* magazine

March 14, 1950. Durango, Colo. Two Colorado businessmen. Said that an object — dark, flat, about 5 ft. in diameter, circled their automobile at tremendous speed, traveling in a 25 or 30 ft. radius about car. The "thing" zipped around the car for about 5 minutes.

March 26, 1950. Washington, D.C. Private pilot, Bertram A. Totten. Saw aluminum-colored disc about 40 ft. in diameter, 10 ft. thick. He was flying at 5,000 ft., saw disc whirling along 1,000 ft. below him. Zoomed up, disappeared in overcast.

March 29, 1950. Unidentified flying objects — full moons with wakes of fire, or strange bodies emitting smoke trails, sighted skittering in all directions above the Mediterranean...in northern Israel, over Acre, over Italy. American seaman reported seeing flying fireballs over Hong Kong. (No one else reported seeing these latter.)

May 29, 1950. Night. Pilot, first officer, flight engineer of American Airlines DC-6, over Mt. Vernon, outside Washington, D.C. Saw torpedo-shaped object silhouetted against full moon. Wingless. Lighted at forward end. When approached, darted east at terrific speed.

March 21, 1950. Crew of Chicago and Southern airliner. Night. Near Stuttgart, Arkansas. Circular craft with strange, blue-white light. Pilots said they observed lighted ports. Craft traveled at terrific speed.

April 18, 1950. Captain Carl Gray, piloting Braniff airliner. Large, round shining object, oscillating at estimated height of 15 miles above earth.

March 12, 13, 14, 15, 1950. Mexico City. Meteorologists. Veteran pilots. Hundreds of citizens. Four discs of whitish metal like aluminum. Altitude: approximately 35,000 to 40,000 feet. *True* magazine.

April 27, 1950. 8:25 P.M. Trans World Airlines plane, flight 117, over Goshen, Indiana. Captain Robert F. Adickes, pilot; Captain Robert F. Manning, copilot; hostess Gloria Hinshaw, and passengers. Strange, glowing, reddish light, approximated as fifty feet across. Rolled like cartwheel through sky at times. When pilot attempted to get close to it, took off at high speed, estimated 400 mph. Seen edgewise, it was a disc.

May 22, 1950. (As reported in *Arizona Daily Sun*) Dr. Seymour L. Hess, resident astronomer, Lowell Observatory, Flagstaff, Arizona. 12:15 P.M. Saw bright disc, estimated 6 feet in diameter. Observed it through binoculars.

June 21, 1950. Hamilton Flying Field, Oakland, Cal. 1:35 A.M. Disc-shaped object, roaring at estimated speed of 1,000 to 1,500 miles an hour, made five "passes" near a beacon just north of the air field. Observed by Corporal Roger C. Pryor, a control tower operator; verified by Staff Sergeant Ellis R. Lorimer and Staff Sergeant Virgil Capuro. Object shot out blue flame, roared like thunder.

June 27, 1950. Over Las Vegas, Nevada, near Baker. 8:08 P.M. Three United Airlines pilots flying "Mainliner" plane. Saw torpedo-shaped object, bluish with orange tint at center.

Flying at estimated height of 20,000 feet. Very fast. Gerald Heard (check)

July 2, 1950. Springfield, Ill. Chief pilot of Capital Aviation Co. 11:00 P.M. Blue streak with reddish tail struck propeller of plane. Explosion of light. No sound. No shock. No damage to plane.

July 2, 1950. Torpedo-shaped object. Observed over 400 miles of route, between the states of Washington and Montana. Flying east.

July 30, 1950. Sioux City, Iowa. U.S. Weather Bureau station. Leo Jeske. Disc-shaped, or round object, estimated height 10,000 — 12,000 feet. Hung stationary for a while, then disappeared. National Guardsmen at Sioux City air base reported on the same day that they saw a "white, round something," evidently following an airplane.

August 2, 1950. 1:30 P.M. Pacific Coast, from San Rafael to San Francisco. Moving object. Estimated height: 15,000 feet. Gave off green, red, orange and blue light.

Sept. 20, 1950. Nashville, Tennessee. Explosion in sky. Apparently a meteor, exploding in the air. Jarred an area between Paducah, Ky., and Memphis, Tenn. Brilliant flash of light, burning with orange, blue, yellow flame.

January 20, 1951. Sioux City Airport. 8:30 P.M. Captain Lawrence C. Vinther, co-pilot James F. Bachmeier, Mid-Continent Airlines. Ordered by control tower to investigate bright light over field. Light dived at plane, then flew parallel. Both men reported seeing cigar-shaped craft with glider-type wing. No exhaust glow. No sound. Confirmed by civilian employee.

Feb. 14, 1951. Capt. J.E. Cocker, All-Weather Flying Division, Capt. E.W. Spradley, Aerial Photography Laboratory, Wright Field, Dayton, Ohio. Tracking weather balloon over Alamogordo, New Mexico. Saw strange object in sky. Flat, like a dime. Milky color. Just hovering. Estimated alt.: bet. 50,000 and 60,000 ft. Three brilliant flashes, then object disappeared.

May 22, 1951. Rainy Lake, Minn. 50 residents. Saw “crystal ball” flash across heavens at est. 700 mph. Stopped. Hung motionless over lake. Shot upwards at terrific speed. Joined by second “crystal ball.”

May 22, 1951. Capt. W.R. Hunt, American Airlines pilot. Bluish white “star.” Dashed about his plane at est. 500-1,000 mph., near Dodge City, Kans.

May 29, 1951. Downey, outside Los Angeles. 3:48 P.M. Three technical writers for North American Aviation. Saw 30 glowing, meteor-like objects. Estimated diameter of each: 30 feet. Estimated speed: 1,200 mph. Made right-angled turns at this speed. Moved with skipping motion. Intense blue light from each. No noise. No exhaust. No vapor trail.
Note: These observers were Edward Sullivan, Weiner Eichler, and Victor Black, mentioned elsewhere. Sullivan later started a monthly news sheet on saucers, and also took part in the formation of Civilian Saucer Investigation, Box 971, Los Angeles 53, California.

July 14, 1951. White Sands. Two strange objects. Photographed. Film not clear enough to tell clearly what they were.

August 25, 1951. 9:10 P.M. Lubbock, Texas. Dr. W.I. Robinson, professor of geology at Texas Technological College; Dr. A.G. Oberg, a professor of chemical engineering; Professor W. L. Ducker, head of department of petroleum engineering. Observed string of lights racing across sky. Looked like 30 luminous beads, arranged in crescent shape. Saw similar formation a few moments later. Raced through 30_ of arc in one second. Estimated speed: 18,000 mph. Many different flights observed between August and November of that year.

August 30, 1951. Lubbock, Texas. Night. Carl Hart, Jr. Photographed the "Lubbock Lights." Got five exposures. Photographs published in several periodicals, including *Life* Magazine. (Note:Dr. R.S. Underwood of the Department of Mathematics at Texas Technological College later wrote Robert E. Ginna, Jr., co-author of article in Life that he was able to triangulate Lubbock Lights on a September night in 1951 and concluded that their altitude was 2,100 feet, estimated speed: 750 mph.)

Sept. 9, 1951. Phoenix, Ariz. Lights over city, changing from green to blue to amber. Hovered. Swooped. Great speed.

Sept. 10, 1951. Two pilots. Mitchell Field, L.I. Saw object in sky. Looked like small fighter plane. Flew at estimated 900 mph.

Oct. 2, 1951. Hogansburg, N.Y. Residents of town. Reported dark, brownish ball about 4 ft. in diameter. Landed in field.

Took off with buzzing sound. Sighters of it decided not to get too close.

January 29, 1952. Wonsan, Korea. B-29 on solo mission. Flying less than 200 mph, somewhat above 2,000 feet. Both tail gunner and fire-control man saw luminous object with bluish halo and pulsating effect. Followed plane for about five minutes, then pulled ahead and shot away at high speed. Similar globe seen by tail gunner and waist man of another B-29, over Sunshon, 80 miles away. This globe also followed plane, then disappeared.

February 18, 1952. Albuquerque, New Mexico. Just before sunup. C.E. Redman, photographer. Saw two bright objects in sky over Tijeros Canyon. Bluish white. No sound. No vapor trails. Estimated diameter: 136 feet. Hung motionless, then dropped behind mountain. Looked like two bell peppers in shape.

March 29, 1952. Just before noon. U.S. Air Base, Northern Japan. Lt. David C. Brigham. Saw disc about 8 inches in diameter. Closed to within 20 feet of his Thunderjet plane. Altitude: 6,000 feet. Disc shot up out of sight. Disc looked like chromium. No apparent projections. No exhaust. No vapor trail.

April 10, 1952. Singapore. Hundreds of persons. Strange cigar-shaped object flying at great height, leaving long, fiery trail in its wake.

May 11, 1952. Seattle, Washington. An unidentified missile, possibly a giant meteor, rumbled across the sky and exploded with a force that knocked citizens from their beds. The explosion bathed the city in an eerie, blue-white light, was visible 60 miles away. Fireballs fell straight down from the exploding object like fireworks. No reports of damage. No recovered fragments.

December 29, 1952. Near Denney, Colorado. About 5:00 P.M. Blazing object streaking across sky. Flared brilliantly as if it had exploded. Left faint black object hanging in sky.

July 2, 1952. Steep Rock Lake, Ontario. Saucer landed on Sawmill Bay, an arm of lake. Manned by "little men." Took off at high speed.

July 11, 1952. Herr Linke. Western Germany. He and his 11-year-old daughter saw landed saucer. It was round, with windows or ports, had conning tower ten feet high. There were "men" inside the saucer. They wore metallic suits.

June 19, 1952. Labrador. Goose Bay Air Force Base. Right after midnight. Red light, holding southwest course. Hovered at 4,000 feet, changed from red to white. Vanished from radar scope.

July 13, 1952. Kirksville, Missouri. 9:00 P.M. Air Force radarmen. Unknown object, estimated size of B-36. Tracked at 1,700 mph.

July 14, 1952. 8:12 P.M. 1st Officer William B. Nash, 2nd Officer William H. Fortenberry. Ferrying a Pan-American World Airways DC-4 from New York to Miami, crew of 3, ten passengers. Cruising at 8,000 feet over Chesapeake Bay. Night clear. Visibility unlimited. Saw 6 glowing red discs approaching at tremendous speed. Watched discs flip sideways, perform sharp turns. Discs flew echelon. Estimated diameter of discs: 100 feet. Estimated speed: in excess of 1,000 mph. Made 150 degree change of course almost instantaneously.

July 19 — July 29, 1952. Washington, D.C. Harry G. Barnes, senior air route traffic controller for the Civil Aeronautics Administration, and many other radar observers. Strange pips on radarscopes. Strange lights off the wings of commercial airplanes. The lights, planes, U.F.O., or whatever they were, played over Washington at high speed, making acute turns. Performed gyrations no known aircraft could perform. Caused a nine day sensation in the newspapers and weekly magazines.

July 24, 1952. Two Air Force Colonels, flying at 11,000 ft. near Carson Sink, Nev. 3:40 P.M. Saw three silver objects shaped like arrowheads, sharply-defined outlines, definite ridge on top. Passed at high speed in a continuous bank.

July 29, 1952. Near Fort Huron, Mich. Pilots of two F-94's making practice runs on a B-25. Radar station picked up UFO, asked for investigation. One jet went up to 20,000 feet, pilot spotted UFO visually. Chased it. Both jet and UFO showed up on radar scope. Object kept ahead of jet without effort.

July 29, 1952 (Check Cleveland, Ohio papers). Several Cleveland newspapers printed reports that an Air Force plane had shot down a saucer that had "repeatedly" attacked it.

August 5, 1952. Haneda AFB, Japan. Shortly after midnight. Two airmen. Saw large round, light-bearing object in sky.

Watched it through 7X 50 binoculars. Saw brilliant light around edge of object. Called radar, and radar got a fix. Jet went up, got a radar lock-on, but lost it. Ground radar showed that object broke into three pieces which flew formation for some distance, then disappeared.

August 19, 1952. West Palm Beach, Fla. Night time, in a wooded rural area. D.S. Desvergers, Scoutmaster and former Marine. Saw object "shaped like half a rubber ball," on ground, after he had stopped to investigate lights in woods as he was taking three Boy Scouts home. Desvergers reported that he flashed his flashlight on object and was overcome by a blast of fire. Hair was said to have been singed off Mr. Desverger's arms, three tiny holes burned in his cap. (His personal account of this encounter appeared later in American Weekly Magazine.)
His whole story was discredited by Captain Ruppelt, former head of Project Blue Book, writing as a civilian in TRUE magazine.

August 20, 1952. Congaree-Air Base near Columbia, South Carolina. "Blip" on radarscope. Estimated distance: 60 miles southeast. Estimated speed: 4,000 mph.

August 31, 1952. Herbert Long, Kutztown, Pa. Reported seeing landed saucer.

September 1952. How to see flying saucers. K. Sivezy. il diags Pop Sci 161: 167-170 S '52. Kenneth M. Sivezy demonstrates Dr. Donald F. Menzel's theories with diagrams. This is a duplicate of the Lubbock Lights, mentioned elsewhere, made with milk bottles, flashlight, etc., with an explanation that such light could be caused by lenses, fluctuations in air density, etc.

September 2, 1952. A Signor Manguzzi and his wife. Saw saucer land on glacier inn Bernese Alps at altitude of 10,000 feet. Saw "man" emerge. Signor Manguzzi took photograph of craft and occupant.

Sept. 1, 1952 (or thereabouts). (Reported in TIME, Sept. 8, 1952.) Bill Squier, radio performer. Reported in Wichita, Kansas, Beacon. In nearby Pittsburgh, Kansas, saw machine about 75 feet in diameter, hovering 10 feet above ground. Machine looked like two large platters cupped together and ringed with small propellers. Squier's story said that he got out of car, walked to within 100 feet of saucer, saw bluish light through portholes, saw figures in saucer that looked like "human beings." As he walked toward it, the machine rose straight upward at great speed and disappeared. Several of Squier's colleagues at the radio station where he works went to the spot and found grass and weeds flattened in a rough oval area as if a heavy wind or weight had crushed them. (Note: reported in TIME that the Associated Press state wire refused to put the story on the wire.)

September 12, 1952. Flatwoods, West Virginia. 7:00 P.M. Mrs. Kathleen May, Eddie May, Fred May, Ronnie Shaver, Tommy Hyer, Neil Nunley, and Gene Lemon. The children of Mrs. May told her they had seen a flying saucer land. She and the children walked up a hill to investigate. Reported seeing a globe-like ball of fire, a luminous, giant "monster" of man-like appearance. They also reporting being practically overcome by nauseating stench. All were terrified and fled. Widely reported in newspaper. See FATE, Jan. 1953). (Captain E. J. Ruppelt, after becoming a civilian, writing in TRUE Magazine, casts considerable doubt on the authenticity of this sighting. He asked for a call from municipal authorities at the site if they found anything to support the claim. Mr. Ruppelt reports that there were no calls.)

Oct. 9, 1952. Roy Messmore, U.S. Civil Aeronautics Administration official. Hulman Municipal Airport, Terre Haute, Ind. Saw huge metallic sphere speeding over field.

October 17, 1952. Orange, Texas. 3:30 A.M. Captain E.G. Sparks, Orange Police Department. Ball of fire, trailing smoke, going around in circles at incredible speed in sky. At 4:10 A.M. exploded with brilliant flash seen from Texas to Tennessee. At 9:48, there was a second explosion that shook the ground with the force of an earthquake.

October 27, 1952. French customs official. Marignac airdrome. Saw torpedo-shaped craft land and take off. (See notes on French aircraft elsewhere in this book)

November 25, 1952. Canal Zone. Radar sighting. Two unidentified objects observed for five hours, at altitudes of from 1,000 to 28,000 feet. Estimated speed: 250 mph. *Fate*, January 1953

November 28, 1952. Bluesky, Alberta, Canada. Fred Clarke, wife and granddaughter. Strange object, shaped like boat, with circular-shaped discs on arm protruding from fuselage. No wings. Object hung motionless, then moved away at high speed. No sound. (Reported in Edmonton Journal from Fairview Weekly Post.)

November 29, 1952. Korea. Night. Major Mack W. Dollahan, St. Petersburg, Florida. Ball of fire with ten foot tail of flame. Crossed in front of bomber. Blew up and disappeared.

November 30, 1952. Italian farmer named Ferrari. Saw disc, near at hand, over his head. Disc opened like clamshell. Ferrari saw and heard humanoid types in craft.

December 14, 1952. Charlottesville, Virginia. 11:45 A.M. Roy Franke, manager of University of Virginia Airport at Milton, his wife, and a student pilot, Harry Pond, Jr. Saw disc with orange glow hovering. Discharged a number of leaf-like objects. Whole group hung motionless for a while, then moved off at tremendous speed.

January 6, 1953. Dallas, Texas. M. F. Fetchenback, traffic controller, Love Field; Linwood Martin, Dallas. Saw swept-back winged object, red-glowing front, blue wings, white center. Observed through binoculars and telescope. Estimated speed: 600 MPH.

January 26, 1953. Radar site, New Mexico. Air Force people. Saw bright, reddish-white object. Watched it for 45 minutes visually and by radar. It was nine miles away, traveling very slowly — and traveling against the wind.

January 28, 1953. 9:35 P.M. Jet pilot near Albany, Ga. Saw brilliant white light. Light then changed constantly from white to orange and back to white again. Changed shape from circular to triangular, split into two triangles, one above the other....disappeared. Both object and jet picked up on ground radar. Object kept lead on jet.

June 18, 1953. Three people in Houston, Texas, reported seeing bat-like man land in tree.

June 25, 1953. Brush Creek, California. Two miners, John Q. Black and John Van Allen. Mr. Black reported that flying saucer had landed twice near the gold mine they operate in remote Marble Creek area, once on May 20, once on June 20. Each time, a little broad-shouldered "man" got out, scooped a bucket of water from a creek, and handed it inside saucer to companion. Saucer used 3-legged landing gear that retracted when they took off. Gear left marks on sand the size of elephant tracks. (Check this story against New York Herald Tribune's article of June 28, 1953, describing landing gear of Canada's planned flying saucer. Note resemblance.) As a sequel to this report, a vast array of observers, armed with still and movie cameras, gathered at Brush Creek on July 20, 1953, to record the expected third appearance of the "little men" and their saucer. No saucer, no little men appeared.

October 16, 1954. Ex-French customs inspector, Damien Sigueres. Saw saucer land, "man in diving suit" steps out, re-enters craft, take off.

Fall, 1954. France. At least seven landings of strange craft and "Little Men" reported by Frenchmen. See LIFE Magazine, Nov. 1, 1954.

Fall, 1954. Italy. Many sightings. Many reports of landed craft, "Little Men," metallic costumes, uniforms or pressure suits.

Fall, 1954. In woods near Tuscan village of Bucine. Two dwarfs popped out of a spindle-shaped craft, robbed a Signora Dainelli of one silk stocking, one bunch of carnations.

CHAPTER 8
WHAT HAS BEEN SAID ABOUT FLYING SAUCERS

It is extremely interesting — and perhaps enlightening — to go back and trace the record on what has been said about flying saucers. Who said what — and when? Who came out first with the extraterrestrial theory? What publications later came to this conclusion? What publications scoffed heartily at the whole thing?

It is not too difficult to trace this record. It is all in print. It is available to anyone who has the time, the patience and the facilities to trace the record back to the very beginning. It is a long, long trail, and it takes persistence. And it takes the facilities of a New York City, with its great central public library, its back issues of magazines, its old files of newspapers. It calls for source materials not available to everyone everywhere. But it is available. And it is in the public record.

In tracing this record, various sources are available. The newspapers, that have published first-hand reports from individuals who have claimed to have seen "saucers." The magazines, that have either reported, or made editorial analysis and comment. Books, that have been written by various authors on the subject of saucers. Photographs that have been published in periodicals and books. Statements, by spokesmen of the Air Force and other military and governmental bodies. Statements by scientists. Statements by foreign writers and spokesmen for foreign governments. Radio and television broadcasts. Aviation industry trade magazines.

As far as newspaper reports go, this writer has collected them for thirteen years. This collection is by no means complete. Many reports of saucer sightings have been published locally by newspapers all over the country, but never given national mention. My sources are limited principally to the publications I read regularly — the New York metropolitan newspapers.

With regard to magazines, the easiest way to check the record on what has appeared in this country is to refer to the *Readers' Guide to Periodical Literature*, which is to be found in any public library.

This monthly guide lists articles and stories that have appeared in practically every major publication in the United States. It does not list "pulps." It does not list some important publications in which articles on "flying saucers" have appeared. But it does give the most comprehensive check list of articles on "saucers" that have been published.

Even here, on the subject of saucers, there is reason for some bafflement and amusement. No article on flying saucers was listed by Readers' Guide until May 1949. At that time, the subject was listed under: *Illusions and Hallucinations.*

Sometime between January 1951 and March 1951, however, the Guide changed its listing to plain *Flying Saucers.*

The *Encyclopedia Britannica*, font of information, at latest check does not mention flying saucers at all.

In this book, you will find a complete listing of all mention of flying saucers made by *Readers' Guide*, from its May 1949, issue until the publication date of this book. The record given is chronological, with each article listed in the order in which it appeared, together with a brief digest of the article. The author has read every one of the articles listed, in many cases not just once, but several times. He has attempted to give you here a factual, truthful, unbiased summary of each.

There are several publications, important in the reporting of saucer material, not listed in *Readers' Guide*.

Three of these are TRUE, LOOK, and FATE.

Neither TRUE nor FATE is listed in the Guide. LOOK now is, but it was not listed until May 1953.

LOOK is a weekly news-picture magazine that practically everybody knows. It needs no introduction.

TRUE, *the Magazine for Men*, is a well-known monthly magazine published by Fawcett Publications, Inc. It specializes in stories and articles that are completely factual, non-fiction. Its appeal is basically to men. TRUE's first article on flying saucers, authored by Major Donald E. Keyhoe, USMC (ret.), appeared in the January, 1950, issue of this publication. Titled *The Flying Saucers are Real*, It was billed as the most important story ever to appear in the magazine. The article advanced the theory that saucers are from outer space.

FATE is a monthly publication published by Clark Publishing Company, Evanston, Illinois. FATE's editor is Robert N. Webster. Clark Publishing Company was originally owned by Raymond Palmer. It was originally published quarterly. A recent statement of ownership of FATE, appearing in the January, 1955 issue of the magazine, on the newsstands early in December, 1954, stated that the publication is owned by Mary Margaret Fuller, Curtis Fuller, Raymond A. Palmer and Marjorie Palmer.

FATE made its initial appearance in the spring of 1948. It stated itself as dedicated to "True stories of the strange, the unusual, the unknown." It has since changed that to read: "True stories of the strange and unknown."

By its very nature, FATE must report mysteries, seek mysteries. In its issues since first publication date, it has dealt with the inexplicable. Poltergeists. Ghosts. Haunted places like famous Borley Rectory. Talking mongooses. Even odder subjects, subjects that most academic scientists wouldn't touch with a ten-foot pole.

In its pages, you will find, intermixed, articles on bleeding saints, black magic of India, the vision of the Virgin of Guadaloupe, "Lady Wonder," the famous typewriting "psychic" horse, apparitions, fairy crosses, phantom lights, mysterious ship and aircraft disappearances, and the true mystic experiences of readers.

In its pages, you will also find advertisements for esoteric and occult books, Tarot cards, crystal balls, lucky charms, books on ancient wisdom, advertisements for astrologers, courses of the Rosicrucians, the Brotherhood of the White Temple, Inc., and various other similar organizations — with advertisements that most magazines would not touch with a ten-foot pole.

Increasingly, through the years, FATE has become more filled with the writings of spiritualists, with many a Rev. tacked before a name, although the magazine published excerpts from the *Power of Positive Thinking*, by the eminently respected Dr. Norman Vincent Peale, minister of Marble Collegiate Church in New York City.

Increasingly, FATE has carried the advertisements of Venture Bookshop, Evanston, Illinois, offering everything from crystal balls to beads containing water from the fountain of Lourdes.

FATE has a sister publication, *Other Worlds*, an out an out science fiction magazine published by Clark Publishing Company. This latter makes no pretense of being other than what it is — a straight science fiction publication.

When you look for FATE on a newsstand, you will generally find it on that part of the stand devoted to science fiction publications.

It is interesting to note that it was FATE, in its initial Spring 1948 issue, that published the article of Kenneth Arnold, the man whose sightings triggered the whole saucer mystery, on what he saw on June 24, 1947.

It is also interesting to note that it was FATE, in its initial issue, that first advanced the theory that the saucers might be interplanetary. This theory was advanced in an article by "John C. Ross." John C. Ross was a pen name of Curtis Fuller, then editor of aviation magazine *Flying*, who later went to work for FATE, and who, as we have seen, is listed as one of the owners of FATE.

It is also interesting to note that Kenneth Arnold, whose report to the newspapers on June 24, 1947, started the whole saucer mystery, again pursued the theory that saucers are from outer space in the second issue of this magazine, and, in the third issue of the publication, contributed an article on phantom lights seen in Nevada.

In the beginning, it was the attitude of FATE that the U.S. armed services, particularly the U.S. Air Force, was doing a "cover-up job," on news about flying saucers — not to suppress news of secret weapons, either of this country nor some other, but to keep the BIG NEWS, news of visitors from other worlds, from a possibly panicky public.

FATE's great stock in trade, over a period of many years, in its pages, and often illustrated on its front covers, has been "flying saucers."

The theory of craft and visitors from outer space, which FATE advanced in the very beginning, was later arrived at through their own investigative facilities by TRUE and then LIFE, and was left open for such a possibility by LOOK, despite its article explaining saucers as natural phenomena by Dr. Donald E. Menzel, professor of astronomy and mathematics at Harvard University, and director of Harvard Observatory.

Month after month, in the face of official denial of the existence of saucers, FATE kept the pot boiling, reporting on sightings, expressing complete skepticism with regard to landings, bits of saucers or whole saucers being found, "little men" emerging from sauces, and other such lurid details.

From the beginning, FATE has insisted that no one knows what saucers are and FATE editor Robert N. Webster has, in appearance, practically leaned over backward in trying to do an honest, factual, straightforward reporting job.

Raymond Palmer, however, in some of his writings in the magazine, of which is an owner, and in his book that he wrote with Kenneth Arnold, is, however, a bit less temperate.

In the listing of publications not listed in the *Readers' Guide*, in order to avoid confusion, and to place all articles by all magazines in proper context and perspective, the digests of articles of FATE, LOOK and TRUE have been collated, in chronological order, with articles of other magazines. So have been books on saucers, in proper chronological order.

There are other sources of information on saucers which are more difficult to trace than newspapers, magazines, and books. Two of these are radio and television. A great deal of mention about saucers has been made in both of these mediums, but since it is impossible to monitor all radio and television programs, no attempt has been made here to trace what must have been voluminous mention on the air, except for one or two instances where such broadcasts were personally seen or heard.

Nor has there been any attempt to check the European press, magazines, radio or television, with the exception of saucer articles carried by French and Italian magazines in the fall of 1954, described elsewhere in this book, and a couple of books by foreign authors.

Such reporting would take, not just the efforts of one person, but of a whole battery of research workers and writers.

It can be assumed that such unreviewed flying saucer mention, no matter where made, parallels what has been said and re-said in other publications listed in this book.

As you read this chapter on what people have said about saucers, you are going to find the names of many people that come bobbing up regularly in the picture: The name of "Professor" George Adamski, leading exponent of the space-ship theory, an amateur astronomer who claims to have photographed such ships near the moon, as long ago as 1929, and who says that he talked to a man who arrived in such a ship from Venus in 1952. You'll find the name of Frank Scully, humorist and *Variety* columnist, who wrote a book on flying saucers in 1950 that told about saucer crashes in the American desert, and the emergence from those saucers of "little men."

You'll find the name of Major Donald E. Keyhoe, USMC (ret.), who has written numerous articles and two books on saucers, claiming that the craft are extraterrestrial, and that the U.S. Air Force is keeping the truth of this from the people. You'll find the name of [MISSING PAGE OR WORDS HERE] and occult subjects, and on strange happenings on the earth; the name of Gerald Heard, known chiefly for his writing of weird stories and scientific fiction; the name of Ray Palmer of FATE; the name of Sidney Shallet, who wrote an "expose" of saucers for *The Saturday Evening Post*; the names of H.B. Darrach and R. Ginna, who wrote the article in LIFE that concluded that saucers are from outer space.

You'll find the names of various Air Force spokesmen and other governmental authorities; the names of scientists; the names of aircraft manufacturers.

For here is the record, the wild, wooly, wacky, wonderful record of the flying saucer furor. Nothing has been invented. Nothing twisted. Here is what happened, when it happened, who said what — and when.

Here is entertainment, if you want it. Fantasy fiction, if you want it. Fantastic science, if you want it. And conceivably, chicanery, gobbledegooking, double-talking and muddle-headedness, as well as honesty, sincerity and forthrightness.

As a record of human dopiness, whether on the part of believers, or non-believers, it is superb. As an example of human gullibility, or human pig-headedness in the face of facts, or even as a magnificent cover-up, it has no equal.

Here it is, the fantastic chronicle of one of the most amazing — perhaps the most amazing event ever to take place in human history.

You may not find the answers here. Only time will give the answers. And it may take a long, long time for the real answers to be given to a waiting world. Especially if the saucers are piloted by a race, or races, from other worlds.

Until all the answers are given to us — if ever — I am trying to save you a great deal of research, a great deal of legwork, a great deal of poring over old records, going through all the laborious — and perhaps senseless — effort of putting the record together.

And perhaps it is senseless.

Captain E.J. Ruppelt, once head of Project Bluebook, official USAF investigating body for flying saucers, has written that once he found himself thoughtfully studying a piece of a "mysterious substance" that had fallen from the sky into a farmer's pond. Scientific evaluation revealed it to be a piece of cow manure.

Unless this author is sadly mistaken, he is very, very much afraid that, in reading the record of what has been said and written about flying saucers, you are going to find yourself staring in bewilderment at pretty much this same substance in many places in this book.

But here is the record — or one small segment of it—that has been given to the public — from the very beginning. I hope you have fun reading it. I had fun collecting it.

Flying saucers before their eyes. Newsweek 30:19, J1 14, 1947. A first report on sightings and speculations as to what "saucers" might be.

Flying saucers; the somethings. il Time 50:18 J1 14, 1947 A rather skeptical report on some of the sightings. "All over the U.S.A. last week, people turned curious or uneasy eyes toward the skies.

The sky is haunted. Wesley Price. Sat Eve Post Mr 6 48. This short article in the Post tells of "Gizmos," pips of light seen on radar screen that indicate solid bodies there. Mr. Price stated that these pips of light — with no apparent mass — had been spotted for almost a year. He mentioned Kenneth Ehlers, employed at the Landing Aids Experiment Station near Arcata, Cal., as the best-informed person on the subject. "Gizmos" were reported as flying in any kind of weather, flying with the wind, across the wind, against the wind. Experts had explained them as ionized masses or air inversions, although there could be concentrated, group flying of massed ions, mystified Mr. Price. He wrote that the pips had the sharply defined outline that an airplane might make — but that there were no aircraft there. (NOTE: You will read later of the appearance of such "pips" over Washington, D.C., in July 1952, where they caused a national furor. As you will see, they were explained as ionized masses or air inversions in the Post in 1948, four years before USAF officials explained them in the same terms.)

FATE. Volume 1, No. 1., Spring, 1948. This first issue of FATE carried Kenneth Arnold's story in his own words. He told what he saw on Tuesday, June 24, 1947. A quite lengthy and factual article.

FATE. Volume 1, No. 1. Article by science writer John C. Ross. This was a pen name used by Curtis Fuller, then editor of the magazine, *Flying*. In this article, Ross — or Fuller — stated that he was very familiar with a great many U.S. experimental, and even top secret aircraft, and that none ever approximated what Kenneth Arnold reported seeing. He mentioned the Chance-Vought V-173, the Northrup Flying Wings, the German Jaeger P-13, long before these experimental craft were mentioned by *U.S. News and World Report* in the article, Flying Saucers, The Real Story, 28:13-15, April 7, 1950, with the statement that these craft were prototypes of flying saucers. Almost two years before this date, Curtis Fuller, in FATE, gave as his reasoned belief that these experimental craft, none of which was ever known to have been flown successfully, could not have been in any way connected with what Kenneth Arnold reported seeing. It was also Mr. Fuller's opinion that, if Kenneth Arnold saw what he thought he saw, he was seeing something not of this earth at all, but probably from another planet. Thus, it was Curtis Fuller, not a science fiction writer but the writer and editor of an aviation publication, who first advanced in print the belief that the saucers were from another place than the earth. (This statement has an exception or two. Charles Fort and "Professor" George Adamski, among others, had long since claimed that the earth had been visited by outsiders. Mention of these men and others is made elsewhere in this book. But for all practical purposes, Curtis Fuller seems to have been the writer who connected the 1947 saucer sightings with visitors from outer space.)

FATE. Volume 1, No. 1. Another article, the Mystery of the Flying Discs, a round-up of the sightings reported from various places. In this article was also a report by Kenneth Arnold of an investigation he had made, in collaboration with Air Force Intelligence Officers, of the controversial sighting at Maury Island, Washington. In this article, Mr. Arnold tells of interviewing Harold A. Dahl and Fred L. Chrisman, members of the Tacoma Harbor Patrol, who reported the story (given elsewhere in this book) of a saucer out of a group that jettisoned hot slag, damaging their boat and killing a pet dog. Mr. Arnold was instrumental in getting the Air Force to investigate this story that had a tragic aftermath. The plane of the Air Force

MISSING PAGE 103

FATE. Sept. 1940. My Encounter with Flying Discs. Article by John H. Janssen, aviation editor of the *Morristown Daily Record*, Morristown, New Jersey, as reported in that paper on July 10, 1947. Photographs of discs, taken by Mr. Janssen. Mr. Janssen states in this article that was "held up" by a disc which stopped the engine of the airline he was flying over New Jersey and held the plane suspended motionless for a while.

FATE. Sept. 1949. *Tribal Memories of Flying Saucers.* Article by Oge-Make, a Navajo Indian. He tells the Paiute legend of the flying saucer. According to this legend, the saucers are flown by a "lost race" of higher intellect than contemporary man, called Hav-Musuvs, who live in great caverns in the Panamint Mountains. The guardian priests of this race wear white robes and carry long tubes (ray guns) with which they can inflict paralysis or death at a distance. According to an old Paiute medicine man, a Paiute warrior, ages ago, in seeking death, invaded the Hav-Musuvs' mountain vastnesses, only to have the lost race invite him to live with them, rather than giving him the death he sought.

FATE. Nov. 1949. What the Air Force Believes About Flying Saucers. FATE's own digest of the official report of studies made by "Project Saucer" at its headquarters at Wright Field, Dayton, Ohio. Most of this is a direct quote from the "Project Saucer" report. It is an excellent summary and analysis of Air Force findings up to the FATE publication date in the fall of 1949.

FATE. Winter 1949. The Mystery Ship. Article by L. Taylor Hansen. Asks if "flying submarine" pilots Witted and Chiles saw over Alabama could have been from Mars. Ties in with the writing of astronomer Percival Lowell's observations of that planet years ago. A speculative, rather than an informative article.

What you can believe about flying saucers. S. Shalett, il Sat Eve Post 221:20-1 Ap 30; 36 My 7 '49. This is a very carefully researched, very carefully written series of two articles by Sidney Shalett. It is excellently done. It is painstakingly written summary of saucer sightings up to publication date in

1949. Mr. Shalett was given Air Force cooperation. Conclusion: flying saucers are weather balloons, normal aerial and optical phenomena. (NOTE: True Magazine and Donald E. Keyhoe stated that it was rumored that Forrestal, then Chief of Staff of the Air Force, requested the Saturday Evening Post to publish the article.) This same accusation is made by Ray Palmer in the Arnold-Palmer book, "*The coming of the Saucers.*"

Things that go whiz; flying saucers. Time 53:98 May 9, '49. Scoffing report on the whole idea that saucers could exit.

FATE. May 1949. Short squib about mysterious "Sky Octopus," a sphere with many rays or arms, seen over Katrineholm, Sweden earlier in year.

January 1950, TRUE. The Flying Saucers Are Real by Donald E. Keyhoe. Donald Keyhoe was hired by Ken Purdy, Editor of TRUE to investigate flying saucers. It was the conclusion of Mr. Keyhoe and TRUE that the flying saucers are real — and that they are from outer space.

Visitors from Venus; flying saucer yarn. Time 53:49 Jan 9, '50. This is another article ridiculing the idea that saucers could be extra-terrestrial. It also stated flatly that the Air Force had announced the abandonment of the "Project Saucer" Group the week before (Jan. 1, 1950), with "Project Saucer's" files to be put on public exhibition at the Pentagon in Washington.

FATE. January 1950. A red-hot letter from Fred L. Chrisman, one of the men who reported the Maury Island sighting. Chrisman was very bitter at FATE for saying that he and

Harold Dahl had "confessed" to the Air Force that their story had been a hoax. He pointed out that he was an active reservist in the U.S. Air Force and that the Air Force had never criticized him for a "hoax" that had resulted in the deaths of two Air Force Intelligence officers. He further stated that the "saucer fragments" from the crashed plane had never been found, that Hal Dahl was flown to Alaska on an Army plane and later disappeared, and that the Air Force had never permitted the crashed plane to be photographed. Mr. Chrisman's letter to FATE seems to be that of a man who had been left holding the bag, and his defense of himself is worth reading. (Incidentally, he did not seem to know that the report that he and Mr. Dahl had "confessed" to a hoax came from the official "Project Saucer" report which FATE had reprinted verbatim.)

TRUE, March 1950. Navy Officer Tells How Scientists Tracked a Flying Saucer. Commander Robert B. McLaughlin, USN. Commander McLaughlin, a rocket expert at White Sands Proving Ground, reports on the White Sands sighting of an elliptical object, approximately 105 feet in diameter, flying approximately 56 miles above the earth at a speed of approximately 5 miles per second. Also mentions other sightings. Commander McLaughlin gave as his opinion in this article that saucers are piloted, extraterrestrial space ships.

TRUE, March 1950. Los Plativolos. Report to the Editor. A report of Mexican sightings of 1949, by correspondent Lowell Harmer.)

Flying saucer mystery. Science N L 57: 188 Mr 25 '50. Saucers are either: the planet Venus; ballrooms, meteors, or radio-controlled jet or rocket aircraft; or a mild form of mass hallucination; or the Air Force is testing a disc of some kind. The idea that saucers might be from Mars is pure wishful thinking.

TRUE. April 1950. Aviation Editor John duBarry's story of the sighting of a strange object over the Carolinas on Wednesday, December 28, 1949. Seen by hundreds of people in North and South Carolina. Object evidently at great distance, at great height, of great size. Reported extensively in local papers on next day, particularly in Charlotte, N.C.

Pies in the sky in Mexico City. il Time 55:36 Ap 3 '50. Scoffing report on Mexican sightings of the latter part of March 1950.

Flying saucers, the real story. il U.S. News, 28:13-15 Apr 7 '50. This is editor Henry J. Taylor's famous article in which he stated that flying saucers were secret U.S. weapons, and that he had positive proof to back up this statement. He also stated that the saucers were of three types, disc-shaped, torpedo-shaped and sphere-shaped, and that all sightings, including the Kenneth Arnold and Chiles-Whitted sightings were of these new secret craft. (This article resulted in categorical denial by the Army, the Navy, the Air Force, and even by the spokesman for the President of the United States. All governmental sources said, following the appearance of this article and the radio broadcast which Mr. Taylor made, that the U.S. had no such craft, even in the experimental stages.)

Saucer-eyed dragons. il Time 55:52-4 Ap 17 '50. This is an article ridiculing the story of Commander Robert . McLaughlin about sightings at White Sands Providing Ground. States that Commander McLaughlin was disciplined for the story. Also has a few barbed thrusts at U.S. News and other publications which have reported sightings.

Flying saucers again. il Newsweek 35:29, Ap 17 '50. Reports on old and new sightings. The broadcast of H.J. Taylor and subsequent denial by all governmental sources.

FATE. May 1950. Space Ships, Flying Saucers and Clean Noses. By Ray Palmer. In this 17-page article, Ray Palmer bitterly takes the U.S. Air Force to task for its "cover-up" on the flying saucers — not because the saucers are secret weapons, but because they may be extraterrestrial craft. Mr. Palmer, in his own words, is "hitting back" against what he believed to be a smear campaign against him.

He takes first of all, a recent (Spring 1950) newspaper story quoting Army Intelligence, a story ridiculing reports of "Little Men," and then he proceeds to jump all over it. A quote from the Intelligence report:

"A Popular magazine now publishes a report by two Death Valley prospectors, of a 24-foot disc landing in the desert at a speed of 300 miles an hour.

"The prospectors, Buck Fitzgerald and Maze Garney, asserted they chased two 24-inch gents over a sand dune before losing them.

"Army Intelligence refused to swallow that one. Magazines such as this," it said, "seldom have any evidence to support their fantasies."

Mr. Palmer then angrily pointed out that it wasn't FATE's report, but one that had been published by International News Service.

Mr. Palmer then goes on, remarking on certain reports of landings in Wisconsin, and the report of one farmer who said that "out of one disc came a bunch of little men. They were dressed in gray uniforms with red shoulder bars and wore red caps."

The Army Intelligence report had said: "Investigation revealed that the Wisconsin farmer had been discharged from the Army for mental reasons." The probe was dropped right there.

Mr. Palmer said that he personally investigated reports of sighting around the Waupaca area, Stevens Point, and Wisconsin Rapids. He also stated that dozens of reports were made. Reporters said that discs sighted were tiny and brilliant. At least one person was injured by one. All discs either exploded violently, or exploded low over the ground. Fragments picked up looked like plaster of paris. "What these objects were, FATE has no theory to explain."

The article then goes onto mention at least 15 sightings of early 1950, sightings of spectacular somethings that could not be explained in terms of ordinary phenomena.

The article concludes with a summary of 21 points with regard to flying saucers, in which the final point was: "We don't know *what* flying saucers are."

It is Mr. Palmer's thesis in this article that, if space travelers are visiting us, if some sensational new power source has been discovered, it will be used by the military for war, not given to the world for peacetime advancements.

FATE. September 1950. Flying Saucers as Astronomers See Them. An article by George Adamski. Mr. Adamski in 1950 ran a restaurant on the road leading up to Mt. Palomar observatory. He is an amateur astronomer. He claims that he has photographed "space ships" near the moon for years. He also claims to have talked to a man from a landed flying saucer. This article in FATE advances some of his views. For more of them, read the book, *Flying Saucers Have Landed* on which Mr. Adamski collaborated with Desmond Leslie.

Flying disc aircraft. il diag. Pop Mech 93:114-5, My '50. This is an article about Dr. E.W. Kay of Glendale, California, and the testing of a disc of his own design. The disc was fastened by an arm to a pole, so it would operate.

BOOK. The Flying Saucers Are Real. Donald E. Keyhoe, Fawcett Publications, Inc., May 1950. This book was an expansion of Mr. Keyhoe's article in TRUE, articles which he was commissioned to write by the magazine.

This book is one of the best that has been done on the extraterrestrial theory. Its material was carefully researched. The book itself carefully written. It was written only after many conversations with eyewitnesses of saucer sightings, talks with Air Force officials, pilots, scientists and “Project Saucer” personnel.

It is a fascinating book. It reviews many 19th Century sightings, many modern sightings. It caused a furor when it hit the newsstands in a 25¢ Gold Medal edition with an initial printing of 500,000. One Congressman demanded its recall on the basis that it might cause public confusion. Some of the fastest sales on record were said to have been made at the Pentagon, where, it is reported, 1,200 copies went like hotcakes.

A new printing was ordered by the publisher the week of publication.

This is the book that convinced thousands of people that flying saucers are piloted by visitors from outer space — and that the truth of this is being kept from the American people by over-zealous censorship by the Air Force. Among others who have quoted Major Keyhoe for their belief that flying saucers are extra-terrestrial: Air Chief Marshall Lord Dowding, Commander in Chief of the British Royal Air Force.

Aeronautics: Flying saucer is good news. H.J. Taylor. il Readers Digest 57:14-16 J1 '50. This is a condensation from the radio broadcast of Henry J. Taylor, editor of U.S. News & World Report.

LOOK. July 18, 1950. Flying saucers, myth or menace. An article by Bruce Bliven. It reviews various sightings. It speaks of Navy "Skyhook" balloons as the big reason for saucer sightings. Speaks of the fact that Columbia Broadcasting company succeeded in locating Mr. Charles A. Zimmerman, builder of an apocryphal "flying saucer" which some guessers believed to be prototype of present saucers, and which Mr. Zimmerman himself said had never flown. The article reports the ostensible closing down of "Project Saucer" as of Jan. 1950 with the closing remark that "Scientific probability runs heavily against saucers."

Aeronautics: Flying saucer . H.J. Taylor. il Readers Digest 57:14-16 J1 '50. This is another resume of the H.J. Taylor broadcast and article.

Flying saucer, fact or fiction? C. Fuller. il Flying 47:16-17 J1 '50. This is Curtis Fuller who also wrote for FATE. It is rather complete report on the sightings by Arnold, Smith, Chiles, Adams, and Adickes with their own drawings of what they saw. High worthwhile reading. "But what the strange phenomena are, the editors of Flying do not pretend to know. We can only say what they are not. They are not anything the glib radio commentators and the sensational magazines say they are. They are a mystery and a contradiction, and we know little more about what they are than when we started our investigation."

TRUE. August 1950. Flight 117 and the Flying Saucer. Donald E. Keyhoe. This is a complete, detailed report of the sighing of a red globe on April 27, 1950, by Adickes and Manning, of Trans World Airlines...one of the "classic" sightings.

Flying, Sept. 1950, p. 64. Letters from readers of the July article. A report from Dr. L.J. Alger, M.D., that he had seen a saucer over Acapulco, Mexico. Also a report from Capt. W. T. Sperry, American Airlines, of his sighting of an unknown aerial object on May 29, 1950.

BOOK. Behind The Flying Saucers. Frank Scully. Henry Holt & Co., September 1950. This was the second book on saucers to be given to an eagerly-waiting public. Its author, Frank Scully, a *Variety* reporter and author of the books *Fun In Bed, More Fun In Bed*, and *Just What The Doctor Ordered.*

This book was published as a factual account of what lay behind the mystery of the flying saucers. It stated that the saucers were from Venus, that a number had crashed in the Southwestern desert country, and that little men in blue suits — dead — had been taken from them, and that other little men in blue suits — alive — had been seen escaping in the desert. The book stated that the saucers used magnetic and gravitational forces for flight.

The book was angrily reviewed by *The Saturday Reviews of Literature*, in the September 23, 1950, issue, and denounced as a hoax. Not only that critical publication, but many others, followed suit.

Two years later, in 1952, TRUE Magazine commissioned J.P. Cahn, a reporter in *The San Francisco Chronicle*, to investigate the story from top to bottom, and to sift the facts. In the September 1952 issue of TRUE, you'll find Mr. Cahn's article in which he presented evidence to show that the whole book was a hoax.

More flying saucers. Review of Behind The Flying Saucers by F. Scully. Science N L 58:181 S 16 '50. An unflattering preview of the Frank Scully book. It notes that Scully's previous books were *Fun In Bed*, *More Fun In Bed*, and *Just What The Doctor Ordered*. S.N.L. says: "Matter traveling at the speed of light would have a mass that is infinite. Using the kind of thinking that is in the book, Dr. Gee's flying saucers traveling on their way to Earth from Venue, at greater than the speed of light, ought to be bigger than all the universes put together, bigger than infinity."

In a flying saucer from Venus. Review of Behind The Flying Saucers by F.I. Scully; R. Gelatt, il Sat. R. Lit. 33;25 0 21 '50. Roland Gelatt rips into Scully's book. States that he did some checking on Scully's story. Calls whole thing a colossal hoax. Winds up review with: "To the first little man from another planet who walks into this office, with or without Frank Scully, SRL (*Saturday Review of Literature*) will present $100,000."

Those little men from Venus. Reply to R. Gelatt. C. Carson, Sat. R. Lit. 33:25 0 21 '50. This is a letter from a reader, Charles Carson, of Los Angeles, Cal., agreeing with Gelatt that the Scully book is pure yarn.

FATE. Dec. 1950. Saucers Over Baltimore. A short article on saucers over Baltimore, Md., said to have photographed by Jack Engeman of Baltimore.

FATE. Jan. 1951. New Report on the Flying Saucers. An article by Ray Palmer. A new listing of eye-witness reports, some taken from the magazine *Flying*. Many new sightings reported. Palmer's final remark: "Nobody knows what they are."

Saucers, secrecy and security. R.H. Wood. Aviation W 54: 50 F 19 '51. This is an editorial by Robert H. Wood. He sets down as gospel the Lidell explanation that saucer sightings are due to "Skyhook" balloons, and issues a ringing challenge for a freer press in America. This editorial congratulates LOOK and states that *Aviation Week* nearly had pulled a scoop itself on "Operation Skyhook." (Author's note: News of "Operation Skyhook" had been publicized fully in LOOK in its July 18, 1950 issue in the article by Bruce Bliven...and by Sidney Shalett in *The Saturday Evening Post* in 1949. Yet, the Liddell report gave the balloon theory out as a great news in 1951.

Flying saucers again. Scholastic 58:12 F 21 '51

Belated explanation of flying saucers. il Time 57:22 F 26 '51. A report on Dr. Urner Liddell's release of "Skyhook" story. Time calls it best explanation yet, but points out that public had not been kept in dark about "Operation Skyhook."

Saucers? No. Skyhooks. il Newsweek 37: 17 F 26 '51. A brief review of saucers again. Dr. Urner Liddell's belief that saucer sightings are attributable to "Skyhook" balloons.

Flying saucers. Balloony, not baloney. Aviation W 54:13 F 19 '51. This is merely a review of the LOOK article that appeared a week previously.

LOOK. Feb. 27, 1951. A nuclear physicist exposes flying saucers. Article by Richard Wilson, Chief of LOOK's Washington Bureau, reporting on Dr. Urner Liddell's 10-page report that saucers were Navy "Skyhook" balloons. Dr. Liddell is in the Nuclear Physics branch of the Office of the Naval Research. The widely-publicized Liddell report based its case heavily on the statement that: "No saucers were reported before "Operation Skyhook" began in 1947." It gives a good description of "Skyhook" balloons and why sighting of them in stratosphere, reflecting sunlight while earth below them is in darkness could lead to reports of saucers.

The Harper Edition was published April 1951, second printing, October 1952. Bantam Edition published April 1953, 1st printing March 1953. Excerpts from chapter. 12 of book published in Catholic Digest, issue of July 1951.

BOOK: *Is Another World Watching?* Harper & Brothers. Copyright 1950-51 by Gerald Heard. First published in England under the title: The *Riddle of The Flying Saucers.* The Harper Edition was published April, 1951, second printing, October, 1952. Bantam Edition published April, 1953, 1st printing March, 1953. Excerpts from chapter 12 of book published in Catholic Digest, issue of July, 1951. Mr. Heard is a well-known author, a broadcaster, and a lecturer. He was born in England, educated at Cambridge. He was once editor of the *London Realist,* once broadcaster for BBC, held the chair of historical anthropology in the 1930s at Duke University.

A special edition of this work revised and with new material by the author, was published in newsstand edition by

Bantam Books. It appeared on the newsstands in the last week of June 1953.

Mr. Heard's former writings have sometimes been on the mystical and fantastic side. Some titles taken at random from our local library in Old Greenwich and the New York Public Library's main branch at 42nd Street and Fifth Avenue, are as follows: *Gabriel and the Creatures, Great Fog and Other Weird Tales, The Lost Cavern* and *Other Tales of the Fantastic.*

In his book, Is Another World Watching?, Mr. Heard, who is heralded as an expert on the front cover, does a careful researching and annotating job. He even quotes George Gallup findings in the twentieth Gallup "Polls of Opinion" report to the effect that the public was neither frightened nor skeptical of flying saucers — and mentions 5% of the people saying saucers are "from another planet or star" to prove his point about the lack of skepticism.

After a careful setting down of the record, both in old sightings and current ones, Mr. Heard goes into his deduction: that the makers and pilots of the saucers are a race of super insects, specifically, bees. The reason that Mr. Heard goes this route is because he had evidently fallen completely in love with the work of the great entomologist, Karl von Frisch. von Frisch definitely proved, to the amazement of fellow scientists, that bees think, exchange information, and have a definite way of telling others in the hive where and at what distance honey-bearing flowers are found. His findings are fantastic — and true.

But Mr. Heard, in applying von Frisch's findings to flying saucers comes up with such odd assumptions that bees have just now — with Frisch's discoveries — arrived at the ability to communicate. For all that is known, the pattern of bee behavior was established millions upon millions of years ago — and hasn't changed one whit since.

The reason that Mr. Heard takes this extreme approach is seemingly because he is baffled by the G-pull — the pull of gravity — on whatever might be within the flying saucers, spheres, torpedoes or what have you. This one stumps him, and leads him to the conclusion that only an insect-type being, with its skeleton on the outside, not inside, could take this gravitational pressure developed by right-angled turns, or even sharper turns taken at speeds of from 1,000 mph up to 18,000 mph.

More about out there; review of Is Another World Watching? Riddle of the flying saucers by G. Heard, W. Ley Sat Rev Lit 34:20-1 Ap 28 '51. Willy Ley's evaluation of Gerald Heard's book: "a very fine fiction story...reading time well spent...It is much easier to believe in a tight-lipped AEC than interplanetary visitors." (Mr. Ley is a famous science writer; co-author of "Conquest of Space" with Chesley Bonstell.)

FATE. April 1951. Saucers Over England. Article. Reported sightings over the British Isles.

FATE. April 1951. 1,000 Years of Flying Saucers. Article by Harold T. Wilkins. Historic reports of saucer phenomena. A number of listings reported in books by Charles Fort.

FATE. May-June 1951. The Saucers Aren't Balloons. Articles by FATE editor Robert N. Webster. An accusation that Dr. Werner Liddell's statement that all saucer reports were due to sightings of the Navy's "Skyhook" balloons was a cruel hoax on the American public.

Aviation Week, June 25, 1951, p. 74. Robert H. Wood, writing on editorial page, asking, "Where are the flying saucers?" says magazine has received no new reports. Also ends with: "But there still remain some reports from apparently trained or competent observers that cannot be explained or discredited easily. We are open-minded, but the next move seems to be up to the saucers."

Another saucer mystery. L.W. Vinther. il Flying 48:23 Je '51. This is a report on the sighting of Jan. 20, 1951, on Flight 9, Mid-Continental Airlines plane, over Sioux City, Iowa. This is a first-hand, first-person account of an sighting of an object as big as a B-29. No jet. No exhaust flame. (In this same issue, *Flying* reports that in the past 11 months, it had reported the observations of strange craft by 5 veteran pilots, and would keep on going so, in the belief that there was something to the saucer sightings.)

What were the flying saucers? il Pop Sci 159:74-5 Ag '51. Various theories advanced to explain what people probably saw when they reported seeing flying saucers. Leaves question open to doubt.

FATE. Oct. 1951. The Navy's Saucers. FATE's monthly report on the saucers. Included in the report: one month after Dr. Werner Liddell's report on Skyhook balloons, the Navy itself reported the sighting of two mysterious smoke-trailing objects by a warship off Korea. Competent observers aboard the seaplane tender *Gardiner's Bay* watched the two objects strike the water at great speed. "Identification remains a great mystery."

FATE. January 1952. Let's Get Up To Date on Flying Saucers. An article by FATE editor Robert N. Webster. This article is a review of the saucer situation with Mr. Webster's final, baffled statement: "As we get deeper and deeper into our investigation of strange aerial phenomena, we feel we have less and less of an idea of what this is all about."

FATE. Feb-March 1952. The Steep Rock Flying Saucer. This tells of a saucer landing, or series of landings, on Steep Rock Lake, Ontario. The article is a reprint taken from the Steep Rock Echo, the house magazine of the Steep Rock Mines, Ltd., one of the big and long-established Canadian companies. According to FATE, Mr. B.J. Eyton, editor, published the account, which was anonymous, with the explanation that he could not vouch for its accuracy, since he was not present at the sightings, but that it was written by one of the company's senior employees who did not wish his name used for fear of ridicule.

This article describes the saucer seen and looking like two saucers put together. It had aboard it a crew of little humanoids. These midgets came out on the lake, put over a brilliant green hose that looked like transparent plastic, and evidently took on water or pumped out residue through the hose. These little characters, according to the article, acted a little like robots. They seemed to walk backwards at the same gait humans use in walking forwards. Ezikiel reported something similar. Seeing itself observed, the saucer closed its top port and took off in a flash. The observers thought the saw one poor unfortunate fall off the saucer into the water. One observer later went back with a friend to try to take photographs of a saucer. They saw one, but were so excited they did not succeed in getting photographs. They have not gone back since.

FATE. Feb.-March 1952. The Mystery of the Crawling Fireballs. Article by Henry C. Golus. Tells about the fireballs that terrorized Europeans for 150 years, up to the early 1900s.

Korean saucers. Newsweek 39:44 Mr 3 '52. Report on Korea sighting. Jan 29-30, 1950. Conclusion: "Old time pilots suggest that saucers are perhaps like St. Elmo's fire."

More saucers over North Korea. il *Time* 59:92 Mr 3 '52. A much less scoffing review of saucers than previous ones by this publication. Gives some pros and cons. Says flying saucer phenomena will continue to fascinate *psychologists*, as well as physicists.

Have we visitors from space? H.B. Darrach, Jr. and R. Ginna. il *Life* 32:80-2 Ap 7 '52. This was the famous article in which Life declared itself for the belief that the saucers are from some other planet. The article reviews ten of the most baffling sightings, including those of Arnold, Gorman, Whitted and Chiles, and others listed in this book. And the conclusion drawn was that the only place the saucers could be from was outer space.

TRUE. April 1952. The Editor Speaking. Reports that since last TRUE article: "in Los Angeles a group of highly reputable scientists learned in physics, in astronomy, in the behavior of guided missiles and related matters, have formed an independent agency for the investigation of saucer sightings." The men: Edward Sullivan, Werner Eichler and Victor Black, all of the North American Aerophysics Laboratory. The name of the civilian investigative agency: Civilian Saucer Investigation, Box 1971, Los Angeles 53, California.

Flying saucers are old stuff. il *Pop Sci* 160:145-7 My '52. A write-up on Robert L. Unger, technical writer for Republic Aviation Corp., Farmingdale, L.I., who traced saucer sightings of the past. The article said that Unger is convinced that saucers are visitors from another world. It also states that Dr. Walter Riedel, the rocket expert, and Dr. Maurice A. Biot, a top U.S. aerodynamicist, believe the same thing. This article reports the beliefs of these men, with no editorial comment.

FATE. June 1952. I See By The Papers. A column by Curtis Fuller. The column is a review of newspaper articles on saucers and allied phenomena. The article at hand is on the green fireballs sighted with increasing frequency in Southwestern United States.

Those flying saucers. il diags. *Time* 59: 54-6 Je 9 '52. Explanation of saucer phenomena as given by Dr. Donald F. Menzel of Harvard.

Saucers elude astronomers. C.C. Wylie Sci N L 61:375 Je 14 '52. Dr. C.C. Wylie, Professor of Astronomy, University of Iowa, "Not one saucer has been reported as the result of astronomical observations." Saucers have been reported from only one point — therefore are probably spots of reflected light.

LOOK. June 17, 1952, pp. 98-9. This is the first of two articles on flying saucers. Chester Morrison, of LOOK, interviewed Dr. Donald F. Menzel at his home in Cambridge, Mass. The article contains some of Dr. Menzel's explanations of saucers, later expanded into his book, which is outlined elsewhere in this volume.

Saucer reactions. R.E. Ginna, Jr. il Life 32:20 Je 9 '52. Mr. Ginna states that his article in Life, 32:80-2 Ap 7 '52, drew wide response, prompted many people to report what they had seen to U.S. Air Force to assist its investigations.

BOOK. *I Rode A Flying Saucer.* George W. Van Tassel. Copyright 1952. Published by New Age Publishing Co., Los Angeles, California. Subtitled: The Mystery of The Flying Saucers Revealed, this book claims that the author received many "vibrations" from beings that fly the saucers. Their purpose in sending the messages: to warn earthmen to stop playing around with atomic weapons.

Names of some of the beings: Lutbunn, senior in command first wave, planet patrol, realms of Schare. Elcar, 6th projection, 42nd wave, 4th sector patrol, realms of Schare. Totalmon, 4th projection, 7th wave, space patrol, realms of Schare. "Elevation 750 miles from you, speed 170,000 miles per second."

Other names: Leektow. Oblow. Locktopar. Melca. Clatu. Singba. Kletarc. Tonla. Tolta.

The craft these people fly: ventlas.

LOOK. July 1, 1952. P. 37. The second part of two articles on flying saucers, this part written by J. Robert Moskin. This one tells of the seriousness of the Air Force's search to find the answers. It gives the Air Force graph of sightings in 1952, reproduced elsewhere in this book. Also tells of the new Air Force Program to set up grids at key points.

The title of this article is: "Whatever it is, the Air Force must HUNT FOR THE FLYING SAUCER." And the subject is: "Fearful of danger from the skies, the United States Air Force is launching a secret scientific search to discover once-and-for-all what is the mysterious, unbelievable thing Americans keep sighting overhead."

Round up on the flying saucer mystery. I. Have we visitors from outer space. H.B. Darrach, Jr. and Robert Ginna. Flying saucers, new in name only. J.R. Aswell, Reader's Digest 3-9, J1 '52.

This is a series of the two articles, presented without comment, by The Reader's Digest. The first, by Darrach and Ginna, is a condensation from their article in LIFE. The second, by Aswell, points out the similarity between objects sighed for years and recent sightings of "saucers." The article describes the sighting of Frank Schofield, of astronomer E. Walter Maunder, the Chicago sighting of 1897, that of the *Lady of The Lake*, the formation of lights that flew across Saskatchewan, the U.S. and Bermuda in 1913 — all of which are described elsewhere in this book.

FATE. August 1952. I See By The Papers. Curtis Fuller. A new and current round-up of saucer and fireball sightings.

Blips on the Scopes. Time 60:40 Ag 4 '52 Report on blips seen on Washington radarscopes, July 26, 1952. Quote: "Oddest fact was that no radar outside ten-mile radius in Washington reported seeing anything unusual at any time."

Washington's blips. il Life 33:39 (check) Ag 4 '52. A report on the radar sightings over Washington, D.C., beginning Sunday, July 20, 1952 at 12:45 A.M. and resumed one week later. "oddest fact was that while civilian aircraft reported sighting lights, Air Force aircraft said they saw nothing."

What's going on in the skies. U.S. News 33 13-15 Ag 8 '52. Explanation of saucers in terms of mirages, cloud layers, reflections, deflected radar beams.

Saucer season. Newsweek 40:56 Ag 11 '52. A tongue-in-cheek report on saucers. Rather tartly points out that even Life and its sister-magazine, Time, don't agree.

Something in the air. il Time 60:58 Ag 11 '52. Report of Major General Roger M. Ramsey, Director of Operations, and Major General John Samford, Director of Intelligence. States that after 6 years of study, both are "reasonably well" convinced there is no such thing as "flying saucer." Explanation of sightings: air inversions, birds, meteors, balloons, etc. But these things accounted for only 80% of sightings. To probe still further, the Air Force plans to distribute 200 special cameras to competent observers and has ordered some powerful new Schmidt telescopes that will scan sky continuously from horizon to horizon.

Saucers under glass. Newsweek 40:49 Ag 18 '52. Report on Noel Scott's production of "saucers" in bell: Space ship notions are more exciting than dull, jar. Conclusion: "Military books on subject are still wide open."

New saucer epidemic. New Republic 127:7 Ag 18 '52. This article reports on Noel Scott's report of producing saucers artificially at Ft. Belvoir, Va., also on Dr. Donald F. Menzel's laboratory reproductions of flying saucers. Concludes *New Republic*: prosaic scientific probability.

No visitors from space. Sci N L 62: 143 Ag 30 '52. No reason to believe flying saucer phenomena are extra-terrestrial.

Opinions expressed by Dr. Otto Struve of the University of California, at the Convention of Western Amateur Astronomers at Berkeley, Cal. While it's possible other intelligent beings exist on other earth-like planets, possibilities of their visiting earth is virtually zero.

BOOK. Saucers First Contact Revealed. Orfeo Angelluci. Mr. Angelluci, a metal fabricator in the Burbank plant of Lockheed Aviation Corporation, at the time he wrote of his experience, writes that he was taken aboard a flying saucer on the night of July 23, 1952, and was taken 1,000 miles out in space. He also met a spaceman, named Neptune, for whom Mr. Angelluci bought a bottle of lemon pop, but Neptune disappeared before he could drink it.

In his writings, Mr. Angelluci refers to himself in the third person as Orfeo.

A sample: "Orfeo now knows why they made the choice of contact which they did. It will never be dishonored or slighted." "Arise, you Children; for of you is the New Era. Let your voices ring out in song, "WELCOME SPACE VISITORS."

Mr. Angellucci's name for the flying saucer: crystal discs. But he doesn't claim to know where they come from: "Their actual names were never even alluded to. Their place of origin is a complete mystery as yet. The age of the visitors is not known. The maximum velocity of their ships in voyage can only be conjectured."

Mr. Angellucci evidently founded a newspaper, the 20th Century Times, on the strength of his experience and solicits manuscripts from: "Writers of the future. Humane writers with blood in their system. Writers with ideals, backed with enthusiasm."

(AUTHOR'S NOTE: In early February 1955, I received a broadside entitled: HERE IT IS AT LAST! The second book on flying saucers to be published by Ray Palmer. The Secret of the Saucers by Orfeo Angellucci.

A quote: *"A psychic adventure backed up by actual witnesses relating an aircraft worker's utterly strange and thrilling experience."*

"This argument has raged for seven years: Are these saucers from other worlds? Are they from other dimensions? Are they psychic experiences? And if the latter, can they be proved?

"Ray Palmer set out to dig up that proof, and with the most astounding success! Yes, the saucers are from other worlds. They are also both real and psychic. They are actualities, not mental visions. They are both visible and invisible. Their physical reality was proved in THE COMING OF THE SAUCERS; (by Ray Palmer and Kenneth Arnold) now their psychic reality is proved in THE SECRET OF THE SAUCERS.

"HERE IS A BOOK THAT WILL STAGGER YOUR IMAGINATION!"

It sure does, pals.)

BOOK: The Coming of The Saucers. By Kenneth Arnold, Member Idaho Search and Rescue Mercy Flyers; Flying Deputy for the Ada County Aerial Posse; Acting Deputy Federal United States Marshall; Aerial Salesman and Originator of the Great Western Fire Control System; and Ray Palmer, Editor and Publisher; Owner Clark Publishing Company, Publishers of Fate Magazine and Other Worlds Science Stories; Author and Traveler; Amateur Archaeologist and Ethnologist. Copyright 1952 by Ray Palmer, Amherst, Wisconsin. Privately published by the Authors. (The above is taken verbatim from the flyleaf of the book.)

The first part of this book is an accounting of what Kenneth Arnold reported seeing on Tuesday, June 24, 1947, over Mineral, Washington. Arnold then tells of going on a fishing trip to Sekieu, Washington, with Colonel Paul Wieland, who had served as judge on the Malmedy case and at the Nuremberg trials. At Sekieu, on July 4, 1947, there was a "red tide" that was killing Chinook salmon. In Arnold's words: *"It looked to me rather like a gob of something had fallen out of the sky. Even though the scientists had a name for it, I admitted red tides into my collection of phenomena along with flying saucers."* (AUTHOR'S NOTE: red tides have been seen in the oceans of this country for over a century. They are caused by a micro-organism of some kind. Fully written-up in *The Saturday Evening Post.* See Guide to Periodical Literature.)

On the next day, Arnold reports, he met Captain E.J. Smith and co-pilot Ralph Stevens and learned of the saucer sighting of the night before, observed by Captain Smith, supported and verified by the entire crew of his DC-3. He met Captain Smith and Ralph Stevens in the anteroom of the Seattle offices of the International News Service.

During July, Arnold reports, he was requested to send a full report of his experience of June 24 to the commanding officer of Wright-Patterson Field.

On the 1th of July, Arnold received a letter from Ray Palmer on the letterhead of *The Venture Press.* Arnold (and Palmer, co-author of this book) state that neither Arnold nor his friends had ever heard of Ray Palmer before. Mr. Palmer wanted to publish Mr. Arnold's story and pay him for it.

In a subsequent letter, Mr. Palmer told Mr. Arnold that he had heard that two harbor patrolmen at Tacoma, Washington, Mr. Harold A. Dahl and Mr. Fred L. Chrisman, claimed that they had not only sighted a group of saucers, but that they had some fragments from one of them.

In the meantime, Mr. Arnold states he was visited by two representatives of A-2 Military Intelligence of the Fourth Air Force, Lieutenant Frank M. Brown and Captain William Davidson. These members of Intelligence had flown to Boise in a military A-26 bomber especially to see Mr. Arnold.

While in Boise, they also met Captain E.J. Smith, and Dave Johnson, aviation editor of *The Idaho Statesman*, who had tried to photograph a disc-like object over Anderson Dam, near Boise, a few days previously.

The men from Military Intelligence, Mr. Arnold writes, advised him not to talk to outsiders about his experiences.

In the meantime, Mr. Arnold decided to take up Ray Palmer's offer of $200 expense money to investigate the Tacoma sighting of Dahl and Chrisman. He took off for Tacoma in his own plane on July 29, 1947.

From this point on in his book, Mr. Arnold's story becomes cloak-and-dagger. He invited Captain E.J. Smith in on the investigation. They talked to Dahl and Chrisman. They saw and handled fragments said to have fallen from a saucer. Then they called in Lieutenant Brown and Captain Davidson of Air Intelligence again.

Arnold felt that they were being menaced by something or somebody. He and Captain Smith tore their room (Room 502 in the Winthrop Hotel in Tacoma) practically to pieces, thinking that dictaphones had been planted on them. They were suspicious of the Dahl and Chrisman story. Arnold reports that he sent a number of wires to his wife, Doris, in Boise, "that frightened her as to my safety." "I called long distance to my mother in Albany, Oregon, telling my brother who answered the phone that I didn't know if I would see them again but wanted them to know where I was. In fact, I was so suspicious of somebody recording my conversations that I asked my brother to take my mother out in the yard and tell her that I felt in extreme danger of some kind."

On August 1, 1947, Arnold learned from the Tacoma Times, that the plane of Intelligence officers carrying the "saucer fragments" had crashed, killing Lieutenant Brown and Captain Davidson.

On August 3, at 2:00 P.M., Captain Smith brought Major Sander of S-2 Army Intelligence of McChord Field, to Room 502. The Major remarked that he was positive Messrs. Arnold and Smith had been made the victims of a hoax. Then the Major, according to Mr. Arnold's book, collected all "saucer fragments" left in the room and took them away with him. Major Sander then drove Messrs. Smith and Arnold out to a smelting plant near Tacoma, showed them samples of smelter slag, intimating that it was identical with the fragments in the Major's car. At this point, Mr. Arnold reports his feeling that the Major was trying to cover up.

Leaving Tacoma, Messrs. Arnold and Smith decided to say good bye to Harold Dahl. When they went to the house where Arnold had talked to Dahl before, according to Mr. Arnold, not only did no one live there, but the house looked completely deserted, and was "as if it had not been lived in it for three months...I had never heard of anything like this except in dreams. I was panicky."

(Note: It would seem evident that, with the conclusion of Arnold's account of his subsequent return home to Boise from this trip, the writing the rest of the book is Ray Palmer's.)

The rest of the book consists of a chapter on the "project Saucer" report of April 27, 1949; a chapter of comments on the "Project Saucer" report; a chapter on one thousand years of flying saucers; a chapter on Foo Fighters; a chapter on foreign sightings; a chapter on reports from American observers; a chapter "Analysis Versus Opinion;" and a number of photographs on the camera story of the saucers.

In this part of the book, it is claimed that Intelligence "was busy cooking up a two-part article in *The Saturday Evening Post* (presumably authored by Sidney A. Shallet) which was designed to pooh-pooh the whole business and laugh it all away."

The book also claims that Crisman and Dahl have "mysteriously disappeared." It submits a qualitative analysis of original fragments from Maury Island sent to Ray Palmer, and a similar analysis of fragments from the "particular slag piles pointed out by Major Sander." The analyses, the book states, were quite different.

The book also brings out the fact that Crisman had been in touch with Palmer before. He had warned Ray Palmer to "lay off what was then known as "the Shaver Mystery," a secret underground menace, in which a fantastic story was told by Crisman of being in a cave in Burma in search of this "underground menace" and being "rayed" by an unseen being and having a hole the size of a dime burned in his arm. A letter which Palmer "believed not at all."

In the chapter, Analysis Versus Opinion, Ray Palmer sums up his opinion that the saucers are real, that they are not the product of a United States military arm, that they are not a development of the Russian government; that no claims that they are from another planet have been substantiated. The authors of the book present no theory as to what saucers really are.

The photographs in the book, including photographs of Ray Palmer and Kenneth Arnold, are rounded-up from many sources. the authors claim that newspapers would not supply original prints or addresses of photographers who took the pictures, and that efforts to obtain sundry photographs proved fruitless. Among the photographs are a number by Mr. George Adamski, averred to be luminous discs and other aerial objects at distances from 50,000 to 210,000 miles from the earth, flying between the earth and the moon, some within 100 miles of the moon's surface. The photographs also include pictures of a wooden bridge across the Salmon River in Oregon that burned on July 24, 1947. "How could this bridge have burst into flame along its entire length at the same instant?...Upon later investigation by the F.B.I., the steel cables of the bridge were found to be melted in several places. Ordinary steel melts at 2,800° F., and, according to opinions, an ordinary wood fire in the open air could not generate enough heat to melt such cables...Forest rangers in Oregon, in this period, reported seeing glowing objects land in the forest and start numerous fires. Early in 1952, small flying discs were observed to dart from Snake River canyon, follow a B-29 for several minutes, then dart back again. Did the burn this bridge?")

(Note: Final conclusion: This book may not present any theories but it certainly brings up a lot of unanswerable questions, and certainly lets the reader conclude that the answer to saucers is space ships.)

TRUE. September 1952. The flying and the mysterious little men. Article by J.P. Cahn, of the San Francisco Chronicle, who was assigned by True to sift the facts — if any — behind Frank Scully's book, *Behind the Flying Saucers*. According to Cahn, there were no saucers, no strange metals, no "little men in blue suits." The Scully book, according to Cahn, who did a thorough job of investigating, was a hoax. Reason for the hoax: not obtainable.

FATE. Sept. 1952. Wheel of Light in the Sea. Commander J. R. Bodler, U.S.N. ret., reports on a rotating wheel of light with spokes, seen in ocean, Nov. 14, 1949, 1830 GTM, in Strait of Hormuz, off Iran, on ship bound for India. (Such wheels of light have been reported before — in books by Charles Fort; in book, Oddities, by T. R. Gould, published in England. The Persian Gulf evidently abounds in such wheels of light.)

FATE. Sept. 1952. I see by The Papers. Curtis Fuller. More saucer sightings.

Wind is up in Kansas. Time 60:86 S 8 '52. Story about the notice on bulletin board of Wichita, Kansas, *Beacon.* (About Sept. 1, '52.) Story old of a radio performer named Bill Squier who reported seeing, near Pillsbury, Kansas, the landing of a saucer. He said he got near enough to see human-like figures in saucer. Then it took off at high speed. Friends said they had visited spot later and saw grass and weeds beaten down as if by high wind.

New theory on flying saucers. D.H. Menzel. il *Sci Digest* 32:11-6 S '52. Dr. Menzel's belief that saucer sightings are due to natural phenomena.

Magicians scoff at flying saucers. J. Mulholland il *Pop Sci* 161: 96-8 S '52. Flying saucers are a state of mind, brought on by suggestion.

Reporter at large. D. ang. *New Yorker* 28:68 S 6 '52. Something in the sky. An article by Daniel Lang. This is one of the very best of all saucer articles. It is soberly factual, soundly researched, written after many conversations with authorities in Washington. It doesn't attempt to present anybody's theories, rationalizations, or deductions. Conclusion: What are saucers? Unknown.

Scientist diagnoses flying saucers. I.M. Levitt. *Pop Mech* 98:95 S '52. Dr. I.M. Levitt, Feld Planetarian, Franklin Institute, Phila., Pa. Saucers are apparitions. Radar discrepancies. Meteorological balloons. Particles of dust. Mirages.

How to fly a saucer. il *Collier's* 130:50-1 04 '52. Description of miniatures used by Director George Pal in filming H.G. *Well's War of the Worlds.*

Flying saucer hoax. V. Black. *Am Mercury* 75:61-66 O '52. Author Victor Black tells about Ed. J. Sullivan of Los Angeles, and "his religio-scientific" cult of the saucer. States that saucers are "electrical whirlwinds of cosmic dust. The earth, whizzing through space, is constantly passing through electrically-charged fields of meteoric dust or cosmic debris...these can result in a rotating field. Under the right conditions, this rotating field can develop a tremendous force." The article goes on to speak somewhat slightingly of Ed. J. Sullivan, Dr. Lincoln La Paz, and the formation of the Civilian Saucer Center. It winds up with a quote the author says was made by Mrs. Ed. J. Sullivan regarding money coming in to her husband for a monthly flying saucer bulletin: "We can afford a Cadillac now, where before we couldn't." (Article also mentions three technical writers for the Aerophysics Department of North American Aviation's plant at Downey, California, near Los Angeles. Ed J. Sullivan is one of those writers and flying saucer observers.)

TRUE. October 1952. p. 65. We flew above the flying saucers. W.B. Nash, W.H. Fortenberry. Eyewitnesses account of sighting on July 14, 1952, listed elsewhere.

FATE. October 1952. Canadian saucer sightings. Observations on sightings by Canadian scientists.

Logging time. H. Sheridan. Flying 51:51 N '52 Logging Time is a column written by Hy Sheridan in this publication. In this particular column, he wrote that the most reliable reports on saucers have been night sightings. And these sightings have been of *lights*. As for an explanation, Mr. Sheridan writes: "This is my guess. These lights are from gases in the atmosphere that are caused to glow by excitation, such as by electrical excitation...The exciting means may be converging oscillating electrical fields."

"It may be an intensive cosmic ray shower. It may be a concentrated squirt of electrons from the sun. It may be caused by radio waves, electro-magnetic waves from outer space, the "black star radio waves" that we have been hearing about lately, or wave lengths too short to penetrate our atmosphere. According to theory, such spots of glowing gas would show up on the radar screen, for they would be highly ionized. And they would glow like the aurora, usually pale blue, but sometimes orange, green or another color."

Mr. Sheridan, to support this belief, cites the case of a free-floating green ball of fire that drifted around in, and finally out of an aircraft cabin. One of the crewmen, of an experimental nature, put his fingers in it, reported it as feeling cool, and that it raised the hairs on his arm, like a charge of static electricity."

Hollywood builds flying saucers. il *Pop Sci* 161: 32-4 N '52 Tells how George Pal, director for many science-fiction movies, built saucers for film version of H.G. Wells' *War of The Worlds.*

Flying saucers, myth or menace? picture story. L. Elliot. Coronet 33:47-54 N '52. A somewhat lurid summary of saucers with highly imaginative illustrations. Repeat various suppositions: saucers are from Venus...from Russia...from a "lost" race of men who live in ice caves near the North Pole...from "Etheria," one of 7 mysterious spheres between Earth and Venus...or — they are U.S. Navy space craft. Conclusion: "May be the greatest story of all time."

Saucers? M. Thompson. Science 116: 640 D 5 '52. Malcolm Thompson, Thompson Laboratory, General Electric Company, West Lynn, Mass., describes luminous cloud he saw at Hutchinson, Minn. Asks if such phenomena might not be ball lightning or bead lightning. (Author's note: What Mr. Thompson saw would appear to be the same kind of luminosity this author saw over Marietta, Ohio in 1925.)

Flying saucer hoax. R. Gelatt. Sat R. Lit 35:31 D 6 '52. Roland Gelatt reports that in Denver recently, Silas M. Newton, who figured in Frank Scully's book, and Leo A. GeBauer, were charged by the District Attorney with operating a confidence-game swindle involving oil exploration test with "doodlebugs."

Temperature inversions cause flying saucers. Sci N L 68:388 D 20 '52. A report that the Civil Aeronautics authority confirmed that "blips" seen on Washington radarscopes were the result of temperature inversions bending radar rays.

Of spots before the eyes. E.F. Mauer. Sci 116:693 D '19 '52. Asks if saucers may be *muscae volitantes*, spots before the eyes. Edgar F. Maurer, M.D., references: May Ed. Manual of the Diseases of The Eye. Alvarez, W.A. Oxford System of Medicine. "In the opinion of the writer, saucers are motes in the eyes of a dyspeptic microcosm."

FATE. Dec. 1952. Let's Get Straight About the Saucers. Curtis Fuller. A new and lengthy report on saucers with the statement by Mr. Fuller: "I do not know what they are...I believe that the Air Force does not. The "flying saucers" may turn out to be several as yet unknown things."

TRUE. Dec. 25, 1952. p. 25. Donald E. Keyhoe. What radar tells about flying saucers. Article, with photographs of hovering object caught on radar. Discusses reports issued to TRUE Magazine by the Air Force. Explains why temperature inversion could not have been responsible for Washington sightings of July 20, 1952.

Mentions number of sightings from official Air Force files, given Mr. Keyhoe by Air Force officials. Discusses why saucers created under laboratory conditions under glass could not account for sightings. Mr. Keyhoe is careful gatherer of material, checking with noted physicists, astronomers, pilots, and Air Force officials. His conclusion: saucers are space ships visiting the earth.

How to expose flying saucers; air force's project for photographing them. R.Steiner. il Pop Sci 152:226-9 Ja '53 This article, by Ralph Steiner, tells of the Air Force plan to set up diffraction-grating cameras in order to discover the source of light in saucers. It describes the type of camera to be used and tells readers how they can make their own cameras into diffraction-grating types for just a few dollars. Mr. Steiner says that a call to the Air Force drew their assurance that they would more than welcome saucer photographs taken by civilians.

Note of instruction: Do not develop the film. Mail it, undeveloped, together with data, to the Air Technical Intelligence Center, Wright-Patterson Air Force Base, Ohio, attention Unidentified Aerial Objects Investigation.

LOOK. January 13, 19; 53, p. 72. Beany and the flying saucers. This is an article about Bob Clampett and his TV show for children, Time for Beany. The show features "saucers" among its other props.

FATE. January 1953. The Monster and the Saucer. The Flatwoods, West Virginia report. This is highly dubious, widely reported in the press. (See sighting dated Sept 12, 1952 under chapter on sightings) Branded a hoax by Captain Ruppelt.

BOOK. *Flying Saucers.* Donald H. Menzel, Professor of Astrophysics, Harvard University. Harvard University Press, 1953. Copyright 1953 by the President and Fellows of Harvard College.

The most lucid, scientific, rational and reasonable of all flying saucer books is the one by Professor Menzel. He is not only Professor of Astrophysics at Harvard, and a noted world authority on aerial phenomena — he is also Director of Harvard Observatory. In addition, Professor Menzel is an authority on radar, and was, as a Lieutenant Commander in the U.S. Navy in World War II, technical advisor on radar. He knows his stuff.

In addition, he has done an outstanding research job on flying saucers. He has traced saucer sightings back as far as the prophet Ezekiel. He lists saucer sightings all through the middle ages, and furthermore, illustrates those sighting with old woodcut drawings made by *men who saw* history's great apparitions.

Dr. Menzel does not believe that *any* saucer sighting, whether by the ancients, the medievals, or the moderns, was the result of visitations from Mars, Venus, the moon, or from anywhere else in outer space. He believes that there are perfectly logical explanations for saucers in terms of known aerial phenomena. He deals with apparitions, rainbow of effects, such as sun dogs and moon dogs, mirages, aurora, air lenses, ice crystals, reflection and refraction, specters, comets, meteors, and aberrations in radar.

Dr. Menzel's book carries reason, logic, profound learning, and the experience of observation of phenomena over many years. It also carries an appendix of mathematical equations which explain the mechanics of mirage, hallucination, etc. In addition, his book is witty.

It is a fascinating volume, thoroughly enjoyable. And it makes good, sound, hard commonsense. Perhaps this is the only writing in the United States that has correctly explained saucers. Certainly anyone trying to understand the mystery should get Dr. Menzel's book and read it.

After reading this admirable book, and reading it as many as three times (as this author did), it is a great temptation to brush flying saucers out of the mind as one of the great hallucinations that have afflicted the human race from time to time.

For Dr. Menzel has a sound explanation of the saucer sightings of Kenneth Arnold, Captain Mantell, Gorman, Whitted and Chiles, Smith, and all the other "classic" sightings. He has an excellent explanation for the Foo Fighters, and it is not St. Elmo's Fire.

Here is a book written by well-known scientist, and sponsored and published by a great institution dedicated to truth, to the advancement of learning, to the dissemination of learning.

One ought to believe every word of it.

And yet—

Two months after the publication of Dr. Menzel's book, the U.S. Air Force, in its March 1953 issue of *Air Training*, official publication among trainee flyers, published a two-page article requesting help in solving the saucer mystery.

On June 25, 1953, there was carried on the UP wire the story that two prospectors of Brush Creek, California had sighted a landed saucer on two occasions, May 20 and June 20. "Little men," reputedly, were in the saucer.

On June 28, the New York Herald Tribune carried as a feature article by Ansel E. Talbert the report that Canada is developing a real flying saucer. A description of the saucer closely follows the description of what the two minders from Brush Creek reported they saw, even to the type of retractable landing gear.

In May 1950, ex-Captain E.J. Ruppelt, once head of the official U.S. saucer investigating project, stated in TRUE Magazine, that Dr. Menzel's explanation did not explain many saucer sightings.

American Mercury. Jan. 1953, page 21. A full-page apology to Ed J. Sullivan, Dr. Lincoln La Paz, and Dr. Walther Riedel for the article in the October 1952, issue of American Mercury. Under the heading, "*In The Mercury's Opinion,*" the magazine stated: “It was a facetious bit about a subject which we find difficult to take seriously.” The magazine then apologized for anything in the article which had offended the men named previously.

Biblical Flying Saucers. Sci N L 63:148 Mr 7 '53. Quotations from Dr. Donald H. Menzel of Harvard about the prophet Ezekiel and what he probably saw — from Dr. Menzel's book, “Flying Saucers.”

Saucers on radar? D.H. Menzel. il diags Pop Sci 162:168-71 Ap '53.

Saucers on radar are due to radar mirages. An air “sandwich” can cause saucers. Layer of cold air, plus layer of warm air causes the mirage.

FATE. April 1953. More saucer sightings.

FATE. May 1953. More sightings.

FATE. June 1953. Special report on saucer sightings by Curtis Fuller. Reports a concentration of sightings, from Japan to Canada in a 10-day period during latter part of January 1953.

FATE. July 1953. Report of mysterious explosion over Niagara Falls on March 23, 1953. A man named Joseph Cloutier, as reported in FATE, stated that he had seen several pieces of wreckage, looking like aluminum, in the river after the explosion in the sky. No U.S. planes missing.

Those flying saucers. C.C. Wylie. Science 118: 114 J1 31 '53

Dr. C.C. Wylie, Department of Mathematics and Astronomy, State University of Iowa, Iowa City, Iowa, does research on meteors, especially spectacular ones. In this work, he often receives reports of "saucer" sightings. Saucers, according to Dr. Wiley — and based upon his years of research — are spots of reflected light, from birds, aircraft and other well-known objects, seen from the critical angle — the only angle at which such reflection can be seen. As to the green fireballs of the Southwest and other parts of the country, Dr. Wiley points out that they were seen just as often eighty years ago as they are now. Resuming on saucers — of the disc-shaped type — they have the following characteristics, according to this mathematician-astronomer:

1. They are seen only when the sun is shining.

2. They are generally seen in a part of the sky opposite the sun.

3. There is only one sighting on each saucer, as the area for the critical angle is small.

4. The "saucer" may disappear suddenly when the plane turns; it may reappear again at a different level.

Dr. Wiley then goes on to assert that the popular concept of a great and odd flight of meteor-like objects over Toronto on February 9, 1903 was completely erroneous — that there were not 200 to 300 lights, but "only one fireball appeared over North America at that time." (This latter statement was vigorously rebutted later in the year, as you will see.)

FATE. August 1953. Article by John Philip Bessor on a mystery light of Australia, called "Min-Min Light" there. It's a huge globe of brilliant light which soars up from the wooded horizon, travels over tree tops and then hovers. "No one has ever gotten close to the "Min-Min Light."

FATE. October 1953. Special saucer issue. This issue is filled with articles on saucers. The leading article "Saucers, Material or Immaterial?", by Robert N. Webster, states that no idea is too fantastic to consider as a solution to the saucers...even the idea that saucers might be "thought forms."

The following article, Fate's Report on the Flying Saucers, by John C. Ross (Curtis Fuller), gives a round-up of current sightings.

The next article, Fate's Report on the flying saucer being built by Canada. Principle said to be so simple it sounds silly.

The article following is a report that Ohio Northern University. Ada, Ohio, has set up a department to investigate flying saucers.

The next article is a condensation of a report on saucers from Ohio Northern University.

And in the following article, Harold T. Wilkins asks the question: Did the Ancient See Flying Saucers? and traces what may have been saucer sightings back as far as B.C. 322.

Note: One interesting item in this article on the Canadian saucer is a quote attributed to Ritchie Calder, science writer of the London News-Chronicle: "Recently miniature flying saucers 40 inches in diameter were tried out under remote control by the Yugoslav air force. And they operated effectively.

LOOK. October 20, 1953. Flying Saucers From Outer Space. A review of the book of the same title by Maj. Donald E. Keyhoe, U.S.M.C. ret. Accompanied by a statement from the editors. They don't commit themselves one way or the other, but state: "Major Keyhoe soberly believes that flying saucers are from outer space and insists that some Air Force officers are attempting to conceal the facts from the public."

BOOK: Flying Saucers From Outer Space, the second book on saucers by Major Donald E. Keyhoe, U.S. Marine Corps (ret.) Henry Holt and Company. $3.00. October 1953. In this 276-

page book, Major Keyhoe states that since July 1952, in a new investigation of saucers, he has been privileged to cooperate with the Air Force. He also states that he has seen most material used in secret briefings of selected groups of high government officials.

A lot of this book is very cloak-and-dagger, with Mr. Keyhoe trying to get the Air Force to admit that saucers are from outer space — and the Air Force still saying is, had no proof.

The book gives a summary of 51 sightings released by Albert M. Chop, Air Force Press Desk, with U.S. Air Force technical information sheets for unidentified aerial sightings, and a great deal of information concerning sightings, possible sources of power for saucers, and finally a letter from the Air Force Press Desk. This letter, Major Keyhoe states, is an official Air Force admission that the saucers come from speed.

Major Keyhoe again reiterates his belief that the saucers are interplanetary, that the Air Force knows they are, and that it should tell this nation and other nations the truth in order to prepare them for saucer landings.

(Note: One odd thing about this book is Major Keyhoe's waspish remarks about George Adamski, who he says "operates a refreshment stand on the road up to Palomar, and his astronomical experience seems to be confined to a small telescope mounted on the roof." Mr. Keyhoe also states that Adamski's report of talking with a man from another world who landed in a saucer reads like a science fiction, and not too good fiction at that." Well, I dunno. Many of the 20th Century's sightings of comets have been made by amateurs. George Adamski has been claiming the actuality of space ships since 1929. And if Mr. Keyhoe is so sure that saucers are about to land, and that some kind of beings are going to step out of them, why doesn't he believe that they have already landed? His eyebrows must certainly have raised on reading LIFE's report Nov. 1, 1954, on the "Little Men." that a lot of Frenchmen said they saw getting out of landed saucers.

And to get one reviewer's opinion of Major Keyhoe's book, read Jonathan N. Leonard's review on the New York Times Book Review, Nov. 22, 1953, which follows: (this review is missing from the text)

Aviation Week. W 59:18 019 '53. ATIC begins study of flying saucers. In this McGraw-Hill publication, the lead paragraph is:

"A statistical analysis of about 3,000 "flying Saucer" reports received between 1947 and 1952 is being conducted by Air Technical Intelligence Center at Wright-Patterson AFB, Dayton, Ohio, in an effort to refute the myth."

The report goes on to say that 90% of all saucer reports received in 1953 can be explained. At least 80% of all those received in 1952 can also be explained.

The center's official analysis within the next few months is hoped to determine definitely the origin of all reported saucers.

In 1952, nearly 70% of the reports came from civilians and about 30% from military personnel. In 1953, so far, 50% civilian, 50% military.

ATIC believes this is due to decline of publicity about flying saucers until recent publication of two books attempting to explain them as warships from another planet.

Balloons are launched from nearly every airfield in the country at 3:00 and 9:00 A.M. and 3:00 and 9:00 P.M. to altitudes ranging from 60,000 to 100,000 feet.

Of 2,000 reports received through military channels since Jan. 1, 1952, ATIC has determined that 15.4% were balloons; 15.2% aircraft; 17.8% astronomical; 6.3% birds, light reflections, etc.; 1.6 hoaxes; 5.8% radar. Insufficient data to evaluate 23.6% of the reports; 14.3% unsolved.

Sources since Jan. 1952: civilians, 39.7%: USAF pilots and crew members while flying, 11.1%; airline pilots while flying, 2%; non-airline civilian pilots while flying, 4%; tower operators, civilian and military, 1%; balloon observers, 2.5%; civilian scientists and engineers, 3.2%; military personnel, 24%; and radar returns, 12.5%.

In addition, the report mentions, in May 1953, the planet Venus, because of hazy atmospheric conditions, appeared to move on an erratic course, appeared to change color, and, at times, was intensely bright. This planet, ATIC figured, accounted for 29% of all sightings in the month of May. The appearance and behavior of this planet confuses even the most experienced pilots.

To our readers. M. Straight. New Repub 129:22 0 26 '53. Michael Straight is editor of the weekly Washington news-analysis magazine, *New Republic.* The article was written in answer to a reader's request to either confirm or deny the landing of a saucer in a field on Mr. Straight's farm, as reported on Frank Edwards radio program. With gentle satire, Mr. Straight "confirmed" by saying that one night in September 1953, two strangers traveling by automobile had driven into a filling station facing the said field on Mr. Straight's farm, shouting "Did you see it?" When the filling station owner asked, "What?," the strangers said, "A huge machine came down in the field, and when it touched, shot up with a blinding light." Mr. Straight then wrote that, naturally, he had reported this to the proper authorities.

Then he goes on to add: "The trouble is that no one is concerned. The National Security Council and the Joint Chiefs seem preoccupied with other problems. I haven't heard a word yet from Project Saucer at Dayton or Project Magnet in the Pentagon; from the Unidentified Objects Sighting Committee in California, or even from my neighbor, Major Keyhoe."

Reply with rejoinder to C.C. Wylie. A.D. Mebane. Science 118: 725-6 D 11 '53. In his short letter in *Science*, Mr. Alexander D. Mebane, of New York City, refutes Mr. Wylie's assertions that the popular conception of the Toronto-Bermuda meteor flight of 1903 was wrong. Mr. Mebane quotes contemporary astronomers to the effect that it was something quite other than an excellent display of shooting stars. He cites Chant, Pickering, W.J. Fisher, W.F. Denning to show that the phenomena was a 5,200-mile *level* flight of unknown lights over Canada, the United States and on south across the ocean.

Plenty going on in the skies. U.S. News 36-27-8 Ja 1 '54. This article is pretty much the full text of the U.S. Air Force report on sightings during the year 1952 and up to the mid-year, 1953. The Air Force reported, among other things, that up to this time, mid-year '53, *no* photographs of UFOs, taken on diffraction-grid cameras, had been received. And then, this report went on the say the following:

1. The Air Force is *not* withholding any "flying saucer" information from the public.

2. While the Air Force does not release the names of people reporting sightings, they are not asked to say anything to reporters, etc. They are free to talk to anybody and to say anything they please.

3. The Air Force does *not* possess photographs which prove their existence of "flying saucers."

4. *No* movie film discloses any proof of a tangible nature to show that there are such things as "flying saucers."

5. No authentic physical evidence has been received establishing the existence of space ships from other planets.

6. All other information with respect to sightings is a matter of public record.

NOTE: Reports which divulge the capabilities of our aircraft, radar, and electronic equipment are classified for obvious reasons.

"When it has completed its analysis, ATIC expects to be able to report that there is no existing danger to the U.S. from interplanetary travelers and that there is nothing to cause undue speculation or hysteria."

FATE. January 1954. Several items relative to saucers in Curtis Fuller's column, I See by The Papers.

Air Force looks at saucers. A Long. Sci Digest 35: 9-10 Ja '54 "Flying saucer hysteria in the United States has been stimulated by sensational sightings reported from time to time in the press. And the mystery apparently is made to grow deeper by an Air Force policy of not discrediting a person or an organization." The article then goes on to say that the Air Force, after investigating a report, no matter how hallucinational, will not call it the bunk. "This assures the Air Force that other people will continue turning in legitimate reports without fear of public ridicule."

The article then continues by pointing out that within our solar system, there is no other planet like Earth that can support life as it exists on earth. It also quotes Rev. Francis J. Heyden, head of the Department of Astronomy, Georgetown University, who said that any spaceship approaching earth at the speed necessary to get from some other solar system to ours would have to decelerate so rapidly that "it would produce a pyro-technic display that would make a meteor look sick. The whole world would know about it...the people on earth would tremble with fear."

On the flying saucer trail. il Am Mag 157 56 Ap '54.This is a one-page article about Mrs. Coral Lorenzen of Sturgeon Bay, Wisconsin, a housewife who founded and heads Aerial Phenomena Research Organization, an outfit said to have 1,000 members all over the world, many of whom have reported odd objects in the sky. The article also said that Mrs. Lorenzen distributes a 10-page bi-monthly bulletin with latest saucer information to APRO members. According to the article, Mrs. Lorenzon classifies saucers into four categories: 1. Disc-shaped; 2. Cigar-shaped; 3. Ball-shaped; 4. Double-ringed type.

FATE. May 1954. Special saucer issue. Robert N. Webster writes that the problem of unidentified flying objects is little closer to being solved then when Kenneth Arnold made his first report in 1947. "We do not personally believe that any person has seen "little men" step out of a flying saucer or has gone on a ride in one — but, nevertheless, we have included a number of these alleged events in this issue." There are eight saucer articles in this issue of FATE. One tells of the establishment of Canadian saucer-hunting station. A second gives official information from other governments and mentions important sightings.

This issue of FATE lauds the Air Corps for its dogged persistence in still investigating saucer reports in the face of orthodox science, reports on the special project of Dr. Clyde Tombaugh, searching the skies for a group of tiny moons believed to be circling the earth at altitudes of from 10,000 to 240,000 miles. (One since discovered. Athalia.) This issue of FATE is also filled with current — 1954 — saucer sightings, with names, dates, and descriptions of objects observed; a report on men who say they have ridden in flying saucers; and a lengthy report on the "little man" and the saucer reported by miners John Q. Black and John Van Allen, of Brush Creek, Cal.

BOOK: *Flying Saucers Have Landed.* Desmond Leslie and George Adamski. New York: The British Book Center. London: Werner Laurie. $3.50. This is quite a book. Both Leslie and Adamski have written on mystical or occult subjects. Adamski has claimed for years that space ships have not only been cruising around and near our earth, but that he has repeatedly photographed them. (He had an article in FATE Magazine, September 1950, and another in FATE Magazine for July 1951, in which some of these photographs were published.) The book have some close-ups of purported scouting ships from Venus and other photographs purporting to be giant carrier ships releasing flying saucers.)

The book traces flying saucers before the Flood, saucers in the ancient Sanskrit writings, saucers in the 18th, 19th and 20th Centuries, saucers in the Mahabarata.

It repeats the arcane legends: "Venus is the home of the gods. From Venus, in the year B.C. 18,617, 841 came the first vehicle out of space to alight on our planet."

In the book, George Adamski states that he was requested in 1949 by the Point Loma Navy Electronics Laboratory to try to get photographs of strange craft moving through spaces.

Also, in the book he states — that on 12:30 P.M., Thursday, 20 November 1952, he made personal contact with a man from another world who landed in a flying saucer on the California desert 10 miles from Desert Center toward Parker, Arizona. This account is accompanied by sworn affidavits of six witnesses.

As a matter of passing interest, it might be noted that two of these witnesses, George H. Williamson and Alfred C. Bailey, are the co-authors of a book on flying saucers, *The Saucers Speak!,* in which they claim to have received messages — through a Ouija board contraption, and by means of radio — messages from the "people" who fly the saucer.

It is also interesting to note that two other books on flying saucers also published by British Book Center, those of Cedric Allingham and of Leonard G. Cramp, cross-praise the Adamski book. the introduction to Mr. Cramp's book was written by Desmond

Leslie, Mr. Adamski's collaborator. *Honi soit qui mal y pens.*

BOOK. *The Saucers Speak!* George H. Williamson and Alfred C. Bailey. A documentary report of Interstellar Communication by Radio Telegraphy. Copyright, 1954. Published by New Age Publishing Company, Los Angeles, California. In their book, Messrs. Williamson and Bailey claim that they received messages — through automatic writing, using something like a Ouija board, and by means of radio, in code — from the people who fly saucers. What are saucers? "Crystal Bells," say the authors. Who flies them? Nah-9 of Solar X Group. Ankar-22 from Jupiter. Regga of Masar (Mars). Zrs of Uranus. Zo of Neptune. Touka of Pluto. Actar of Mercury. Kadar Lacu, head of the Universal Tribunal...on the planet Hatonn in Andromeda. Lomec of Venus.

The book reports that on November 20, 1952, Mr. and Mrs. Williamson with Mr. and Mrs. Bailey "were in company with three other people in the Desert near Desert Center, California, when a cigar-shaped mother ship was observed by all present and a personal contact was made with one of the occupants of a scout-type saucer." This was George Adamski's meeting with the Venusian.

Reason for the communications to Messrs. Williamson and Bailey: Warning to Earth that use of atomic bombs will destroy this planet.

BOOK. *The White Sands Incident.* Daniel W. Fry. Mr. Fry, at the time of writing this account, was a rocket technician at White Sands Proving Ground. His story is that he encountered a space ship at the proving grounds, got aboard, and while talking with visitors from space who flew the craft, traveled to New York City and back in 30 minutes, at a speed of 8,000 miles per hour.

TRUE. May 1954. What Our Air Force Found Out About Flying Saucers. Capt. Edward J. Ruppelt, USAF. From 1952 to 1953, Mr. Ruppelt was in charge of Project Blue Book. The official Air Force investigation of Unidentified Flying Objects. In this TRUE book-length, he tells what the USAF found out about flying saucers. Mr. Ruppelt, now a civilian, believes that flying saucers either do not exist — or are interplanetary.

This account of flying saucers — right out of headquarters — is a 10,000 word report on what Mr. Ruppelt found out during his official investigation over a period of two years. The report is straightforward, factual, believable. It pokes considerable fun at the "little men in blue suit" writers, raises a dubious eyebrow at photographs of the "Lubbock Lights," which he states were not what the college professors saw, explains that the professors saw the lights only from one position, and did not see them in other locations. It casts complete doubt on the Desvergers story of a landed saucer; on the Flatwoods, West Virginia, "Monster"; and mentions by name and date saucer pursuits that were really pursuits of lighted balloons.

Mr. Ruppelt gives a chronological accounting of official Air Force acts, from the very beginnings of the saucer investigation, with many facts never released before.

Facts: There are no good movies of flying saucers. There are no good "stills" of flying saucers in close-up. There are no files bulging with secret information. No one is "killing" newspaper or magazine stories. The stories about "little men" are nonsense. No one is being told not to talk about any saucer sightings. No saucer has ever fallen. No fragments of saucers have ever been obtained. The Air Force is not hiding any information — because the Air Force has no tangible proof of what saucers are.

Among other facts that Mr. Ruppelt gives is one that will stump some of the scientists who have said there has never been a "fix" on a saucer from two different locations. Mr. Ruppelt points out that, not only have there been such a fix by eyewitnesses either on the ground or in the air, but simultaneously by radar as well.

Mr. Ruppelt speaks of Professor Donald H. Menzel's book, as follows: "His explanation failed to account for the many cases where there was a simultaneous radar fix on a UFO and a visual sighting. Mirages and reflections can and do feel the naked eye, but they don't show up simultaneously on a radar scope."

Another interesting comment that Mr. Ruppelt makes is on the "blip" rat race that started over Washington on the night of July 19, 1952. As Mr. Ruppelt explains the bewildering double-shuffling of the Air Force on that occasion — " The story caught the Air Force completely off balance and the handling of it got fouled up beyond all recognition. It finally took a couple of generals and a press conference to straighten things out."

Mr. Ruppelt says that the "blips" were due to an air inversion that *was* present over Washington on the nights the "blips" made their appearance.

Here are some more of Mr. Ruppelt's significant statements.

1. The Air Force has not concealed any secret sensations about the saucers.
2. Project Bluebook was never given any instructions to conceal facts.
3. There is no evidence that the saucers are U.S. secret weapons.
4. There is no evidence that the saucers are of foreign manufacturer.

Then Mr. Ruppelt writes that these four points may bring to you the possibility that the saucers are craft from outer space. "As staggering as the implications may be, to my mind, this is the most acceptable theory — if the saucers exist. There is no other alternative."

"What is the argument that they are non-existent? It was some stubborn facts on its side.

"First, the residue of unknowns shows no common characteristics. Their shapes, performance, times of appearance, colors, locations showed the same bewildering variety as the 80 per cent that we were able to explain. The 434 unknowns included little lights, big lights, multicolored lights, discs seen by day, cigar shapes, orbs and dots of lights...There is a strong belief in the Air Force that the unknowns are unknown simply because we lacked sufficient data on them.

"Secondly, there were no bursts of unknowns. In general, there was no geographic clustering of unknowns. For a time there were more sightings around certain atomic installations and defense areas. Residents of such areas are more security conscious than people living in a non-sensitive area and quite possibly we got more sightings from atomic and defense sections because more people there were scanning the skies."

There has been no time-pattern to saucer sightings. For a while they seemed to be more numerous in July of 1953, then fell off sharply.

In seven years, there has been no physical evidence of the existence of saucers. No crashes. No landings. No fragments. No "hardware" fallen from the skies. No photographic evidence authorities can credit.

Flying Saucer Bounces Off Design Board. Life. May 31, 1954. This two-page article by LIFE gives theoretical working drawings of a flying saucer, and tells how it would operate. It would have a speed of 1,800 mph, combat radius of 1,500 miles. "The flying saucer into which the Air Force is expected to soon sink a wad of money was designed by a shy, 35-year-old English-born engineer named John C. M. Frost...It is the outgrowth of a saucer-like craft called 'Project Y' which Frost designed for his employers, A.V. Roe Canada Ltd. The principle of Frost's flying saucer is based on the 1930s jet-outlet experiments of a Frenchman named Henri Coanda and is expected to work like this: jets of gas are propelled down and out from vents in the edge of the saucer, pulling air down over the saucer's top and diminishing the air on the top surface. When this pressure is sufficiently less than that on the saucer's undersurface, the saucer rises."

Report on Our 'Flying Saucer' Balloons. Collier's, June 11, 1954. Charlotte Knight. Here is another Skyhook balloon explanation of flying saucer sightings. Charlotte Knight explains that she didn't believe this explanation one bit before she started her investigations, because so many reputable observers had reported flying saucers. She also states that flying saucer reports will persist in coming in, since the armed forces themselves are responsible for sending aloft 90 per cent of the objects reported.

Charlotte Knight didn't believe. But then, she made a 1,000-mile trips for Collier's. She talked with scientists and technicians, both civilian and military, at the Air Force's Cambridge research center in Massachusetts, and at some of the country's most secret and carefully guarded Air Research and Command Development sites, including Muroc and Alamogordo. When she got through, ending at the Office of Naval Research at Washington, D.C., she had no further doubts about how and why balloons behave like flying saucers.

Evidence: The balloons go up to 100,000 feet. In the daytime, the look silvery. At night, after sunset, they look like glowing red balls. They can travel at 500 miles per hour in the jet stream, or hang motionless in the sky for hours. One balloon released on the California Coast came to earth just 52 hours later in Badajoz, Spain. That's traveling.

A pilot at 40,000 feet, trying desperately to reach a glowing red globe at 100,000 feet, would be rightly mystified by not being able to get anywhere near it.

Balloons have been drifting over the country since 1947.

Well, maybe the balloons are the whole answer to the mystery of the saucers. Maybe there has never been any mystery. Maybe all the old indications of visitors from outer space, etc., etc., are so much hokum.

But it was certainly some balloon that Captain William Sperry saw over Mt. Vernon in May 1948. A submarine with lights, no wings. "It circled our DC-6" twice and headed off toward Washington."

It was also some balloon that Captain Charles Shipe Childs and his co-pilot John C. Whitted saw July 24, 1948. Flame-spitting aerial monster. Four times as big as a B-29. No wings. 40-foot red flame shot out of its rear end. Made their DC-3 flutter in the "prop-wash, jet-wash, or rocket-wash." "It sent out tremendous shock waves."

Some balloon that reportedly circled the automobile of Lloyd Locke of Durango and Harold Tanner, of Cortez, Colorado, on March 14, 1950. Circled automobile at tremendous speed in a 25 or 30-foot radius.

Some balloon that, roaring like thunder and shooting blue flame, made five passes near Hamilton Air Base, Oakland, California, early on June 21, 1950.

Some balloons in France, in the Fall of 1954, one of which stepped, in skins of a pleasing variety of pastels, a wonderful array of "Little Men."

But why go on...

Maybe Charlotte Knight, writing in Collier's, was absolutely right.

BOOK. *Flying Saucers On The Attack*, Harold T. Wilkins, Copyright 1954 by Harold T. Wilkins, Citadel Press, N.Y., \$3.50. Mr. Wilkins is a well-known English writer with many books and articles to his credit. Among other works by the same author are; *A Modern Treasure Hunter, Panorama of Treasure Hunting Adventures, Mysteries of the Great War, 1914-18, Captain Kidd and his Skeleton Island, Marvels of Modern Mechanics, Great English Schools, Secret Cities of Old South America, Mysteries of Ancient South America.* He has contributed several articles — on historical saucer sightings and on Foo Fighters — to FATE Magazine.

Mr. Wilkin's 329-page book is completely engrossing. Better that anyone else, perhaps, he traces sightings back as far as 222 B.C., are reported by Julius Obsequens, who wrote a book called *Prodigies.*

He also traces apparent saucer sightings through old Irish, English and German chronicles. His research has been exhaustive. His work is painstaking and scholarly. His book's bibliography lists some seventy-five ancient and medieval records that the average person couldn't even lay hands on. No one since Charles Fort, perhaps has gone to such minute pains to establish a credible background for the extraterrestrial theory.

And yet —

Writing of U.S. sightings, Mr. Wilkins says, page 110, "All in all, I have very good reason to assert that well over 250 cases of sightings remain unsolved and unidentified by Project Saucer, although this is something they have most carefully concealed from the public and press."

Nothing could be more inaccurate.

While it is quite conceivable that the U.S. Force may have concealed its *findings* from the public and the press, it has never concealed the fact that a certain number of sightings have remained "unknowns."

Again, in many apocryphal-sounding reports, Mr. Wilkins refuses to give the names of his informants, as in his Appendix, page 303, he prints a "curious" story told by an "official in an official attorney's office" concerned with tracing lost persons in Los Angeles, Cal. This is the story of two men about 6 feet six inches in height, temporarily employed by this tracing bureau. The men were bluish-green in complexion, and with prick ears like certain dogs. One day one of the men leaned over a filing cabinet, "and, with his curiously curved hand, scored an indentation in the steel at least 1/2 inch deep!" Mr. Wilkins reports that the men had said that they came from another planet, out of a saucer that had landed in the Mojave Desert in 1952. The men disappeared from their jobs at the tracing bureau. The filing cabinet was sent to a metallurgical chemist. He said that, to produce the indentation, it would require a force of some "2,000 lb. to the square inch!" "It also added that traces of more than a dozen elements were found in the dents."

Mr. Wilkins concludes: "Obviously, this story can neither be proved nor disproved, and the indented steel has been locked away. (*Communicated to the author, by a correspondent in Los Angeles, Calif., who insists on anonymity.*)"

Oh, Mr. Wilkins!

FATE. July 1954. An article on some strange meteors, by John Phillip Bessor. He mentions some odd things that have fallen from the sky, including a purple globe that landed in a field in Philadelphia in the fall of 1950. When touched by a policeman, *it turned into a shapeless, gelatinous mass.*

BOOK. *Aboard a Flying Saucer,* Truman Bethurum. DeVorss & Co., Publishers. Copyright 1954 by Truman Bethurum. Mr. Bethurum at the time he wrote his book, was a welder and maintenance man for a western construction company. A letter by the treasurer of his union, reproduced in the book, describes him as a Journeyman Engineer. Mr. Bethurum's book is about eleven visits he claimed to have made aboard a landed flying saucer with the saucer's woman captain, Aura Rhanes. This woman, from a planet called Clarion, on the other side of the moon, had the odd habit of speaking in verse to Mr. Bethurum, and in not very good verse at that. As a sample, she describes a wedding with "the families and many friends of the bride and groom from the many planets assembled: My outfit was of modest style; shoes, hat, bag and accessories like my gown, were a gorgeous cinnamon brown. As all the ladies linked up to bid adieu, the gentlemen kissed their hands. Their fingers were fitted with diamond rings. Many had golden bands. Mine was regal, with a silvery hue, and the settings were azure, or royal hue."

Maybe Mr. Bethurum is telling the truth when he speaks of his visits to this enchanting creature who flew her "Admiral Scow" with a crew of 32 little men. But if this race, millions of years in advance of us are going to come here and inflict doggerel like that on us, God help us all.

As a literary gem, Mr. Bethurum's book is perhaps the best. It reads a little bit like a fish fry in "Green Pastures," with the same charming naivete.

It also has the same primitive innocence as a book entitled, "The Palm Wine Drunkard."

Mr. Bethurum states in his book that he had it ghost-written for him by a ghost writer in Los Angeles, Mary Kay Tennison. He also states that he put his adventures on tape for Professor George Adamski at Palomar Gardens. After that, Mr. Bethurum spoke at a meeting of Saucers, International, at the Hollywood Hotel. Finally, someone warned Mr. Bethurum that he had talked too much and that others would try to steal his experience and write books and articles with them. So he saw an attorney about protecting his "property" and so decided to have a book of his own written to protect his interests.

In Mr. Bethurum's own words, I read his book "with pain gripping my very soul."

Flying Saucers Come From A Distance World. *American Weekly*, October 24, 1954. Prof. Herman Oberth, author of *The Rocket into Interplanetary Space.* Professor Oberth is an internationally known authority on guided missiles and the conquest of space. His technical works were of key importance to the Germans in developing the V-2 rocket. While Prof. Oberth's article is hailed on the front cover of American Weekly as a startling new theory about flying saucers, it is not a new theory. It is the same theory advanced by TRUE, LIFE, FATE, and others, i.e.: Flying saucers are from outer space, quite conceivably from solar system other than ours. The author believes that because the saucers are propelled by unlimited power they can travel at the speed of light — 186,000 miles per second. To get to earth from their distant home, the occupants of the saucers go into a fog of suspended animation, and get no older in their passage, or very little older, because of the "contraction" of time. Conclusion: If we can make them understand some kind of message, we should welcome them. "We should try by every scientific mean that seems feasible to get into contact with them."

FATE. November 1954. This issue carries an article on the "Flying Jellyfish," that trailed BOAC's Stratocruiser, the Centaurus, off Labrador on June 29, 1954. Another article, reprinted by permission from the *London Sunday Dispatch* is by Air Chief Marshal Lord Dowding, then Commander in Chief of the Royal Air Force, who goes on record by saying he believes in flying saucers. According to the Air Chief Marshall, "more than 10,000 sightings have been reported, the majority of which cannot be accounted for, by any "scientific" explanation. Lord Dowding in his article mentioned Major Donald E. Keyhoe's book, "Flying Saucers from Other Space," as giving the best available evidence of the saucers' existence.

The Air Marshal further ruled out the idea that saucers are new types of aircraft of either Russia or the U.S. "They have been tracked on radar screens in America — on one occasion — on three screens simultaneously — and the observed speeds have been as great as 9,000 miles an hour."

Lord Dowding then rules out all earthly materials being able to survive such speeds and such heats — let alone earth men. "I can therefore see no alternative to accepting the theory that they come from some extra-terrestrial source."

The Air Marshal's article then hazards the guess that extra-terrestrial visitors might be far in advance of us spiritually. "But this hypothesis is not universally accepted, particularly in the U.S., where fighters sent up to intercept the visitors have sometimes had unpleasant experiences." And here, the Air Marshall mentions the Mantell tragedy.

Another article in this issue of FATE, *How the Saucers Fly*, is from Major Donald E. Keyhoe's book, *Flying Saucers from Outer Space*. This article gives Major Keyhoe's conversations with certain Canadian scientists and their work with electromagnetism. "These investigations seem to point the way to a new technology in magnetics." And — to powering saucers with a "sink" in the earth's electromagnetic field. The article also explains how a saucer's rim, glowing from high speed, could change colors, from red to orange to yellow to white — or show blue or green from corona effects.

FATE. December 1954. A squib in Curtis Fuller's column: "Dorothy Kilgallen, the columnist, raises this question in a recent article: "Is it possible that new peeps through the telescope on Mt. Palomar indicate that many a scientist — and textbook — could have been wrong about the universe?" (Author's note: this is about like, "When did you stop beating you wife"—or in the case of the first mate writing up the log: "The captain wasn't drunk today."

New York World Telegraph & Sub., November 11, 1954. Two articles on flying saucers sightings in Italy for past 60 days. One article told of reports by many "eyewitnesses" of landed saucer with "little men."

LIFE, Nov. 1, 1954. *Astral Adventurers.* Frenchmen report meeting with unlikely creatures. Report on sightings in France, in fall of 1954, of craft dropping out of the skies — and "little men" hopping out of the craft. Craft left skid marks, gashed railroad ties in one place. Craft and dwarfish occupants reported by good, solid French citizens. ("Little man" at Brush Creek, needing water for his sources? "Little men" at Steep Rock taking on water?)

On November 10, 1954, there appeared in *Greenwich Time*, Greenwich, Conn, a syndicated article by Joseph L. Myler, United Press Staff Correspondent, which pointed out the possibility that the atom will be most easily harnessed for peacetime use when atomic power is taken direct from water, rather than from rare minerals. The article quotes Dr. George R. Harrison of the Massachusetts Institute of Technology to the effect that if the thermonuclear-fission reaction can be slowed down — water itself can become the fuel that inventors have long dreamed of."

Each water molecule consists of two atoms of hydrogen and one of oxygen. If hydrogen fission can be tamed, Harrison said, "humanity should never need to worry about its energy supplies again."

LIFE. Nov. 29, 1954. Now They're in Italy. Report on two dwarfs from landed “saucer” near Tuscan village of Bucine, Italy. Dwarfs stole silk stocking and bunch of carnations from a Signora Rosa Dainelli. This issue also has a photograph taken by Angelo Cozzi, in the Dolomites, of a glowing sphere that Signor Cozzi said sped away after he had photographed it.

Flying Saucers on My Ranch. W.C. Hall, *Sir! A Magazine For Males*, February 1954. W.A. Hall, a young Australian rancher, owner of a 15,000 acre ranch in North Queensland, writes that on a dull, grey day in October (1953?), six saucers came to earth. Out of them got a group of men in uniforms resembling those of U.S. paratroopers. When they saw Mr. Hall, who was on horseback, they climbed back into their saucers and took off. The saucers threw off an odd-colored exhaust. This knocked out both Mr. Hall and his horse, put Mr. Hall into a trance in which he saw his barren Australian acres blooming like an Eden, levitated him five feet off the ground, where he floated for a while before he regained consciousness.

The next year on the ranch, things were fantastic. Grass grew where no grass grew before. Cows, sheep, chickens — and rabbits — multiplied prodigiously. Some of the chicks born had two feet; some of the heifers were born with five legs.

There's a photograph with the article — a saucer coming in for a landing over a flock of sheep. It looks just like one of the saucers in George Adamski's photographs. Odd thing about it is that none of the sheep are looking up at it. Most of them are placidly gracing, although a few are looking at the camera.

Mr. Hall states that the saucers were elliptical in shape, about thirty feet tall, white in color, with a streak of blue running like a ribbon across their middle sections.

BOOK. *Space, Gravity, and the Flying Saucer.* Leonard G. Cramp. British Book Center, Publishers. First published February 1955. Copyrighted 1955 by British Book Center, Inc., 122 East 55 Street, New York, N.Y. This book has an introduction by Desmond Leslie, co-author with George Adamski of the book, *Flying Saucers Have Landed.* Mr. Leslie goes into considerable detail about the "Coniston" saucer and the impossibility that Stephen Darbyshire, the boy who took the photograph, had pulled a hoax. Then Mr. Leslie writes: "In the past year there have been a spate of books on the subject (saucers), mainly preoccupied with long lists of sightings taken from sources as varied in time and space as the Annals of Ancient Rome to the secret files of the Pentagon. Though interesting and valuable as documentation or reference, mere catalogues of events are not going to advance the subject much further. What is required now is a serious scientific study of all this data, and from it, the emergency of explanations in terms acceptable to the more intelligent physicist."

Haw!

Mr. Cramp's book, reviewing a number of sightings, first advances the theory that the saucers fly by means of a G-field, or gravitational-field method of propulsion. Then, on page 137 of this 182-page book, Mr. Cramp advances the additional theory that saucers fly by means of "levitation." Their operators levitate them mentally. Mr. Cramp spends considerable time on the levitations performed by the American, Daniel Douglas Home, by St. Joseph of Copertino, St. Teresa of Avila, and by many other mystics. He also describes levitations performed at "seances" in London.

Mr. Cramp, like Mr. Cedric Allingham, devotes considerable space to George Adamski and to Mr. Adamski's meeting, in the desert, with the Venusian. His last chapter is an attempt to show, by "orthographic" drawings that neither Mr. Adamski, nor the boy who photographed the "Coniston" saucer could have been guilty of fakery.

For one book reviewer's comments on both of these books, read John K. Hutchens' review in The New York Herald Tribune for February 11, 1955, which follows: Friday, February 11, 1955. Book Review by John K. Hutchens. *Flying Saucer from Mars*. By Cedric Allingham. British Book Centre. 153 pages. $2.75. *Space, Gravity and the Flying Saucer*. By Leonard G. Cramp. British Book Centre. 179 pages. $3.

"With just a slight break in luck, one Cedric Allingham, Briton, bird-watcher and mystery-story writer, might have been the first person in this world to meet a visitor from another. The way things turned out, he had to settle for being merely the second. As all good flying saucer fans know, the big honor fell to our own George Adamski, of Mount Palomar, Calif., who met up with a stray Venusian on Nov. 20, 19522, in the California desert and told about it the next year in his share of a book called "Flying Saucers Have Landed," by himself and Desmond Leslie.

What's New Up There?

"Mr. Allingham, a gallant man and generous, doesn't resent Mr. Adamski's stunning coup. In "Flying Saucer From Mars," one of two outer-space special published today by the British Book Center, he even grants that Mr. Adamski learned more from his Venusian than he (Mr. Allingham) did from his Martian, Mr. Adamski being gifted with telepathic powers, Mr. Allingham not. Into each life some rain must fall, but, of course, if a spaceman falls with it, all is not so bad as it might be.

"For Mr. Allingham's meeting—about 3:45 p. m., Feb. 18, 1954, near Lossiemouth, Scotland—did have its moments. He took a picture of his Martian, whereas Mr. Adamski let his Venusian get away unphotographed. The snapshot of the Martian is right here in the book—six-foot spaceman, in a one-piece spacesuit, walking in dim light toward his saucer, his back to the camera. Unhappily, the bird-watcher didn't think in time to get a picture of his new friend's face. But then, I guess you'd be pretty flustered yourself if you had just been talking with a man who breezed in from Mars, with a fancy breathing apparatus in his nose, and asked you by way of "gestures" if there was about to be another war on Earth.

All Aboard for Venus

"Just the same, flustered though he was, and lacking Mr. Adamski's telepathic skills, Mr. Allingham managed to ask a few questions in the form of diagrams drawn on a pad. Astronomers will be relieved to hear that he settled forever that question of the Martian "canals." They're canals, all right; the man from up there said so. (The Marian word for "yes," spoken in a tone like "the clear liquid of a hill-side spring," sound something like "qul-1.") Do the Martians and the Venusians exchange visits? Yes, sir, they do—this one had been over to Venus himself. They also drop in on the moon.

"Could Mr. Allingham look inside the saucer? Nothing doing, the Martian indicated, politely but firmly, and then took off into the heavens, with the aplomb of an Earthman catching the 5:23 for Larchmont. But not before Mr. Allingham had taken a picture of the saucer resting on the ground. This picture, too, is in the book, and if it reminds you of what Arthur C. Clarke, former chairman of the British Interplanetary Society, said of a similar picture taken by Mr. Adamski—"uncanny resemblance to electric-light fitting with table-tennis balls fixed underneath"—well, you must remember that Mr. Clarke is one of those mean old scientific spoilsports who don't trust anybody.

"Mr. Cramp, also a Briton, hasn't had Mr. Allingham's and Mr. Adamski's luck, but that hasn't kept him from doing some heavy thinking about our friends out there and how they get around. What, he asks, makes a flying saucer fly? Might be one thing, might be another, he suggests, with numerous diagrams calculated to confound an Earthman who long ago found even plane geometry tough enough. It could be atomic energy, he submits, or maybe that power of levitation which enables the gifted to suspend objects, including themselves, in mid-air without visible means of support.

Watch Out for Those Corners

"A few problems remain. Sometime it almost seems that the space-minded Earthmen ar fighting among themselves, which won't do at all. Mr. Cramp says flesh-and-blood can survive a right-angle turn in a saucer going 1,000 m. p. h. because the saucer moves in its own gravitational field and thus avoids strain. It was Gerald Heard, wasn't it who guess the saucers are operated by large, trained bees? Major Donald E. Keyhoe, United States Marine Corps (retired) believes they are run by remote control from a mother ship. Mr. Cramp, who admires Major Keyhoe, accepts the Adamski story, which Major Keyhoe plainly deems a fake. They all denounce Donald Menzel, the Harvard astrophysicist and major saucer-debunker. And, speaking of Martians, whatever became of Orson Welles, the very first of them?"

FATE. March 1955. This issue of FATE has a special saucer section, with seven articles on flying saucers: *Unsolved Saucer Mysteries*, by Curtis Fuller; *Why Was Frank Edwards Fired?*

by John C. Ross, who is also Curtis Fuller; *Saucers Over Italy*, by Jared Hamilton; *Religion and Saucers*, by Dr. Homer A. Jack, minister of the Unitarian Church of Evanston, Illinois; *Confusion in the Sky*, by the Editors; *Little Men From All Over*, by Curtis Fuller; and *The Saucer That Got Away* by Paul F. Serpas, who claims that he tried to photograph a saucer outside New Orleans on July 18, 1954, but that his camera positively wouldn't work.

In one of these articles, *Confusion in the Sky*, by the editors there is still the "admonition to all saucer fans to study the Air Force's statements most cautiously — most cautiously indeed — and to have a salt shaker handy."

But in this same article, there is mention of Robert S. Allen's syndicated Washington column and a statement therein, on September 4, 1954, that the U.S. was getting ready to take the wraps off some of its flying saucer secrets with a prediction that the Air Force would reveal fantastic new guided-missiles which were responsible for speeding fireballs stories. It also reported a Winnipeg *Free Press* report that the Canadian government knew all about UFO's flying all over Manitoba one weekend, with an unidentified spokesman saying: "We know all about them; they are under our control," with a refusal to give details.

Other Sources of Saucer Information

In addition to regular magazines and books, there were—in 1955—a great many saucer "bulletins." These are mostly mimeographed, multigraphed, or photo-lith jobs, published under the names of various saucer-watching "societies."

Among these are 'SAUCERS,' published by Flying Saucers International. P.O. Box 35054, Los Angeles, Cal., editor, Max B. Miller; NEXUS, published by James W. Moseley, Box 163,

Fort Lee, N.J.; URANUS, bi monthly, Markham House Press, Ltd., 31 King's Road, London S.W.3, England; THE SAUCER SENTINEL, bi-weekly, Olympic Publications, 6 Holland Court, Saginaw, Michigan; CRIFO NEWSLETTER, Civilian Research, Interplanetary Flying Objects, P.O. Box 1855, Cincinnati, Ohio. Ouranos, Revue Internationale pour l'etude des SOUCOUPES VOLANTES et problemes connexes (Bondy, Seine): Marc Thirouin; E. Biddle (London, N. 20); THE SAUCERIAN, Clarksburg W. Va. Another such bulletin was published bi-monthly by Mrs. Coral Lorenzen, Aerial Phenomena Research Organization, Sturgeon Bay, Wisconsin.

There have also been Flying Saucer Conventions. The first was held August 16th to 18th, 1953 at the Hollywood Hotel, Hollywood, Cal. Among the speaker: Orfeo Angelucci; Silas Newton, Frank Scully, Jeron King Criswell (syndicated columnist, "Criswell Predicts"); Truman Bethurum, George W. Van Tassel, and George Adamski.

The "World's First Interplanetary Spacecraft Convention" was held by George W. Van Tassel at Giant Rock, Cal., on April 4, 1954. Speakers: George W. Van Tassel, Frank Scully, Orfeo Angelucci, George H. Williamson, Truman Bethurum and Daniel Fry.

The convention after that, called "First International Flying Saucers Convention," was held for three days, June 4, 5, and 6, 1954, at the Cathay Circle Theater in Los Angeles, and was sponsored by a new saucer organization: Saucer Research Foundation of Los Angeles. Among the speaker: Daniel W. Fry, Orfeo Angelucci.

Flying Saucers International, publishers of 'SAUCERS,' also sells life membership to the organization for 25 cents.

You can also buy yourself a membership button, appropriately bearing a sketch of a flying saucer and a streak of lightning, for another 25 cents.

The European Sightings of 1954

In the fall of 1954, literally scores of sightings of "flying saucers" were reported, first in France, then in Portugal, Italy and Yugoslavia. They caused a sensation, since people of the Continent had believed that the American furor over the saucers had been mostly hot air.

But there were so many European sightings, and by so many competent observers, that Europeans, for the first time, began to take the saucers seriously. But even among Europeans, opinions on the strange apparitions were mixed. Comment on the earliest sightings provoked the same kind of semi-hysterical outbursts, the same kind of awe and mystery that were present in American reportings. Later comment took on a more earthly tone, as editors reported new European and American developments in aircraft that had never been reported in the American press, and about which only an infinitesimal number of Americans knew.

It is interesting to follow this Continental comment, and what follows here is a boil-down of the most important articles that appeared in French and Italian magazines shortly after the sightings.

In France, the magazine Paris MATCH, issue of September 25-October 2, came out with an article entitled, "The passengers of the flying saucers intrigue the French." This article started out by saying that Miss Edith Jacobsen, Mrs. Aasta Solvang, M. Antoine Mazaud, and M. Marius Dewilde were the only persons to make personal contact with the passengers of the soucoupes volantes (flying saucers.)"

The article then went on to quote la grande autorite (the great authority) George Adamski, on extraterrestrial creatures, drags in the names of Scully and Keyhoe, quotes Vishinsky to the effect that saucers originated in Scotch whisky, quotes some 1948 figures from Air Intelligence at Wright Field, and

Professor Einstein's note to the effect that he had no desire to know what saucers were. End of article.

In its issue for October 25-October 30, MATCH devoted five pages to saucers in an article by Raymond Cartier.

Epoca, November 14, 1954. French aeronautics has developed a flying tube, a new kind of aircraft with circular wings that fit around a central fuselage. The pilot's cabin is in the rear. The flying tube or cigar takes off vertically, can climb to 22,000 meters, and reach a velocity of 2,500 kilometers an hour.

Oggi, November 25, 1954. In a letter to the editor, reader Robert Foppiano wanted to know if (real people actually flew the discs) and some earthling killed a visitor from space — would he be guilty of murder or manslaughter. The editor replied that it was subtle question of law, but that he didn't believe that any Martians had landed, and furthermore, he doubted that letters he had received signed "X22K" were from Martians.

L'Europa, November 14, 1954. Letters to the editor. A Signor A.S. of Rome wrote that he believed that a civilized state might exist on Mars, but that the vehicles people were seeing were earth-made. He stated his belief that earth men in disguise or in outlandish garb had emerged from the craft in order to keep a real secret in the realm of mystery. Another letter from Amilcare Ramponi of Rimini wrote his opinion that if flying discs were from other planets, governmental authorities would have done something about intercepting them. But discs had been around for seven years. One fell near Marietta and no one bothered to go and get it. Another reader, Giovanni Carletti of Milan, advances a spiritual hypothesis: "Could it not be that the means that "non-earth" beings are using to come among us is "metempsychosis?"

La Domenica del Corriere, November 28. This issue has two articles on flying saucers. The first, by Maner Lualdi, reports on some fantastic new craft invented by the French and the Americans — the French flying tube, or flying cigar, perfected after eight years of experimentation, and American craft, notably *supersonic* helicopters. Signor Lualdi explains saucers in terms of these recent revelations — which were revelations to Europeans only, not to citizens of the U.S.A. The writer also pointed out that the attributes of the new French and American craft — hanging stationary and flying perpendicularly — were attributes of saucers.

In one interesting paragraph, he stated that the U.S. Senate was debating the building of an artificial satellite in order to move to the *assault* of Mars in 1970. The italics are mine, not his. And the word *assalto* in Italian means assault or attack. Perhaps he meant merely to write explore, and used an unfortunate choice of word. For why should we wish to assault Mars — unless Mars has been trying to assault us? Here's another little paradox to mull over.

The Signor also writes that the U.S. has hundreds of supersonic helicopters, called the "Gone" — and has probably had such craft for eight or ten years!

The other article in this issue of La Domenica del Corriere, was by v. Beonic-Brocchieri, a university professor. His conclusions were that he would not believe in flying discs, even if he saw one in the sky. He would believe in them only if he could touch one — and the mathematical possibilities of that, he felt, were zero.

The professor pointed out that the discs don't have one millionth of a chance of being real. In areas where they were reported, hundreds of thousands of people, not just a few, should have glimpsed them. This is discounting all the people who were not in a position to see them — those people asleep, etc. The professor then stated his belief in mirages — people didn't have to be lying. But s to the reality of saucers — far too many people (those who didn't see them) would have to be wrong to make far too few (those who had seen them) right.

CHAPTER 9
VISUAL PROOF

What proof do we have, other than the reports of a great many people, that flying saucers really exist — not as mirages and rainbows — but as real, actual "somethings" that fly very fast, that maneuver, that are seemingly piloted, or guided by remote control, by "intelligences"?

We have photographs — or what are alleged to be photographs.

Among the best of the photographs of flying saucers were those that appeared in TRUE Magazine, in its July 1950 issue. Some of these same photographs have been reproduced in FATE Magazine, in the book by Kenneth Arnold and Ray Palmer, and the book by Harold T. Wilkins.

A partial list of photographs, as they have appeared chronologically, follows:

FATE. Vol. 1, No. 1. Photo by Al Hixenbaugh that appeared in *Louisville Times*. Two objects seen over Kentucky on July 7, 1947.

FATE. Vol. 1, No. 1. Newspaper clipping from *Arizona Republic*, Phoenix, Ariz, July 9, 1952. Taken by William A. Rhodes.

FATE. Vol. 1, No. 2. Photo of disc-like object that fell into Crow River, Ontario. Shows mostly splash.
(Later branded an absolute fake by Ray Palmer of FATE.)

FATE. Sept. 1949. Photos of 2 discs taken by John H. Janssen, aviation editor, *Morristown Daily Record*, Morristown, N.J. Appeared in that paper on July 10, 1947.

FATE. Sept. 1950. Photographs of objects purported to be space ships near moon. Taken by George Adamski.

LIFE. June 26, 1950. Photo of flying saucer taken by Paul Trent, McMinnville, Oregon, on May 11, 1950.

TRUE. July 25, 1950. Seven photographs of unidentified flying objects.

FATE. July 1951. More photographs by George Adamski of objects he believed to be flying near moon, more than 200,000 miles from earth.

BOOK. *The Coming of the Saucers*, by Kenneth Arnold and Ray Palmer. Many photographs, some of which had been in newspapers and reproduced before in FATE Magazine. Other photos of sightings over Battle Creek, Catalina Island, Chicago, Ft. Worth and other spots in the United States. In all, there are close to 30 photographs in the book.

TRUE. Dec. 25, 1952. Photographs of hovering object caught on radar.

BOOK. *Flying Saucers Have Landed.* Desmond Leslie and George Adamski. This book has a great number of photographs — pictures of what purports to be a "scout ship" leaving a rocky valley at Desert Center, Cal., on Nov. 20, 1952; photos of some odd-looking cigar-shaped "craft releasing flying saucers;" a photograph of a flying light over New York. Others are "close-ups" of hovering saucers that Robert N. Webster, writing in FATE Magazine, said "looks like the upper half of a singing top with a few ping-pong balls glued to the underside."

BOOK. *Flying Saucers On The Attack.* Harold T. Wilkins. This book has ten photographs of saucers, shown either as flying lights or disc-like objects with turrets. It reproduces some of the shots included in the Arnold-Palmer book, also other photos that have appeared in U.S. newspapers, TRUE, etc.

Paris Match, Paris, France. Oct. 2, 1954. Picture of a landed saucer.

'SAUCERS.' Monthly bulletin. Various pictures in different issues since June 1953. Two especially interesting are in the June 1954 issue — one taken by a group of amateur astronomers in California, one taken in Torver, England. Both objects shown appear identical — discs with turrets.

New York World Telegram & Sun, December 1, 1954. *New York Herald Tribune,* December 10, 1954. This is a photograph of two discs, caught motionless, by photographer Giuseppe Grasso over Taormina, Sicily. The Telegram published the picture on the afternoon of December 1. Its caption was: "FLYING SAUCERS? Amazed spectators at Taormina, Italy, sight objects in sky resembling oft-reported flying discs. Italy recently has been flooded with reports of the flying 'mysteries.'"

Nine days later, this photograph was published as front-page news by the *New York Herald Tribune,* with a four-column story headed: "Air Force to Probe New Flying Saucers Over Europe." The caption under the picture said: "one of the pictures seemingly showing flying saucers, which are being studied by the defense agencies. It was taken at Taormina, Sicily. Similar photographs were taken in Sweden and Yugoslavia." Then, the article, which was written by Ansel E. Talbert, the Herald Tribune military and aviation editor, followed.

The article said that photographs taken in Sweden, Italy and Yugoslavia were being studied by defense agencies to determine whether they could be inhabited vehicles, natural phenomena or frauds. The U.S. Air Force plans to investigate also. Air Force still says it has no opinion on what saucer, cigar-shaped and disc-shaped objects moving through skies since 1947 might be. They "are not any plane, missile or weapon" developed or under development by the United States and that "no authentic evidence exists that they are space ships from another planet."

The article continued by saying that Dr. Rafaele Bendani, Italian astronomer, believed they are "human-made." In Yugoslavia, Dr. Milorad Protic, another astronomer, said that they could not be meteorites. Clair Booth Luce, American Ambassador to Italy, among the hundreds who had seen unusual phenomena in the skies, had no idea what they might be.

In France, the magazine "Express," regarded as the voice of Premier Mendes-France, offered a standing reward of 10,000,000 francs, about $28,570, to the first person to bring a visitor from outer space to its offices. (Our American Saturday Review of Literature offers you a better offer than this — $100,000.00 to the first "little Man" to walk into their offices.)

The French National Committee for Festivals outlined a day of festivity for welcoming such a visitor, with a special gold medal to be struck "For having the courtesy to land first in France."

The United Press, that received the photographs featuring the articles from its Rome Bureau, said that the negative had been examined carefully. No hint of fraud, tampering, or retouching was found.

SIR! A Magazine for Males. February 1955 issue, p. 17. What is claimed to be a photo of a saucer coming for a landing over a flock of sheep; ranch, Queensland, Australia.

BOOK. *Luers sur les Soucoupes Volantes*, Aime Michel (In French). Contains many, many pictures of saucers, many of which have never appeared in the U.S.

BOOK. *Flying Saucers from Mars*. Cedric Allingham. Photograph of what Mr. Allingham claims was of a Martian he saw and talked with. Martian has his back turned towards camera, walking away.

BOOK. *Space, Gravity and the Flying Saucer*. Leonard G. Cramp. Photograph of the Coniston saucer, and of George Adamski's saucer, with a comparison of the two.

Ray Palmer, writing in the book on which he collaborated with Kenneth Arnold, said that original prints of photographs published in newspapers are practically impossible to obtain. The newspapers have "forgotten" the addresses of the photographers who took them.

It doesn't make any difference.

If you will look at all available photographs, you will see one thing. You will see visual corroboration of what sighters of flying saucers have described orally in great detail. Most of them boil down to discs, often discs with shock waves preceding them. Some also look like flying charges of controlled electricity. Some look translucent, or semi-transparent. Fakes? Real? Make up your own mind.

Captain Ruppelt, of the Air Material Command of Dayton, Ohio, has been quoted in the newspapers to the effect that no negative of a flying saucer picture has ever been received by governmental investigators of flying saucers.

You look at the pictures yourself — and be your own judge.

Then look at the pictures of sketches made by French farmers and artisans of what they saw in the fields of France in the Fall of 1954 — LIFE Magazine, Nov. 1, 1954 — and see what they add up to.

Look at the photographs of Farmer Trent's flying saucer, the photograph taken by Giuseppe Grasso over Taormina, Sicily. Compare them. Note their similarity. Observe the clear-cut, sharp outlines that denote reality.

Then make up your own mind as to what you think.

(Editorial comment by R. M. Wood: The following notation was added in black ink, dated by a forensic laboratory as ink from a pen manufactured after 1977. "Good comparisons. Notes were analyzed at NPIC (National Photographic Intelligence Center?) and show similar characteristics of those seen in N.M. (New Mexico?). Photos in White Hot folder are not available as they are TS (TOP SECRET) Restricted Data. AS-2 (Assistant Chief of Staff Number 2) required letter of authority before removing. Much have Majther (Majestic poorly written?) review before visiting blue room (the "famous Blue Room"?) facility.

Suggest you call Nate (Nate Twining?) for appointment to W.P. (Wright-Patterson?). Would also recommend prior approval from Van (Vandenberg?) before you make official inquiries. Wish I could be of more help to you in your follow-up investigation.

Ben

P.S. I will be at ADC for a while. Why don't you visit and will show you around?")

CHAPTER 10
THE LANDINGS

Have there been landings of flying saucers?

According to the reports of those who claim to have seen landings, there have been quite a number of them.

You'll have to accept or reject these on hearsay evidence alone. So far as is known, no saucers has ever malfunctioned and crashed. No fragments of anything resembling a sphere there as exploded have ever been recovered, according to the Air Force.

But landings? Yes. A respectable number of them. Let's not start with one of these claimed to have taken place since 1947. Instead, let's start with a landing mentioned by Charles Fort.

It took place in 1909. This was just six years after the Wright brothers had flown something that was little more than a kite with an engine — and a jeering world disbelieved.

To be exact, it was 11:00 P.M. May 18, 1909, near a road, close to Caerphilly Mountains, in Wales. A gentleman named Lithbridge, of 4 Roland Street, Cardiff, Wales, saw on the grass at the side of the road a large, tube-shaped object. In it were two men, in heavy fur overcoats. When the saw Mr. Lithbridge, they spoke excitedly to each other in a foreign language — and the craft they were in took off and sailed away into the air. Newspaper men who visited the place found the grass trampled. They also found a scattering of torn newspapers and other debris.

We haven't yet, so far as is known, arrived at a piloted, tube-shaped craft in this year (1954) — although the French evidently have, as judged by an Italian newspaper report

December 1954 — but here was this thing, reportedly seen 51 years ago. (Recent newspaper reports have indicated that we will buy patent rights from the French.)

Coming up to date — rumors of saucer landings — and stories of "little men" coming from them alive, or being found in them dead, began circulating shortly after the report by Kenneth Arnold. These reports centered principally around the American deserts.

In the January 1950 issue of FATE, this publication reprinted on AP story reported by two prospectors. This story said that on August 19, 1949, the two prospectors, Buck Fitzgerald, who claimed he had lived in the Death Valley region long enough to recognize a flying disc when he saw one, and Mase Garney, his partner, saw a flying disc about 24 feet in diameter whiz past them at about 300 mph and crash land in the desert. They said that then two little men jumped out and started running when they saw the prospectors. The "little men" looked human, but were very small, like dwarfs. Fitzgerald and Garney said that they chased these little fellows over a sand dune, but lost them.

Fate asked a few questions with regard to the report, such as: "If they couldn't have found the little men, certainly they could have found the crashed disc?" It was at this point that FATE expressed a skepticism about crashed saucers and "little men" that it has expressed every year since 1950.

Sometime around March or April of 1950, a newspaper report, ridiculing landed saucers with little men, which was inspired by an interview with Air Intelligence officers of Wright-Patterson Air Field, appeared in newspapers.

This news story said that the Army was tired of reports of little 30-inch men. "From the phone calls, and scattered reports, it would sound as if the Wellsian invasion of men from Mars is at hand."

"At least three reports of these little guys landing in flying saucers have now been made, in one case, a bunch of them wearing gray uniforms and armed to the teeth spilled out of a flying disc. Where are they?"

"When Army Intelligence officers investigate the possibility of an interplanetary invasion, the little men are not there."

The article then stated that "previous to the report of six 30-inch men burned and charred in a flying turtle disc in the Sierra Madre Mountains in Mexico, Army Intelligence started a similar report in Wisconsin. A farmer said he watched a disc land. "Out of the saucer came a bunch of little men," he reported. "They were dressed in gray uniforms with red shoulder bars and wore red caps."

The Army Intelligence report then said that investigation revealed that the farmer had been discharged from the Army for mental reasons.

The newspaper report then quoted Army Intelligence as saying "A popular magazine now publishes a report by two Death Valley prospectors of a 24-foot disc landing in the desert at a speed of 300 miles an hour."

"The prospectors, Buck Fitzgerald and Mase Garney, asserted chased two 24-inch gents over a sand dune before losing them.

"Army Intelligence refused to swallow that one. Magazines such as this, it said, seldom have any evidence to support their fantasies."

In the May 1950 issue of FATE, under the heading of Space Ships, Flying Saucers and Clean Noses, Ray Palmer lashed back at the Air Force for what he considered to be a slur against the magazine. The news story quoting Army Intelligence, was reprinted. Then Mr. Palmer went on to say that FATE only repeated the story about the Death Valley prospectors, taking it from an International News Service article that had appeared in hundreds of newspapers.

As for the Wisconsin incident, Mr. Palmer stated that he personally investigated reports in and around the Waupaca area, Stevens Point, and Wisconsin Rapids. He states that dozens of reports were made, simultaneously, by farmers and small city folk, of "flying discs." All agreed, according to Mr. Palmer that they were "tiny and brilliant," flew both swiftly and slowly, maneuvered in a way that eliminated the possibility of meteoritic phenomena. At least one person, said Mr. Palmer, was injured by one. "They either struck the ground and exploded violently, or exploded low over the ground. Fragments picked up looked like plaster of paris." "...and," wrote Mr. Palmer, there were no little men, in uniforms or otherwise."

In this same article in FATE, Ray Palmer then went on to give the complete newspaper report of the "earlier incident" alluded to by Army Intelligence. This report, according to Mr. Palmer, was by Sam Petok, Free Press Staff Writer, who got his information from Alma Lawson, a Los Angeles business woman, who got her information from "sober conservative scientist friend," whose name she refused to divulge.

"Pretty lousy evidence," wrote Palmer, "but since Army Intelligence chose to mention the matter in showing how little evidence FATE has to support its fantasies, we'll have to present the matter with as exact information as it is possible to secure."

The newspaper clipping, headed "Interplanetary Saucers Discovered in Mexico," was then reprinted in full. According to the report, a Mexican shepherd had found a landed disc in the lonely reaches of the Sierra Madre mountains. Inside, he said, according to the report, were the charred, burned bodies of six men, all no taller than 30 inches.

U.S. military and medical men, according to this second-hand report, had been summoned to the Mexican capital to study the remains of the little men. All was top, top secret.

The landed disc was described as about 100 feet in diameter, brownish in color, made of metal so hard it could not be cut with a hacksaw. The disc was described as turtle-shaped, with a cabin about fifteen feet long suspended from it.

"FATE," wrote Mr. Palmer, "has no faith in this story. The story as it stands, is hearsay. If it is true

PAGE MISSING 194

Walter Winchell reported on a saucer landing, on June 30, 1950. His report to the nation stated that scientists at Palomar Observatory were said to have seen a "space ship" land in the Mojave Desert in May — that four figures stepped out — took one look — and vamoosed.

In the early fall of 1950, considerable "news" about landings was given to the American public. This was in Frank Scully's book on flying saucers. It went into great detail about saucer crashes in the desert, the emergence of "Little Men," of Air Force studies of new metals, new devices, etc., etc., etc.

On October 21, 1951, natives of Hogansburg, N.Y. reported the landing of a dark, brownish ball about four feet in diameter. It landed in a field, too, off with a buzzing sound. Everyone was afraid to get close to it.

In FATE Magazine, Feb-March 1952, there appeared an account taken from the Steep Rock *Echo*, the house magazine of the Steep Rock Iron Mines, of a landing, or series of landings, that took place on Sawmill Bay, a part of Steep Rock Lake. One date given was July 2, 1952. What was seen is described previously in this book.

On July 11, 1952, a Herr Linke, of Western Germany, has reported to have made affidavit to western intelligence officers that he and his 11-year-old daughter had seen a landed object, round, with portholes, and with a conning tower 10 feet high. Outside it, on the ground, were two figures in some kind of dress that looked metallic. One of them wore a breastplate light. On seeing themselves observed, the figures scrambled back into their craft, which had a cylindrical landing gear, revved her up with a circular burst of blue flames, and took off for the wild blue yonder.

On July 29, 1952, as reported by Cleveland newspapers, an Air Force plane shot down a flying saucer that had repeatedly attacked it. (I have not seen a copy of any of these newspaper reports.)

On August 19, 1952, Paul Desvergers, Scoutmaster, West Palm Beach, Florida, reported his encounter with a landed saucer that was shaped like a helmet. The craft, as he told it, shot a ball of blue flame at him as he approached it closely. The flame singed his arms, burned three holes in his cap. (This story was discredited by Captain E. J. Ruppelt, ex Project Saucer head, writing as a civilian in TRUE.)

On August 31, 1952, Herbert Long, of Kutztown, Pa., said that he saw a flying saucer land, not more than fifty feet away from him.

On September 1, 1952, or thereabouts, Bill Squier, as reported in the *Wichita, Kansas, Beacon,* said that he saw in nearby Pittsburg, Kansas, a disc-like machine, about 75 feet in diameter, hovering about 10 feet above the ground. A bluish light came from the machine's portholes, and inside the craft were what looked like human figures. As Mr. Squier walked towards it, the machine rose at great speed and disappeared. Colleagues of Mr. Squier's who looked at the spot beneath the craft afterwards, were said to have found grass and weeds in a rough oval flattened as if they had been hit by a (MISSING SENTENCES).

On July 30, 1952, Jim Lucas, a Scripps-Howard staff writer, reported in *The New York World Telegram & Sun*, reported that the Air Force was checking on the authenticity of a photograph taken on July 16, 1952, purporting to show five saucers flying formation over Salem Air Station. The photograph, snapped by Coastguardsman Shell R. Alpert at 9:35 A.M. on the 16th, was given (MISSING SENTENCE on page 198.)

On December 1, 1954, *The New York World Telegram & Sun* published a photograph of two saucers over Taormina, Sicily. The same photograph was not published by *The New York Herald Tribune* until December 10, 1954, after checking with authorities for security reasons. Then it was given front-page prominence and a story that USAF was investigating. Also that Sweden, Italy and Yugoslavia were investigating too.

On September 12, 1952, Mrs. Kathleen May of Flatwood, West Va., her two young sons, some other youngsters, and a young National Guardsman named Gene Lemon reported seeing what came to be called the "Flatwood Monster." They reported it to be a fiery, many-like object that seemed to be glowing, or lighted from the inside. This creature had evidently come out of an unknown craft or object shaped like two cones, one on top of the other. All the observers ran from the apparition, had to be treated for shock afterwards. All reported a horrible, nauseating stench in the air around the strange creature and the craft it came from. Observers who visited the spot later reported seeing skid-like marks in the grass, as if something had landed. (This incident was also discredited by Captain Ruppelt in TRUE.)

On November 30, 1952, an Italian farmer named Ferrari, reported seeing a disc about 130 feet wide, only 35 feet over his head. The disc parted like a clam shell, three humanoid figures with masks over the upper part of their faces appeared, spoke in some tongue unfamiliar to Signor Ferrari, closed the saucer again and went straight up in the air, vanishing in seconds.

On June 18, 1953, Mrs. Hilda Walker, Miss Judy Myers and Howard Phillips reported seeing a strange, bat-like figure of a man land in a pecan tree in Houston, Texas. They said that he was dressed like Superman, of the comics, in cape, tight-fitting breeches and quarter-length boots. The figure disappeared as a torpedo-like object flashed into view and then vanished.

On May 20, 1953 and June 20, 1953, reported miners John Black and John Van Allen, a flying saucer 12 feet across with a plastic observation dome had landed on a sand bar beside a creek, near their diggings at Brush Creek, Cal. From the saucer, which had cylindrical, retractable landing gear, and down a rope ladders, came a "little man." He was about four feet high, with long hair and broad shoulders. He had a bucket which he filled with water from the creek and handed it to someone inside the saucer. When he saw that he was observed, the little man rushed to the saucer, entered a port at the bottom of the saucer, pulled himself up inside, and the saucer took off with a hissing sound. It flew tilted sideways to get through a line of trees. Messrs. Black and Van Allen also reported that they had found campsites where the little men had built fires, near the sand bar in the creek, and footprints, about five inches long, that the little men had left. Mr. Black also reported that the little man seen on June 20 was black-haired, fair of skin, wore forest-green pants, a green cap, soft-toed black shoes, and a long tunic, or parka, with a hood. Mr. Van Allen, according to reports, never actually saw the little man; he saw only the saucer, as a silver streak. (As reported before, a vast throng awaited visit of some "Little Men" on July 20, 1953. No "Little Men" appeared.)

Then, there is the western group of writers who have all written books about talking with people from saucers, or of visiting saucers, or of being flown in saucers.

George Adamski, who wrote that at 12:30 P.M., Thursday, November 20, 1952, he made contact with a Venusian from a landed saucer, near Desert Center, California.

Truman Bethurum, who claims that he was permitted to enter a landed saucer and converse with its female captain eleven times during 1952.

Orfeo Angelucci, who claims that he entered a landed saucer on the night of July 23, 1952, and who was flown 1,000 miles out in space where he saw a "mother" ship 1,000 feet long and 100 feet thick. (This revelation was later changed to a "psychic" experience rather than a real one.)

George H. Williamson and Alfred C. Bailey whose book claims that they received a whole series of radio communications from saucer people from Mars, Venus, Mercury, even Pluto.

George W. Van Tassel, who doesn't claim that he rode a flying saucer, but that the intelligences who operate the saucers *claim that he was aboard.*

Daniel W. Fry, who claims that he flew from White Sands Proving Grounds to New York and back in a flying saucer at 8,000 miles per hour.

On January 4, 1954, a guard at the Marigname Airport in France, M. Chesnaux saw a luminous disc land on the field. M. Chesnaux ran inside to phone. The object disappeared. In the morning, scoffers were said to have found metal particles which were turned over to the French government for analysis.

Then there was the landed saucer Mr. Cedric Allingham, wrote that he observed at 3:30 P.M. February 18, 1954, between Lossiemouth and Buckie, Scotland. Mr. Allingham reported seeing a craft about 50 feet wide and 20 feet high. A man about 5 feet 9 inches emerged from it. The man wore a tunic, like coat of mail. The man said he came from Mars. He said the Martians had also visited Venus and the moon. Conversation lagged, so the Martian took off in his saucer.

On September 10, 1954, a farmer named Antoine Mazaud, Plateau of Millevanches, Southern France, reported that he came face to face with a little man wearing a helmet. Mr. Mazaud stuck out a pitchfork he was carrying, but the little man walked up, kissed Farmer Mazaud on the check (Intergalactic queers again?) then climbed into a cigar-shaped craft which took off with a buzzing sound.

On September 24, 1954, at 10:00 in the morning, some Portuguese countrymen reported that they saw, in the Gardunha Mountains near the Spanish border, a sphere which landed not far from them. Two little men in shiny, metallic-like suits climbed out and started collecting specimens of stones and grass. Seeing themselves observed, they invited the earthmen to climb into their machine, which had a semi-transparent center section. The pheasants declined. The little men then entered a hatch and the sphere took off — vertically, as usual.

On September 30, 1954, two Frenchmen, Bernard Goujon and Armand Pichet, who had been working on the road between Maisoncelles and Meaux, said that they saw a flying mushroom about eight feet wide land nearby. The craft, which took off when approached, had retractable landing gear of tripod-type like the saucer observed at Brush Creek, California.

On October 16, 1954, a retired French customs officer named Damien Sigueres reported seeing a saucer land near Perpignan. He said he saw a tall man in a "diving suit" step out. The man saw that he was observed by Mr. Sigueres and his two dogs, so he got back into the craft and it took off. (Note that this man was a "tall" man, and not a "little man.")

In its November 1, 1954 issue, LIFE Magazine carried quite an article. It stated that in the fall of 1954, throughout France, flying saucers and little men stepping from those saucers had been seen by various French citizens. "Out of the autumn skies, from Brittany to the Riviera, dropped a covey of extra-terrestrial vehicles and unearthly men. They were not vaguely-described objects sometime seen by children and frightened old ladies. Good solid citizens: farmers, bakers and other workingmen who had the reputation of being reliable, swore they had seen them."

And from these craft, according to these solid respectable Frenchmen, stepped the most wonderful collection of fairyland characters since the Grimm Brothers wrote their books in which they collected the folklore of Europe.

For here were "little men" in a plethora. And what little men! One of them had a single, solemn eye in the middle of his forehead. Another could change the color of his skin at will, like a chameleon. Still others were of different colors, in pleasing pastels. LIFE reported that they wore plastic helmets, sleeveless diving suits, orange corsets or cellophane wrappers, and spoke English, French or even Latin.

The craft that these little fellows flew were not "infinite power and no mass." They had mass. They evidently were made out of good solid metals or other materials. They left material evidence of their landing, skid marks in the grass, scratches on railroad ties.

Among Frenchmen reporting, according to LIFE, were:

Pierre Lucas, Baker, Loctudy. Saw orange ball fall from sky. Suddenly, small bearded figure with one eye in middle of forehead tapped him on shoulder.

Serge Pochet, Marcoing. Approached by two small shadows.

Gregoire Odut, Wassy. Saw golden disc zoom from Wassy after a two-legged creature leaped out for hasty look.

Francois Panero and Jean Oliver, Toulouse. Saw, near Toulouse, spaceman land in luminous sphere on basketball court.

Jean Narcy, near Wassy. Saw hat-like space ship land. Out of it came a little whiskered man in a fur coat and orange corset.

Yves de Gillaboz and Emile Reynard, Amiens. Saw, in sky near Amiens, "Martian Machine" belching puffs of smoke as it disappeared.

Marius Dewilde, Quarouble. Saw saucer land on railroad tracks. It was rust-colored. Dewilde circled scratches on tie where saucer landed, took tie home as lasting proof that he had actually seen the craft land. Mr. Dewilde reported that he was partially paralyzed by a green light from the machine...also that he saw emerge from it two small, man-like creatures in "divers" suits.

This LIFE article was illustrated with photographs of the Frenchmen and sketches of what they saw. The sketch of the helmet-shaped craft seen by Jean Narcy agrees in detail with LIFE's illustration, in its June 26, 1950 issue, of Farmer Trent's flying saucer, of which LIFE then was completely skeptical, with the description of a landed saucer given by Leslie Desvergers of West Palm Beach, in 1952, with descriptions of others who reported seeing saucers close at hand. It also agrees with everything that had been said about saucers for centuries, including the two different Irish accounts, of the year 213 A.D., which mentions visitors in sky ships, who said they were "drowning," when they got down into the dense atmosphere at our earth's surface.

On November 11, 1954, there appeared in *The New York World Telegram & Sun* two articles on flying saucers. One was headlined: "Italy Sees Things Or Mars Is Here." Rome, Nov. 11. "Italians saw no flying saucers in the skies today, for the first time in two months." Reason: it was raining in Rome on Armistice Day. The article then went on to say that "Men from Mars" popping out of saucers were reported from all over Italy. "Descriptions given by frightened "eyewitnesses" differed somewhat, but appeared to establish that the Martians:

1. Love flowers.
2. Don't do any harm to men.
3. Are about three feet in height and wear armored breastplates and helmets.
4. Seemed to glow.

"The Italian Air Force ministry has officially denied sighting any saucers."

The other article was titled: *"Italian Skeptics Now Eat Words on Saucers."* The article is a pick-up from the *Evansville Press*, a Scripps-Howard newspaper. It was written by a former Evansville resident, now Mrs. James Hogg, III. She then lived in Florence, Italy, where she was secretary to Bernard Berensen, the art critic and writer. Her husband teaches in Florence at an art academy.

Mrs. Hogg's article reported landings, as well as many sightings of saucers in the air. A landing at night, in a little town near Milan. A man returning from the movies on his bike saw a light of great intensity, a luminous body and two small shadows near it uttering strange, guttural sounds. The man raced back to town and told the police. A whole crowd of people went back and saw the figures, described as wearing white pants, grey jackets, transparent helmets, dark colored faces with what looked like "space helmets." The craft the people saw was described as a disc in two parts, illuminated by a green light, that rested on the ground at three points. The upper part was a hemispheric cabin illuminated with a blinding silver light. On the cabin was an antenna.

The ship was in a field with closed gates. When the gates were forced, the humans, who were unarmed, found a box of fruit and threw it at the "little men."

One man, Il Signor Giacomo Stefanoni, tried to sic his dog on the visitors, but the dog bit him in the jacket instead. While Signor was getting himself loose from his dog, the strangers got in their craft and it took off from the ground vertically, with a sound similar to a shrill boat whistle.

Among other reports of "landings" that were reported in late 1954 was one by Cesar Ferriera, of Portugal, who reported two beings out of a "flying cup" who were eight feet tall. They were dressed in pocketless, metallic suits.

In Muenster, Germany, a man named Franz Hoge, reported seeing four little creatures, almost three and one-half feet tall, who emerged from a cigar-shaped craft that hovered right off the ground. It emitted a blinding blue glare.

In Sudbury, Ontario, Ennio la Sarza is reported to have seen a craft come down from the skies and hover just above the ground. Out of it emerged three "monsters" thirteen feet tall with a single eye in the middle of their foreheads. These beings were greenish-blue in color, wore antenna, had claw-like hands. One of them "hypnotized" Mr. la Sarza.

And in Coldwater, Kansas, a 12-year-old farm boy, John Jacob Swain, said that he saw a little man out in a field. The little man was only twenty feet away. He looked at the boy, then ran or flew, to his saucer and took off. The saucer was about fifty feet in diameter, took off without tilting. It had portholes and lights. The little man left tracks—4 and 1/2 inches long, 2 and 1/2 inches across the toes, only 3/4 inches wide at the heel.

And, in December, 1954, there appeared in a U.S. magazine the story of a landing on a ranch in Queensland, Australia, written by the ranch owner, W.C. Hall, described elsewhere in this book.

Now — are all these stories of landings, and particular the details of "little men" popping out of them true? Or are they untrue?

Even FATE Magazine and TRUE Magazine, pioneer exponents of the extraterrestrial theory, have scoffed at such reports. Yet LIFE Magazine, and *The World Telegram & Sun*, have published reports of "little men" as legitimate news.

Is this all nonsense?

No matter how bitterly it is attacked, no matter how much it is debunked, no matter how much saucers are called natural aerial phenomena, or balloons, or optical illusions, or mass hysteria, no matter how much the U.S. Air Force and other nations' air forces say there is no physical evidence to support belief in the existence of flying saucers or humanoid-like creatures flying them, the reports, from honest, conscientious observers, still persist. Reports from French peasants. Reports from Portuguese persist. Reports from

Italian countrymen. Reports from Americans. Reports from Canadians.

Are All these people nuts? Or are the all *agentes provocateur* of their own governments, trying to cover up developments in a new kind of earth craft?

This author cannot bring himself to believe so.

For this is one of the few things that makes sense out of the whole flying saucer mystery. It is the one unique thing that explains *everything* about flying saucers. The unearthly speeds. The fantastic maneuverability. The odd shapes of the craft. Their glowing. The ability to fade, or disappear. The soundlessness. The lack of crashed discs, fragments, or any other lasting physical evidence. The paradox between sightings that evidently go back before the birth of Christ and their parallel to those seen today. The evidence of myth and legend. Odd disappearances of people and objects, including ships and aircraft. All falls into the pattern for explaining the mystery.

But if it is all true — which this writer is perfectly willing, even anxious to concede, the people who fly these craft are certainly a strange race of beings.

What do we know about them — from the record?

For one thing, they seem frightened when they land on earth — as if some of them get here by accident. Most of them choose lonely lakes, or remote-from-civilization mountains, or high glaciers, or lonely farms on which to land. Once they have landed, they don't linger long. They don't go into the local supermarket and buy food or liquor. They don't ask directions, such as "Where is Mars?" or even "Where is the men's room?" They generally take one look around, see that someone is watching them, look startled, as if they had gotten onto the wrong planet by mistake, and then go to a hatch — it is almost always a hatch in the bottom of their saucers, globes, helmets, spheres, torpedoes, or whatever else they are flying — take off forthwith generally straight up — towards outer space. Sometimes their craft are noisy. Sometimes they make a shrill whistle. Sometimes they are soundless. Sometimes they make a slight swish, like the sound of an escaping jet of steam.

If these people carry weapons, they do not use them so far as we know, even to retaliate showers of fruit or whatever else the local inhabitants have at hand to throw at them.

Some of these people wear "space helmets" or "space suits," indicating that they cannot breathe our atmosphere and survive — others observed have worn no such protection. Some have been reported as wearing outer metallic garments, like jerkins. Most reported have been described as wearing uniforms, as if they belonged to the air forces or other military organizations of the places from which they come. A couple have been reported, from different locations — one in Germany and one in France — as wearing breastplate flashlights.

A number of reports have indicated that they speak earth's languages — English, French, Italian, even Latin.

On at least one occasion, these visitors have been observed picking up stones and grass and putting them into a shiny box, as if they were collecting specimens.

On two occasions, "little men" were reported as either piping or carrying aboard water for their craft.

Who are these characters? Are they the "Little People" come back to earth? Did their ancestors once send miners to delve for certain substances on our globe, and are they now back, looking for lost mines?

Or have the Russians and the Americans and the English and the Canadians enlisted every midget on the face of the earth to fly a new kind of aircraft that requires little men?

Is somebody breeding a special race of squat-shouldered, bearded, metallic-armored little fellows to fly these net hot jet jobs? Especially, little men with one single eye in the center of their foreheads — and little men who can change color like chameleons, and still other little men with skins in colors of pleasing pastel?

Or is someone breeding green-skinned monsters with mechanical, claw-like hands?

Here is the heart, the nut, the lasting core of the whole flying saucer mystery.

Granted — as you will see later — that there are such things as real, actual, man-made flying saucers — is there something else? Is it true that saucers are extraterrestrial, as well as terrestrial?

If it is true — -then it is quite easy to understand the Air Force's attitude.

For how can you go out and tell 165,000,000 people who are looking to you to protect them that the Little People have come back to earth again — and that you have no more chance of catching one of them with a jet than you have of catching a sunbeam?

And, if it is true, then it would not be strange if all of earth's governments chose to keep this shattering news from the people. For the arrival of visitors from outer space would change many things on earth.

For one thing, we would have a lot of textbooks that are a bunch of junk. They could be taken out to the ash heaps and burned. The astronomy books, the physics books, the books on the nature of the universe. Books on the nature of matter, books on the physiology of man. Books full of ignorance and misdirection and superstition.

And not only that. We would be faced with tremendous problems in readjustment. Quite conceivably, readjustment in religious thinking. Readjustment in political thinking. And, readjustment in economic thinking.

Just theorize a little bit: Supposing, as others have supposed, that these people, if they exist, have discovered some awesome power that drives these craft? Supposing that it is sunlight, magnetism, or an anti-gravitational power of some sort, such as many writers have presupposed. Or just supposing that it is an entirely new principle of flight, hitched to a known form of power — atomic — made by conversion from earth's most common substance, water itself.

This direct conversion of water to atomic power has long been the goal of the atomic scientists. The present use of uranium is a crude and primitive substitute for ultimate...and that ultimate was long ago pointed out by the scientists, who said that the latent power in a teacup of water could drive the largest liner on a round-trip crossing of the Atlantic.

Supposing visitors have brought that knowledge — or knowledge of some other unlimited power delved from cheap and unlimited resources?

As soon as the secret of this power is obtained, while you might apply it primarily to military purposes, sooner or later you must consider using it for peaceful purposes. And when you do, you must consider the junking of your whole economic system, which is based upon the use of coal mines and waterfalls, petroleum and uranium, and on other crude, primitive, inefficient and costly methods of obtaining power from the resources of nature.

If you have such power and use it, businesses of long standing might well go on the ash heap. Stocks and bonds and investments and endowments and insurance companies and other institutions depending upon the productivity and earnings of such sources of power will require a new evaluation. Millions of people will have to change from one form of employment to another.

The foundation of society might well creak and totter under such as vast step forward because our civilizations are founded upon a system of "scarcity."

And if you junk your economic system, you must junk your political system or systems. For the natural resources of the world will become limitless, inexhaustible. There will be no need for "have nots." There will be no need for "poor countries," or "rich countries."

Unless —

Unless such frightening power got into the hands of those who would enslave the world — not make it a globe of free men. In such case, you might see the world go into a period of barbarism based on science that would make the writings of George Orwell pale into a shadow of the real thing.

This could, of course, be the answer to the mystery of the flying saucers. Perhaps one or more of these craft have malfunctioned, and we have obtained their secrets. Perhaps we have obtained the secrets, but do not know exactly how much information our potential enemies have also obtained. That would account for a suppression of all facts.

Perhaps men in various chancelleries of the world know who these visitors are, where they are from, and what their message is. And perhaps that's why they are so reluctant to take to the human beings whom they govern the secret of the flying saucers — and what it all means.

But, if all this is true, and if there are beings arriving regularly on the 5:15 from Mars and Venus, you would think that all world governments would appraise their people of this fact — and caution them not to throw fruit at the visitors. Or not to venture into their craft, lest they wind up as a specimen, or not to wander across open fields at night, lest they be kidnapped.

We have had no such warnings.

And as for the "Little people" and "monsters" who pilot flying saucers — if they exist, they must know all the furor they are causing. If they can speak our languages, they must be able to read our newspapers, listen to our radio and television. They must be able to read our books. They ought to know a great deal about our civilization. If they had any brains, or were coming here to warn us of impending catastrophe, as so many writers have tried so desperately to prove, you would think that they long since would have called an international meeting at the United Nations headquarters in New York, landing on the top of the building and striding in to the U.N. to state their case.

But do they? No.

Many writers — and laymen — have hazarded the supposition that because these people fly superior craft that they are a superior race, millions of years in advance of us.

But they don't act this way. They act more like half-wits, or the remnant of a once brainy race that has kept its ability to create startling craft, but has degenerated to the point of idiocy otherwise.

Judging by the people they have contacted, people to whom they have entrusted the priceless meaning of their trips to this sphere, the people who pilot the flying saucers are a race of super-jerks.

And we have nothing to fear from them, so long as they continue to impart the meaning of their visitations to people who write books about flying saucers.

CHAPTER 11
WHY AREN'T THERE MORE LANDINGS?

If all these gizmos are "space ships," why don't more of them land?

For one possible explanation, let us turn afield from the direct subject of flying saucers and allied phenomena to an authority quoted on an entirely different subject.

Here is a quite significant and awesome statement from Dr. Lincoln La Paz, astronomer and mathematician by profession, and one of the world's great authorities on meteorites. Dr. La Paz founded and heads the Institute of Meteoritics at the University of New Mexico. He had edited official handbooks of the U.S. Air Force.

This statement is taken from the article about Dr. La Paz, *Mr. Fireball of Albuquerque*, by Neil M. Clark, in the May 16, 1953 issue of The Saturday Evening Post, beginning on page 28.

This is a theory of Dr. La Paz to account for the absence of any fragments whatsoever left from the explosion of the great Russian meteorite that fell on June 30, 1908 in Siberia.

La Paz has proposed an explanation based on a theory of "reversed matter" put forward by two famous nuclear physicists, George Gamow and P. A. M. Dirac. The meat of their theory can be explained in two quick sentences, but the implications have to be imagined.

An atom of ordinary earth matter, physicists believe, consists of a central nucleus with planetary electrons revolving around it, the nucleus carrying a positive charge of electricity and each electron a negative charge. Certain theoretical considerations led Dirac and Gamow to dream up another "inside-out" kind of matter in which the electric charges are reversed so that the nucleus is negatively charged and is circled by positively charged electrons.

This strange kind of matter has been called contraterrene to distinguish it from terrene, or earth matter. If chunks of contraterrene and terrene matter were to collide, complete annihilation of the smaller mass would ensue and the huge amount of energy released would blow things sky-high. La Paz long ago suggested that the Siberian meteorite was composed of contraterrene material and that, for example, Vasily's 1500 reindeer and the 80,000,000 pine and larch trees blown down in the area of fall were charred by the intense radiation released during the annihilation of this inside-out meteorite.

As evidence of the Siberian fall is not the only one wherein contraterrene meteorites have hit the earth, La Paz points out that several other meteoritical mysteries are satisfactorily solved by assuming that chunks of "reversed matter" have from time to time tumbled out of our skies. There is, for example, the puzzle of the beautiful gemlike Libyan Desert silica glass found in an area apparently quite devoid of meteorites. Glassy melts of siliceous materials have been found not only at genuine meteorite craters like those at Hanbury in Central Australia and at Wabra, Arabia, but also at the Trinity A-bomb site near Alamogordo, New Mexico, where the atomic age was ushered in at dawn on July 16, 1945. Evidently radiation from atom-bomb blasts is just as competent to produce silica glasses as the terrific heat generated by the high-speed impact of big meteorites.

This being so, the heat energy released during the annihilation of a contraterrene meteorite that chanced to fall in the Libyan sand dunes would sheathe these dunes, like the floor of the Trinity A-bomb Crater, with silica glass, yet leave no recoverable meteorite fragments.

Are there likely to be many masses of contraterrene matter flying about in space in addition to everything else? La Paz thinks there may be enough to be worth worrying about. He has proved mathematically that some meteorites which strike the earth come, not from our own solar system, which should all be made up of terrene matter, but from outer space; and it is possible, he suggest, that , taking the universe as a whole, "reversed matter" is just as common there as our familiar terrene matter is here.

By permission Neil M. Clark and *The Saturday Evening Post*

Now just ponder that theory for a long moment. Then just imagine a people trying for some reason to communicate us.

The only trouble is, they come from a place where their universe consists of "reversed matter."

As many observes of spheres above the earth have noted

Fragments recovered: none.

Lending some credence to such wild suppositions was the discovery on (date) (refer to news clip) of the "anti-proton" etc.

CHAPTER 12
THE U.S. AIR FORCE AND FLYING SAUCERS

Trying to understand the attitude and actions of the USAF with regard to flying saucers is like trying to unravel the riddle of The Sphinx.

This is not meant to be, in any way, a criticism of the Air Force or its policies.

But trying to understand the actions of our Air Force is part of the problem of trying to understand the nature of the saucers. What is put down here is set down as a matter of historical record, not as criticism.

Every year, from 1947, the Air Force has been accused of a cover-up job — not a cover-up on the existence of real, man-made saucers, which it has every right to cover up — but on the greatest story since the birth of Christ, the appearance of craft and some kind of intelligences from other planets.

Every year since 1949, USAF has stated regularly that, while the possibility that some of the "unknowns" sighted might drift in from outer space, there exists no tangible evidence to prove or disprove this possibility.

And in spite of contradictions, in spite of seeming double-talk, in spite of seeming foul-ups in press releases, in spite of seeming inconsistencies between stories issued by different branches of the services, USAF has hewed to a pretty consisted official line. This line, with waverings here and there, with deviations here and there, is as follows:

1. The Air Force does not know what flying saucers are.

2. The Air Force has no evidence to indicate that they are the products of a foreign power.
3. Whatever they are, they pose no threat to the security of the skies of the U.S.A.
4. The Air Force has never ruled out the possibility that, if they exist, they may drift in from outer space, although no tangible evidence exists to prove or disprove this idea. According to the Air Force, there have been no fallen saucers, no fragments, no little men, either alive or dead. Also, according to the Air Force, no good movies, no good still photographs of saucers exist.

As a semi-official recognition of the extra-terrestrial theory, Captain E.J. Ruppelt, now a civilian, the officer who was head of the Air Force's investigations of flying saucers, or unidentified flying objects, at Wright-Patterson Air Field for two years, wrote in TRUE Magazine that it is his belief that if saucers are not a hoax, then they have to be from some other planet or planetary system.

This is the closest to an official statement of belief by the Air Force — or anyone connected with it that has been published to indicate that there is some reason for thinking that saucers do come from outer space.

Major Keyhoe, working with Albert M. Chop, of the Air Force press desk, tried in one of his book to prove that saucers were state of the art and that our Air Force was always on the verge of admitting that actuality, but there has been no official Air Force pronouncement to that effect as yet.

And maybe there never will be.

For consider the dilemma put to the Air Force by the original — and persistent — reports of flying saucers in the skies: The Air Force is charged specifically with the responsibility of guarding the security of the United States in the air. The Air Force, along with the Army, the Navy, the

Marines, and all other governmental and civilian agencies and individuals, is also charged with guarding the military secrets of the United States.

As is well-known, since the fact has been extensively publicized, the armed forces have done a vast amount of work in developing, testing, and putting into production secret devices of many kinds. Some have been atomic or other fission devices. Some have been concerned with aircraft that are faster than sound. And a great, great many have been missiles of various kinds. Undoubtedly, there are a great many more, about the nature of which or the function of which the public knows nothing whatsoever.

At White Sands Proving Grounds, at Holloman Air Base, at Wallops Island, Virginia, at many other places known and unknown throughout the United States, but principally in the western desert areas, various governmental agencies have been performing various tests and experiments for years.

In the sightings of aerial objects some without doubt, could have been the of secret U.S. aircraft and guided missiles.

What were people reporting seeing that was top secret, and what were they seeing that not only didn't originate in the United States, but which might pose some unheard of threat to the U.S. and its people? Were there things aloft which could belong to an enemy power? Were flying saucers a hoax or an aberration which could leave the Air Force red-faced?

What would you have done, faced with the problem of safeguarding the security of the nation, knowing of a great deal of secret work on aircraft, guided missiles, and who knows what else, yet faced with the puzzling phenomenon of continuing reports of craft evidently not of this country or any other country on earth?

Under any circumstances, USAF could find itself in an embarrassing role. No saucer reported — according to official statements — ever stayed around to have its waist measured or its temperature taken. When they took off for the blue, they went too fast to catch. How are you going to put salt on the tail of something streaking at thousands of miles an hour if your slow-poke vehicles can go only up to 700 miles per hours, and that only in a few experimental planes under ideal launching conditions?:

Are you going to risk trying to shoot them down — and hazard swift and unknown forms of retaliation? And how are you going to shoot down something that can outspeed even the fastest experimental rocket — in fact, that can fly rings around the rocket?

Supposing they were extraterrestrial aircraft? What could you do about it? And how could you announce them positively as such unless you had irrefutable evidence — fragments, landed craft, bodies either alive or dead, temperature readings, exact speeds and altitudes measured under completely scientific conditions, photographs, charts, diagrams and all the other evidences of believability?

Supposing you had strong evidence to believe that they were non-terrestrial? Back in 1938, Orson Welles, in his realistic broadcast of H.G. Well's *War of The Worlds*, created a full-scale panic, a panic that was extremely short-lived, because there was no real basis of fact for its existence? Do you want a full-scale, nation-wide panic that would make the 1938 one a pipsqueak, pale imitation? And, if you trigger a full-scale, country-wide panic, with millions clamoring for you to do something, what are you going to do? Advance your technology by decades or centuries overnight so you can cope with the unknown?

Or, supposing you announced that these craft — if craft they are — are either flown or guided by extraterrestrial intelligences, only to discover that they are something else?

In any case, you could make yourself look extremely foolish.

All of these questions help to explain the attitude of the Air Force on flying saucers.

One reason for so much dubious writing on saucers is that the Air Force policy has been to never discredit publicly any report, any published article, any book, anything said on radio or television. You can say what you please about saucers, call them extraterrestrial as much as you like, populate them with anything from green-skinned gnomes with red, red noses to a new species of super insect that builds machines like man. You can spin tall tales of moon-dust, accuse the Air Force of covering up the greatest story since Christ, write all you want to about visits in flying saucers, flights into outer space, conversations with Venusians, Martians, Mercurians, Saturnians and interplanetary Rotarians. The Air Force will not rebuke you, not restrain you — or even suggest that you be restrained by a straightjacket.

You can tell newspaper reporters that you saw a saucer-eyes dragon drop out of the skies and scuttle under your front porch — and the Air Force won't even raise an eyebrow. It will probably very patiently send someone around to talk to you. Your interviewer might surreptitiously try to smell your breath. And then you might be asked to fill out a 24-page report on what you saw. But you will not be held up to ridicule. Your name will be held confidential, if you wish. No matter what you see, the Air Force would like to hear about it.

That, with few deviations, has been the attitude of the Air Force since the beginning.

But there have been deviations.

To even begin to understand these deviations, other factors than the Air Force itself must be considered. The course of action taken by USAF on different occasions cannot be judged as series of isolated happenings or pronouncements, standing all alone. They must be put in context and considered in the light of many other things — what newspaper and magazines said; what prominent men said in interviews for publication; what foreign governments said in an official capacity.

Part of the exasperation of the Air Force, and it has good reason to be exasperated, may be traced to the pronouncements of others.

In the beginning (and the beginning actually reached back as far as 1938, although few people knew this) the Air Force was faced, or seemingly faced, with something it couldn't understand, something that just wasn't possible. And after the first nationwide, screaming report in 1947, USAF was carrying out its investigations in the face of many sources anxious to know the answers — or to jump to conclusions — and to spill their ideas to an eagerly-awaiting public, long before the Air Force might be willing to give the answers to the public itself.

If flying saucers are a hoax and hallucination, and if such things do not exist, then the annoyance of the Air Force, in the face of repeated articles and books claiming that saucers do exist, and that they are flown or guided by intelligences from outer space, can readily be understood.

If flying saucers are fantastic, new, secret weapons of the U.S. and/or its allies, the Air Force attitude can also be understood.

And if they really *are* extraterrestrial vehicles, the Air Force attitude can be understood even more.

In any case, the consistent denials of the existence of such craft, or of fragments from such craft, or any material proof of their existence by the Air Force would make complete sense.

For if such craft exist, and if they are from Venus, Mars, or some other planet in our own or some other solar system, and if they are flown by "little men," then an awful lot of people are in for an awful big shock. For, despite all the publicity that has been given to flying saucers, despite all the articles and books written about them, despite all the claims that they are extraterrestrial most people will find it very hard to believe, if it is so.

Among the public sources of information that may have been gadflies to USAF — and possibly a prophet of things yet to be revealed — has FATE Magazine fully described elsewhere in this book.

FATE advanced the extraterrestrial space craft and then engaged in a running fight with the Air Force.

Concurrent with the birth of this new publication, things were happening.

For instance, the Air Force, that had been claiming steadily that flying saucers were a form of mass hallucination set up a special project for investigating reports of flying saucers. The order for starting this project was signed December 17, 1947. This was 17 days before the death of Captain Mantell at Godman Field.

Headquarters for this new project was Air Material Command, Wright-Patterson Air Field, Dayton, Ohio.

The project started operations January 22, 1948. Even its name was secret for years. This name was Project Sign. This later was changed to project Grudge. Then to Project Blue Book. But to the public, when the public finally was given news of it, it was Project Saucer.

In the beginning, the project was headed by a lieutenant general. Two years later, it was headed by a captain. At the beginning of 1955, it was headed by a lieutenant.

At one time, the project called upon the services of over 200 specialist in the fields of astronomy, physics, meteorology, aerodynamics and allied subjects. It spared no pains to run down and investigate saucer projects, no matter how questionable.

Flying saucers, in all their myriad shapes and sizes, were classified under one name as unidentified flying objects, or UFOs.

One year later, on December 29, 1948, a new project, The Earth Satellite Vehicle Program, was initiated by the U.S. Air Force with an official announcement by the then Secretary, James Forrestal. Well-defined areas of research were allocated to each of the three military departments, Air, Army, and Navy.

Plans for a moon-rocket were released at this time. The artificial satellite planned would have to reach a speed of 23,000 mph to get away from the pull of the earth's gravity, according to newspaper accounts of the time. (Actually, it's nearer 25,000 mph.)

This idea of a man-made satellite circling the earth out in space was not new. It was a dream of the Germans, specifically the dream of Dr. Wernher von Braun, once a leading technician at Peenemunde, now working as a civilian consultant for the U.S., and in 1954, one of the leading exponents for a “crash” program to get a satellite out in space before the Russians.

The significance of a man-made satellite, tirelessly whirling around the earth, is that the nation which builds it first can rule the earth, for all points on the globe will be subject to minute scrutiny — and atomic attack.

It is well-known that the Russians, who have engaged in rocket experimentation far longer than the U.S., are similarly ambitious to hang a satellite in space.

In April 1950, some fifteen months after the beginnings of Project Saucer, *The Saturday Evening Post* published the first of two articles on flying saucers, beginning in its April 30, 1950 issue. These articles attempted to demolish, once and for all, the myth of the flying saucers. They were an authoritative attempt to give the coup de grace to the whole thing. For the articles were written with Air Force cooperation. They were written by Sidney Shalett, a most competent and reputable writer.

The articles stated that the Air Force had secretly initiated Project Saucer. It also stated that USAF had investigated 250 reports and found that they were based on sightings of "Skyhook" balloons, aluminum-covered aircraft target discs, birds, etc., etc., etc.

Mr. Shalett took all of the "classic" sightings — Kenneth Arnold's, the Muroc Air Field Base's sightings on July 8, 1947, the Portland, Oregon sightings of July 4, 1947, the sighting of Captain E. J. Smith, the pursuit of something by Captain Mantell over Godman Field, the "dogfight" of George F. Gorman over Fargo, N.D., the sighting of a "flying torpedo" by Chiles and Whitted, near Montgomery, Ala.

Mr. Shalett reviewed these sightings as the most difficult to rationalize, but gave an official U.S. Air Force conclusion the opinion conclusion the opinion that such things as flying saucers do not exist.

While he reported the indignation of certain Air Force officials over saucer hysteria — men like Hoyt Vandenberg, then Air Chief of Staff, Lt. Gen. Lauris Norstad, and then Lt. Gen. Curtis Le May and former Air Chief General Carl Spaatz, he also wrote things like this:

"Even Col. H.M. McCoy, who heads up the air Intelligence Division of Air Material Command Headquarters at Wright-Patterson Field, Dayton, Ohio, where saucer reports are screened, once thought he saw a disc while flying a P-51 in broad daylight. It turned out to be a glint of sunlight from the canopy of another distant P-51."

Mr. Shalett's articles contained other interesting bits of information. One, the fact that the Air Force had ploughed through all four volumes of Charles Fort's writings. Two, Mr. Shalett said of the saucer investigating agency: "For some obscure security reason, it is still not possible to mention the name of the project."

And very odd indeed was that these two Post articles concluded with a request for reports on saucer sightings — even though saucers could not exist. In fact, the concluding paragraphs asked for highly specific information: appearances; protuberances, if any; color; whether object reflects or projects lights; maneuverability; whether object makes any sound, spurts flames, sparks, or smoke and gives out an odor. Speed. Direction. How it disappears — whether it explodes, fades, or vanishes behind clouds. Please pick up fragments from any explosion — if any.

(There, if you want it, is a complete capsule of information on flying saucers, if you will read it carefully.)

Following this, readers were given the complete address to write to in reporting saucer sightings: Technical Intelligence Division, Air Materiel Command Headquarters, Wright-Patterson Air Force Base, Dayton, Ohio.

And the final paragraph of all: "If you've really seen something and can prove it, you may scare the wits out of the United States Air Force, but it will be grateful to you."

These Post articles were bitterly criticized by Ken Purdy of TRUE, by Donald E. Keyhoe, and by Ray Palmer of FATE. They stated in their later writings that the articles had been written and published at the direct request of James E. Forrestal, then head of the Air Force.

Shortly after the *Post* articles appeared, there appeared another report on flying saucers.

This one was by the Air Force itself.

It was Air Force report M-26-49, *Preliminary Studies on Flying Saucers*, April 27, 1949.

This report stated: “The mere existence of some yet unidentified objects necessitates a constant vigilance on the part of the Project 'Saucer' personnel, and on the part of the civilian population.

“Answers have been-and will be — drawn from such factors as guided missile research activity, balloons, astronomical phenomena...But there are still question marks.

“The saucers are not jokes. Neither are they cause for alarm.”

The Saturday Evening Post was caught with its articles down.

Perhaps, because of far-in-advance deadlines, it had to get its articles set in type before it knew the nature of the Air Force official report.

The Air Force, telling of its analysis of the 250 sightings, then invited people everywhere to report their sightings, in confidence, to the nearest Air Force installation.

All this was very interesting.

And so was this:

On July 18, 1949, newspapers carrying a Dayton, Ohio dateline, stated that “the Air Force admitted today that people actually see 'something' when they report flying saucers and said that some of the unexplained objects traveling at speeds up to 2,000 miles per hour have been tracked by radar. Captain E.J. Ruppelt, head of the Air Force group studying reports of unidentified aerial objects, said ground radar had tracked some aerial objects at speeds ranging between 1,500 and 2,000 miles per hour.

"Captain Ruppelt said jet fighters equipped with radar have been sent aloft to make contact with the phantom objects, but all efforts to catch up with them have failed.

"Of 1,000 investigated reports, Captain Ruppelt said, 38 per cent were meteors or other heavenly bodies, 13 percent balloons, 22 percent birds or aircraft, 2 percent hoaxes, and 25 percent unexplained."

(Almost exactly three years later, on July 30, 1952, in a press conference in Washington reported by Scripps-Howard staff writer Jim G. Lucas, Captain Ruppelt, commenting on a photograph of some UFOs, taken by Coastguardsman Shell R. Alpert, over Salem Air Station, said that the Air Force had yet to get hold of a negative of a flying saucer picture. He also said that his first impression of the photograph was that it was a fake. He said the alleged saucers appeared to have been painted in.)

(Two years after this, in the May 1954 issue of TRUE, Captain Ruppelt, now Mr. Ruppelt, as a civilian, wrote that flying saucers were either: a) non-existent; or: b) extraterrestrial space craft.)

A little over five months after Captain Ruppelt made his July 18, 1940 announcement, another curious thing took place.

On December 27, 1949, the Air Force came out with a public announcement. As newspapers put it: "FLYING SAUCER MYTH BURIED BY AIR FORCE. Verdict of 2-Year Inquiry: Mass Hysteria. Washington, Dec. 17 (UP) — The Air Force today exploded the "flying saucer" myth. It said an exhaustive two-year investigation of scores of reports of strange, disc-like objects sweeping along at tremendous speeds had established there is no such thing. The reports, it said, resulted from misinterpretation of various conventional objects, a mild form of mass hysteria or hoaxes.

"The Air Force added that it has discontinued a special 'project saucer' set up at Wright Field at Dayton, Ohio to study them because 'there is no evidence the reports are not the result of natural phenomena.

"The Air Force said it checked 375 reports of flying saucers without discovering any verification. It said the Army and Navy agreed there was nothing to warrant continuing the Wright Field project."

It is very interesting to note what provoked the Air Force into releasing this blast and taking such drastic action at this time.

It was an article in a national magazine.

The magazine was TRUE, *The Magazine for Men.* The article appeared in the January 1950 issue of TRUE. The magazine was on the newsstand late in the month of December 1949.

For some time, this magazine, published by Fawcett Publications Inc., had been regarding with fishy eye all pronouncements that saucers were optical phenomena or psychological aberrations. It was keeping files on saucer sightings. Ken Purdy, then Editor of TRUE, had commissioned Donald E. Keyhoe, Major U.S.M.C. (ret.) to investigate and put the results of his investigation into an article in TRUE. Mr. Keyhoe was chosen as a reputable, acknowledged authority on aviation. His article in TRUE stated that:

1. The earth has been observed periodically by visitors from another planet.

2. This observation has increased markedly in the past two years.

The Air Force had been informed of TRUE's intent to publish its conclusions. No attempt was made to block publication.

But when the article appeared on the newsstand, such a furor of publicity was given to it by press and radio, that the Air Force came out with its own press report, denying the existence of saucers.

And, said the Air Force, Project Saucer was kaput. It would be no more. It was not only abandoning the investigation of saucers, it was completely disbanding the investigative body. It also said that all data assembled so far, with photographs, would be put on public display at the Pentagon.

But the data never was.

And, while the original saucer project ended, while the investigative body *was* disbanded, the investigation of saucer reports stopped only for a while. A short time later, it was continued, not with the same staff as before, and with a new name, Project Bluebook. And it was changed from a special investigative project to a standard intelligence function, with a staff of some four officers, two civilians and an airman.

It is interesting to pause here and wonder why USAF radically changed the form of its saucer investigating project at the end of 1949. Did USAF know positively by the end of this year what flying saucers were — and that they posed no threat to the security of U.S. skies, or its population? Was the saucer mystery one of those things where one branch of the armed services was doing work so secret that other branches did not know about it? Had our government discovered that the saucers were of English origin, as has been suggested by one or two writers? And did it merely keep the investigation going — to make sure that no saucer malfunctioned and fell into the wrong hands? Or did the Air Force call off the hunt simply because there was insufficient data to indicate anything real in the skies? Did the Air Force have excellent reasons to believe that the whole thing was hoax and hallucination — and reinstate the investigation just to keep the populace alert — just in case?

No one knows, except the Air Force.

And its action at this time is as big a mystery as anything else connected with the saucers.

And so was this one:

On December 30, three days after its press release announcing that saucers did not exist, the Air Force gave part of a secret Project Saucer report to members of the press in Washington. To this official report, as much as to anything else, aside from saucer sightings, may be given the credit for the continuation of the theory that saucers are from outer space. For this report analyzed possible motives of such visitors and stated:

"Such a civilization might observe that we on Earth now have atomic bombs and are fast developing rockets. In view of the past history of mankind, they should be alarmed. We should, therefore, at this time above all expect to behold such manifestation."

The full contents of this report — *Air Force Project Saucer Report*, December 30, 1949 — were not made public at this time.

On February 22, 1950, the Air Force again said that there were no such things as flying saucers.

On this date, at Boca Chica Naval Station, Key West, Florida, radar observers tracked two glowing objects at great height, estimated

PAGE 239 MISSING

If they are, they have the worst possible shape for speed and efficiency. Mr. Ley's conclusion: "The U.S. may have mastered the secret of sending discs over nation in controlled flights, although it was probable that untrained observers had mistaken balloons for the saucers.

On April 11, 1950, Henry J. Taylor reported that an "enormous and fantastic type of vehicle" is being projected into the high skies by the Navy from an airfield near Minneapolis. "It's an enormous translucent thing with a long tail and flies up to 100,000 feet in the air. Some of these vehicles, Mr. Taylor said, travel all over the country and at an altitude of twenty miles. He said that some carry lights that blink on and off at sunset. The whole contraption glows and can be seen for as long as thirty minutes after darkness, he continued, as reported by *The New York Times*.

Well, Mr. Taylor was absolutely correct. He was describing "Skyhook" balloons, sent up by General Mills and the Navy. He also was reporting, as hot news, and practically in Mr.Sidney Shalett's own words, what Mr. Shalett had previously reported in *The Saturday Evening Post*, in April 1949, exactly one year earlier.

(In retrospect, it looks a little as if Mr. Taylor, to get off the hook from the furor his "expose" had caused, found it necessary to bring out the balloons explanation of saucers once more. It has been brought out successively, year after year, ever since *The Saturday Evening Post* first advanced it.

In the last week of May 1950, Donald Keyhoe's book*, The Flying Saucers Are Real*, an expansion of the article in TRUE Magazine, hit the newsstands in a 25¢ Gold Medal edition published by Fawcett, the publisher of TRUE. According to Mr. Roscoe Fawcett, vice president of Fawcett Publications, Inc., as reported in *Greenwich Time*, Greenwich, Conn., a printing of 500,000 more copies of the book was ordered immediately after its first appearance. Mr. Fawcett said that 8,000 copies of the book were distributed in Washington, D.C., with some 1,200 copies going like hotcakes in the Pentagon Building. Calls had come in for 4,000 more copies for Washington.

On June 1, 1950, Daniel J. Flood, a Pennsylvania Congressman, telegraphed Fawcett Publications in Greenwich, Conn., urging that the book be removed from newsstands. Mr. Flood was afraid Mr. Keyhoe's book might cause alarm and public confusion.

On June 23, 1950, three Air Force observers in the traffic control tower at Hamilton Field, California, reported that a flying disc made three passes over the airfield early in the day. It made a thunder-like roar, buzzed the field at an altitude of 2,000 to 5,000 feet. Estimated speed: between 1,000 and 1,500 mph. Air Force officers at the base had no comment to make.

In July 1950, the aviation magazine *Flying*, with an article by Curtis Fuller, who also wrote for FATE, came out with the belief that there was something in back of all the saucer sightings.

In September 1950, the aviation magazine Flying, with an article by Curtis Fuller, who also wrote for FATE, came out with the belief that there was something in back of all the saucer sightings.

In September 1950, the flying saucer book by Frank Scully made its appearance. This book published by Henry Holt & Co., was heralded by the publisher as a true and factual account. The book stated that flying saucers were from Venus, that they were piloted by little men in bell-hop-like suits. It also said that the saucers' source of power was magnetic and that several saucers had crashed in the desert country of the Southwest. It told fantastic stories of tiny radios, new kinds of metals, new kinds of textiles never seen before on the earth.

This whole book was labeled a barrage of nonsense by most reviewers. It was later investigated by J.P. Cahn *of The San Francisco Chronicle,* on assignment from TRUE, and branded a complete and heartless hoax, with a couple of the key figures in the book later being prosecuted — and convicted — of attempt to swindle, in the Colorado courts. On December 29, 1953, Silas Newton, a Denver physicist, and Leo A. Gebauer, a television dealer, were found guilty to conspiring to commit a confidence game. Perhaps the book can be judged by these "authorities" quoted by Scully in his book. And then again, perhaps not.

On February 14, 1951, two Air Force officers at Wright-Patterson Air Field reported having seen, over Alamogordo, New Mexico, a strange, unknown object, at an estimated height of 50,000 to 60,000 feet.

In February of 1951, the magazine *Aviation* came out with an editorial expressing belief that saucers were "Skyhook" balloons, not anything mysterious.

On February 26, 1951, a former Air Force scientist, Dr. Anthony O. Mirachi, Scituate, Mass, who in 1950 had investigated more than 300 reports of flying saucers as head of the Air Force's Atmospheric Composition Bureau of the Geophysical Division, said that saucers might be missiles launched to photograph the nation's atom-testing grounds.

On May 5, 1951, Australia was flooded with reports of a cigar-shaped object that flashed across the sky over Sydney shortly after dawn.

On August 27, 1951, the famous "Lubbock Lights," two strange formations like strings of beads in crescent shape, hurtled through the sky at a speed that carried them from horizon to horizon in three seconds. They were photographed by Carl Hart, Jr. The photographs were widely published.

On September 9, 1951, two Air Force jet pilots chased as disc-shaped something over Delaware. Air Force spokesman described their reports as the usual flying saucer story.

On October 16, 1951, the Navy announced to the press that it had launched rockets from giant balloons, high above the north magnetic pole, and that the rockets went twenty miles up.

In its April 7, 1952 issue, LIFE Magazine declared itself for belief in saucers as visitors from outer space, in an article by H.B. Darrach Jr. and R. Ginna. The authors reviewed the most baffling of the "classic" sightings, came to what they felt was the inescapable conclusion that saucers are space craft.

In its July 1, 1952 issue, LOOK Magazine came out with some interesting news. Its article said that the Air Force was deadly serious in its attempt to get at the bottom of the saucer mystery. It said that USAF had been trying to find a pattern in saucer sightings — and had found it. The magazine reproduced an official Project Bluebook map that showed how sightings for 1951 and the first half of 1952 were grouped in clusters around atomic installations, heavily industrialized areas, and over the U.S. Capital. The article, quite evidently written with Air Force assistance and released with Air Force permission, went on to say that USAF was buying diffraction-grid cameras to place in strategic areas about the country, in the hope of getting good photographs of the unknowns overhead.

On July 19, the greatest furor about flying saucers since Kenneth Arnold's report touched off the big mystery was turned loose when "blips" from unknown objects appeared over Washington, D.C.

The "blips" appeared again — this time, one week later, at 9:08 P.M., on the night of July 26, 1952.

This whole Washington affair of the blips was one of the wackiest and most hilarious in the whole confused history of flying saucers. The first time the blips appeared, at 12:45 A.M. on the night of the 19th, the Air Force did not send up jet interceptors because "Air Force radar operators at Andrews Field were wholly unable to confirm Civil Aeronautics Administration's sightings by radar at Washington National Airport."

The second time the blips appeared, they caused a 7-days wonder. The blips had a wonderful time for themselves. They flitted over the White House. They darted over air installations. They cruised above the Pentagon.

Radar operators of Civil Aeronautics Administration described them as "purple polliwogs."

Every time a conventional plane got close to them, they disappeared. It was as if they — whatever they were — were gleefully thumbing their noses at anything the U.S. might put into the air.

The second time the blips appeared, they caused such a furor they even rated a call from the White House to USAF headquarters in the Pentagon. According to Captain E. J. Ruppelt, writing in TRUE Magazine in 1954, he was the man delegated to talk to the White House caller. According to Captain Ruppelt, President Truman listened on an extension, but said nothing.

On this second occasion of the blips' appearance, it took the Air Force more than two hours to "scramble" two jet interceptors over the capital. This second time, Air Force radarmen reported seeing spots in front of their eyes fully fifteen minutes before the alarm came in from C.A.A., but then, the Andrews Field men were unable to locate the "objects" where the C.A.A. men said they knew they were.

Of the jet men aloft, one reported that he had seen four lights about ten miles in front of him and slightly above him, but that he could not overtake them before they vanished. On a little later attempt to intercept, he said that he saw a steady white light about five miles ahead of him and ten miles east of Mt. Vernon, but that the lights disappeared in about a minute.

The other jet man reported that he had seen nothing.

This whole affair evidently so rattled the Air Force — which had been taking a shellacking in the newspapers for lack of vigilance at the time of the blips' first appearance — that it began making statements, some of which contradicted each other, and none of which made complete sense.

For instance, the Air Force was quoted as saying: "We have no concrete evidence that they are flying saucers. Conversely, we have no concrete evidence that they are not flying saucers.

Then Air Force spokesmen said that reports had been relayed to intelligence officers in the Pentagon and to the Air Force technical information center at Wright-Patterson.

Other statements were to follow. Captain Ruppelt, writing about it later in TRUE, had this to say: "The story caught the Air Force completely off balance and the handling of it got fouled up beyond all recognition. It finally took a couple of generals and a press conference to straighten things out.

All was confusion. Everything was as clear as mud.

On this same night, July 26, 1952, the Associated Press reported that police and military observers, as well as hundreds of civilians, said that they had seen saucers flying over south-central Indiana between midnight and dawn. Observers had watched their gyrations for several hours. One viewer reported that one of the lights he saw was bluish, another white, another orange. It was also reported that the lights sailed into view from the south, east and north, respectively, and chased each other all over the sky.

(These sightings are not mentioned at all by Captain Ruppelt, who states positively that the sightings over Washington were due to radar aberrations. Captain Ruppelt also states that the jets sent up to investigate blips over Washington had been unable to find anything. This does not agree with newspaper and magazine reports.)

To continue with the record:

On July 28, 1952, the Air Defense Command released the news that it had alerted jet pilots to take off instantly in pursuit of any flying saucers sighted anywhere in the country.

Newspapers also reported on this date that more than 60 reports of flying saucers had been made to the Mitchel Air Force base from all parts of the New York Metropolitan area to be forwarded to air intelligence at Wright-Patterson Field.

Concurrent with this report, the Air Force stated that, of 1,000 sightings reported in the past few years, "only a small percentage of those received from reliable sources remain unexplained." The unexplained case could be "misinterpretations of various conventional objects, a mild form of hysteria, meteorological phenomena or hoaxes."

On July 29, 1952, a Tuesday, *The New York World Telegram & Sun*, in a UP report from Washington dated the same day said: "Air Force brass has decided to get to the bottom of the mystery. "Forsaking an earlier attitude that 'there 'ain't no such animal,' they are enlisting top scientists in a new study, it was learned.

"The Air Force will rely primarily on physicists for its flying saucer investigation. This is in line with the tentative opinion already reached in some Air Force circles that variously described mystery objects in the sky are physical phenomena, however, imperfectly understood up to now, rather than actual flying discs."

Please read on.

"A high Air Force officer, who informed the United Press of these developments, said: "We are fairly well convinced that the so-called flying saucers are not anything posing a threat to the air defense of the United States."

"Air Force spokesman insisted there was no military secrecy veiling the quest for saucer data. Any seeming reluctance to give out information was based unhappily on ignorance, not on military secrecy, they said.

"Observers who have followed the saucer saga through five years asserted with renewed vigor that the glowing, vari-colored objects sighted visually all over the land, and recently by radar, were not secret aircraft, weapons developments or of interplanetary character.

"Sightings so far unexplained and increasingly regarded as physical phenomena 'show a pattern which would indicate that the objects are being controlled by a reasoning body,' the Air Force said."

Said which, again? A little more slowly this time.

Everything was fouled-up. So the Air Force called a special press conference, the biggest since the end of World War II, in Washington on July 29, at the Pentagon. Those present for the Air Force, according to Captain Ruppelt, were: Maj. Gen. John A. Samford, Air Force Director of Intelligence, Maj. Gen. Roger Ramey, director of operations, and four technical men from ATIC, Col. Donald Bower, Capt. Roy James, Burgoyne Griffin, and Captain Ruppelt.

It is curious to observe what different reporters and their publications got out of this press conference. The *N.Y. Daily News* seems to have gotten one thing, *The World Telegram &*

Sun, a slightly different shading, *The New York Times* something a little different still.

A full account of the conference appeared in *The New York Times* which headed its story, by Austin Stevens, as follows: "AIR FORCE DEBUNKS SAUCERS AS JUST NATURAL PHENOMENA...*Intelligence Chief Denies a Menace Exists* — 'Objects' Believed To Be Reflections, But Adequate Guard Will Be Kept. Washington, July 29 — Air Force Headquarters skimmed away into the broken dish ware bin today the latest wave of 'flying saucers.' It called them 'natural phenomena,' and announced through high-ranking officers that henceforth the Air Force would treat reports of the discs with adequate but not 'frantic' attention."

At the end of one hour and twenty minutes of exchange between a large group of reporters and the Air Force's chief "saucer" students, Maj. Gen. John A. Stamford, Chief of Intelligence, agreed to the following summary of his views, according to Stevens:

- So-called flying saucers constitute no menace to the United States.
- None of the several thousand "saucer" reports checked by the Air Force in the last six years has disclosed the existence of any material flying object, except where the report emanated from an observer's sighting of a United States plane or missile or his mistaking it for something else.
- The United States has nothing in its arsenal of weapons, either existing or developmental, that has an unlimited speed and no mass, characteristics attributed to many alleged "saucers". Radar is capable of playing tricks for which it was not designed; so is the human eye.

"Appearing before the press is by no means a scoffing mood, but instead, in an agreeable atmosphere of willingness to discuss anything they knew, the Air Force said they considered it the service's 'obligation' to continue to investigate saucer reports.

Out of the press conference came a new theory of "temperature inversions" — the existence of a cool layer of air stretched between two hot layers which Air Force spokesmen said could cause reflections of lights — both in human eyes and on radar screens.

In announcing that the investigation of "saucer" phenomena would continue, the Air Force said it was purchasing cameras equipped with diffraction grids that would be used to discover the source of light in the flying phenomena. The news that the Air Force was also considering the purchase of a special telescope with a wide-angle lens to photograph large sections of the sky was also announced at this time.

Neither of these pieces of news was news. Both had been publicized by LOOK Magazine in its July 1, 1952, issue, out sometime in late June.

What LOOK had also publicized was the Project Bluebook map showing concentrations of saucer sightings at key points in the country.

At the July 29 conference, Air Force officers expressed the opinion that no special significance could be placed on such geographical groupings. Such spots could be regarded as "sensitive areas," where people would be more apt to report anything in the air.

At this same time, Major Jerre Boggs of the Air Force was reported as having said by Daniel Lang of *The New Yorker Magazine*:

MISSING PAGE 251

to the Air Force for study. Reporter Lucas discussed the picture with Captain E.J. Ruppelt. Captain Ruppelt said that he was skeptical, since he had not obtained a negative for the photograph, and said that the Air Force had yet to get hold of a negative for a flying saucer picture. According to Mr. Lucas, Captain Ruppelt said that the alleged flying saucers appeared to have been painted in. Their somewhat irregular, wavy edges indicated as much, he said. On this date, Captain Ruppelt took a plane for Dayton, Ohio, taking Coastguardsman Alpert's photograph with him for further study.

On this same date, *The Cleveland Press*, another Scripps-Howard paper, had an article about a veteran Air Force pilot whose plane was repeatedly "attached" by a flying saucer. This incident was said to have happened over a year ago over Augusta, Georgia, on a warm, sunny, clear day. The full story, according to the *Press*'s aviation editor, was said to be in the Air Force's top secret files in Washington.

On August 1, 1952, the photograph of "saucers" taken by Coastguardsman Shell R. Alpert was reproduced widely in the nation's newspaper. It was an official release by the U.S. Coast Guard.

August 2, 1952: Harvard astronomer calls picture worthless. No accompanying scientific data. No temperature distribution. No measured altitude.

On August 3, 1952, Maj. Gen. Roger Ramey further deflated the flying saucer "scare" by saying on a television show on which he was interviewed that he did not rule out the possibility that the objects were interplanetary visitors, but that he was exceedingly skeptical. As for the Russians — "Russia has no ability to produce an object that can make such fantastic power that its speed can't be tracked by radar."

To continue:

In August 1952, John J. O'Neil, writing in the editorial pages of *The New York Herald Tribune*, called flying saucers a farcical tag for ancient phenomena. Mr. O'Neil's thesis was that modern science is laboring under the burden of archaic views held by former scientists — and that what people see when they see saucers are genuine atmospheric phenomena. For one significant quote: “A more useful picture of the earth's atmosphere will present it as a gigantic electronic tube...in which they may act as anodes, biasing grids, screen grids...outer interplanetary space...is a region charged with energy at a very high potential and in a variety of forms, which we may learn some day to extract and apply to useful purposes.”

To continue:

On August 5, 1952, it was announced by a spokesman for the Army Corps of Engineers that physicist Noel Scott had succeeded in making “flying saucers” in a bell jar at Ft. Belvoir, Va. These fiery objects were made by introducing molecules of ionized air into the partial vacuum of the bell jar.

August 9, 1952: International authority on the atmosphere said: “I know of no conditions in the earth's atmosphere, high or low, which would duplicate those conditions needed to make the laboratory models.”

On August 22, 1952, Glenn L. Martin, aircraft builder, speaking at a Kiwanis dinner at Johnstown, Pa., said that the United States had fantastic new weapons in bird-dog missiles capable of overcoming an enemy with a 20-to-1 numerical superiority.

On August 27, D.S. Desvergers, hardware salesman and Scoutmaster reported seeing a landed saucer near West Palm Beach, Florida.

On August 29, the British came out with an announcement that said their scientists had developed a guided missile that can take off automatically and chase an enemy plane wherever it goes.

(NOTE: A curious U.S. vs. Britain bragging about their missiles and other aviation advances starts right here. You will see more of it as you continue with the reading of the record. Right now, notice this paragraph.)

"Reliable quarters believe the British plan to try out some of their guided missiles, regarded by their designers as having 'smarter' electronic brains than those produced in the United States."

Again, a quote of Sir Frank Spriggs, managing director of the Hawker-Siddeley group of companies. He said the new weapons are so fantastic that "it takes a madman even to order them — but we've ordered."

On September 10, 1952, the U.S. Senate was told by Senator Jos. C. O'Mahoney, D., Wyo., that the United States is acquiring highly secret weapons that can conquer the atmosphere. After his speech, the Senate tentatively approved an extra $5,000,000,000 (5 billion).

On January 28, 1953, the Air Force revealed, after suppressing it for almost a year, a pilot's story of being buzzed by a flying disc over Japan, just before noon, March 29, 1952. This news was released from a United States air base in northern Japan. In Washington, a spokesman at Air Force headquarters said that the technical intelligence officer of the Air Materiel Command at Wright-Patterson had received none of this incident. "It was indicated there probably would not be a request sent to the Far East for such a report."

On February 12, 1953, the Marines stepped forth. They reported that a Marine jet pilot chased a mysterious glowing object through the skies at more than 500 mph over Cherry

Point, N.C., Marine Corp Air Base. Pilot Marine Lt. Ed Balocco reported silvery object, looking like an airplane with red lights; "moved from below me to 10,000 feet in a matter of seconds."

On February 11, 1953, there appeared in newspapers a news note from *The Toronto Star* that a 1,500 mph flying saucer may be built in Canada. "The proposed craft would be able to take off vertically, fly horizontally at 1,500 mph, and use the gyroscopic effect of a revolving power plant to acquire stability." The article was then quoted as saying: "Reports have been so persistent and apparently consistent concerning the Canadian craft that western scientists consider the possibility that Soviet Russia has carried similar developments to a more advanced stage." The craft proposed by the Canadian was to have a diameter of about forty feet.

On February 20, 1953, the U.S. Army reported to newspapers that it has guided missiles so good it is almost impossible for them to miss a target. The article was about the guided missile "Nike."

In its March 1953 issue, Air Training, official trainee's publication of USAF, published an article: "*you can help solve the saucer mystery.*" The article carried a reproduction of the Project Bluebook map that had been published in LOOK Magazine, and air trainees were given instruction as to what to look for and how to report the sighting of a UFO. There was nothing secret about this. I received a copy of Air Training in request to the Air Force.

By this time, the Air Force had printed very comprehensive forms for reporting the sighting of unknown flying objects.

On May 5, 1953, government scientists at Langley Field, Va., disclosed that they were doing research on guided missiles "that may attain speeds up to 15,000 mph, almost 20 times the speed of sound."

On May 15, 1953, Robert Ruark, Scripps-Howard columnist, reported that he had seen a real flying saucer, a silver ball in the sky, while hunting big game in Africa, in January 1953.

In June 1953, writer Gerald Heard's book *Is Another World Watching Us*? was brought in Bantam Books edition in the United States.

On June 11, 1953, the U.S. Army announced that it had a guided missile ready for battle.

PAGE 257 MISSING

semi-permanent basis. The article said: “One sign of how it has settled is that it started in 1948 under a Lieutenant General and is now headed by a First Lieutenant.”

On September 17, 1953, it was announced in The New York Times, among other newspapers, that a 1,500 mph disc-shaped fighter was being studied in blueprint by the U.S. and Canada.

On the same date, the U.S. Air Force “cautiously lifted the secrecy” curtain today from its 'flying stiletto,' a dagger-shaped research plane designed to fly at 2,000 mph at extremely high altitudes.” A jet-propelled job, practically wingless, but operating on conventional principles.

On November 3, 1953, it was reported in the newspapers that an Italian navy officer, Giuseppe d Nitto, working secretly under government supervision, said he had developed a system *of beaming electricity through space without wires*. “Scientists say such an achievement would be the most sensational since atomic fission.”

On December 12, 1953, Canadian Air Force radar experts scanned the skies for a “thing” after the crew of a trans-Canada Air Lines plane reported a greenish-blue light over

Lake Ontario. It brightened the clouds as it descended slowly from the skies. (Author's note: sounds like the greenish-blue cloud of stuff I saw descending over Marietta, Ohio, back in 1926.

On December 17, 1953, the U.S. Air Force permitted news to be released that Maj. Charles E. Yeager had flown an airplane, the Bell X1A at a speed of 1,600 mph. The craft was dropped from the belly of a B-29 at 30,000 feet.

On December 28, 1953, the Soviet press, following a sensational Swedish saucer sighting attributed to the Russians, came out with a blast accusing "aggressive forces" in the U.S and other western countries of inventing flying saucers to fan war hysteria and get bigger armaments appropriations.

Somewhere around this time, the late Andrei Vishinsky, Soviet U.N. representative, said that flying saucers were shipped to the U.S. in Scotch whisky. Very, very funny.

In March 1954, there was a Martin Aircraft advertisement that the Martin Matador, first successful pilotless bomber, had been released to the officially joined NATO 4th Allied Tactical Air Force in Europe, under 12th Air Force.

On February 3, 1954, there appeared in the Greenwich, Conn., *Time* a report that two local boys, Waldo Morrell and Roy Moshier, 11 and 14 years old, respectively, had seen a flying saucer over the Mianus River. It was like a balloon, with a light shining inside. "It was a couple of thousand feet high, like clouds," said the boys.

In April 1954, *The New York Herald Tribune* reported, in an article by Robert S. Bird, that Soviet Russia is working on a "fantastic" lightweight rocket engine which might be used to either propel a 5,000 mph guided missile, or to give 2,000,000 (that's right, 2 million) horsepower blast-off to a passenger-carrying earth satellite that would girdle the earth every four hours in outer space. This news was based on a report by an American rocket expert, George P. Sutton, head of North American Aviation's aerophysics department. Mr. Sutton, who privately specialized in co-relating rocket data from behind the Iron Curtain, told the Third Symposium on Space Travel at the American Museum's Hayden Planetarium that the evaluation of the Russian experiment was his own personal appraisal and was fitted together from many sources.

The new super-rocket, Mr. Sutton said, according to the report, is called Model 103 and is amazingly small and light for its enormous power...it throws an exhaust flame 160 feet long at a temperature of more than 6,000 degrees Fahrenheit, measures fifty feet in length and five and one half feet in diameter and can develop the power of 10 battleships of the Missouri class. "The Russians appears to be thinking of a satellite vehicle, which would rise to a predetermined altitude a few hundred miles above the earth and thereafter would circle around the earth every few hours at this altitude."

On April 16, 1954, Ansel E. Talbert, writing in *The New York Herald Tribune*, said that the development by the American aircraft industry of practical devices to reverse instantly at a pilot's will the thrust of a powerful jet airplane had been disclosed yesterday at the closing session of the national aircraft production forum in the Hotel Statler in Washington, on April 15, 1954.

On June 1, 1954, the U.S. Air Force announced that reports of flying saucers had fallen off swiftly since 1952. The Air Force release said that 1,700 sightings were received in 1952, but that the figure fell off to 429 in 1953 and that only 54 sightings had been reported to date in 1954.

"The Air Force is still unable to explain 10 per cent of the sightings. The idea that some drift in from outer space still gets attention, but the Air Force says that it has no such evidence. It also has no evidence that they come from a foreign government."

On the same day, and in the same New York newspaper, it was reported that Capt. Charles J. Kratovil, Trans World Airlines pilot, reported that he saw a large, white, disc-like object, moving against a 60 mph wind near Boston, Mass. Jets were sent up. At 10,000 feet, pilots saw the object 10,000 feet above them, and rising fast.

On June 3, 1954, the Navy issued the first news on its XFY-1 plane, a vertical take-off aircraft that takes off from its tail and lands on its tail, the first propeller-driven aircraft designed to take off and land like a helicopter and fly and fight like a jet interceptor.

On June 4, 1954, with a Cleveland dateline, newspaper reported that "governmental scientists guardedly revealed evidence of American progress in a global race for development of trans-ocean guided missiles and atomic aircraft engines. Urgent research goals disclosed at the laboratories of the National Advisory Committees for Aeronautics: lightweight atomic power plants able to drive warplanes at supersonic speed to any point on the face of the earth and return; and intercontinental guided missile with speeds up to 6,000 mph; or ten times the speed of sound. "Problems just as formidable appeared to face the inter-continental guided missile researchers. At the 6,600 mile-an-hour speeds now being investigated, temperatures from air friction would be enough to vaporize diamonds and melt presently known missile materials. High-melting-point ceramic and metallic materials, water cooling and insulation are now being studied."

On June 7, 1954, it was reported in the newspapers that the U.S. has a new small jet designed to attain supersonic speeds in combat well above 1,000 miles per hour.

On June 30, 1954, it was reported in newspapers that a British Overseas Airways Corp. pilot had said that a large UFO and 6 smaller ones accompanied his Stratocruiser for 80 miles as it crossed the Atlantic, headed for London. Capt. P.R. Howard, a veteran of 250 Atlantic crossings, said the object resembled a large burst of flak and six smaller ones. Incident occurred at midnight, June 29, 150 miles southwest of Labrador. An American jet from Goose Bay tried to intercept the objects, but they "faded" as the jet approached. Mr. Howard was quoted as saying: "All appeared black and I'll swear they were solid. Sometimes the big central object appeared wedge-shaped, sometimes like a dumb-bell, sometimes like a sphere with tail-like projections." All 10 members of the crew agreed with his description, as did those of the 51 passengers who were awake at the time of the sighting.

On July 13, 1954, in the column *Europe's Lighter Side*, in *The New York Herald Tribune*, Art Buchwald, Paris correspondent for the Tribune, reported an interview with Professor Henri Coanda, "a Romanian-born inventor who has spent the adult part of his sixty-nine years solving some of the most complex problems man has been faced with."

Read carefully: "But the principle which Professor Coanda will be remembered for in future years is the "Coanda Effect," a discovery he made in 1937 that has made it possible for people living on this planet to build flying saucers.

"The principle is that by driving one side of a nozzle, a stream of air can be curved to follow the same side. By using a jet engine in the center of a flying saucer and sending out the blasts to ports all around the saucer, and by controlling the air, the Coanda effect can be used to lift a multi-ton machine vertically and land it vertically. A flying saucer now being built by the Canadians will use the Coanda-effect principle.

"The Professor says that the flying saucers seen over Scandinavia are Russian ones and many intelligent people are quite sure the Russians are ahead of the Western allies in flying saucer experimentation. Coanda said that flying saucers can fly at 2,000 miles an hour."

Read on, please.

"The only future in the air, "Coanda said, "is the flying saucer. The present-day airplane is a kite. All we have been doing for forty years is improving kites.

"But there is an air phenomena which is much more interesting than pulling a machine by motors against friction. the flying saucer can overcome the problem of friction became of the vacuum over it. There are no shock waves to disturb control of your ship, and with less skin friction your metals will be able to withstand the pressures now working on the ordinary type of plane."

Well, if that isn't clear enough, what is?

But, go on.

On August 2, 1954, Herman Oberth, wartime V-2 rocket expert, one of the German rocket staff, said in Nuremberg that he was convinced that the things called flying saucers are real and perhaps are manned by "the Vikings from another planetary system. We cannot produce such saucers yet and we are fairly certain that the other planets of our solar system lack civilizations capable of their manufacture," Oberth was reported as saying. "Thus, one concludes that these flying objects are the exploring ships of another solar system, or even of a far-off fixed star."

It is very interesting that, as a rocket authority, formerly stationed at Peenemuende, Mr. Oberth had evidently not heard of Professor Coanda.

On August 16, 1954, Joseph and Stewart Alsop, in their syndicated column, had some very disturbing words for

Americans. The gist of their column was that "The Pentagon intelligence analysts have reluctantly concluded that the Soviet Union is already producing a jet engine about twice as powerful as any yet produced in the United States.

"This is the biggest shock, the bitterest pill, in a development that was generally shocking and unexpected. Until a few months ago, the official forecasters were convinced that the Soviet aircraft industry would at least two years more to turn out planes comparable to our B-47 and B-52. But now such planes are already in the air...one can see why Donald Quarles, Assistant Secretary of Defense for Research Development, recently warned that the Soviets were challenging the American lead in weapons development."

On August 22, 1954, the Air Force released the news that a U.S. test plane had recently broken the all-time world altitude record by climbing to a height more than 15.5 miles in the air. Air Force specialists in high-altitude research said that a piloted aircraft capable of operating successfully above 75,000 feet is in effect a model "space ship" providing a flying laboratory for solving many of the problems of future journeys into outer space.

Two days later, on August 24, the Air Force named the pilot and the height to which he flew his plane in the greatest distance straight up ever flown by man. He was identified as Major Arthur Murray. The height he flew was announced as 90,000 feet, or more than 17 miles above the earth.

On October 9, 1954, Defense Secretary Charles E. Wilson ordered a "new look" at the nation's guided missile program to speed up the output of robot weapons of all types. "About 700,000,000 worth of robots were produced in the last five fiscal years, while an estimated $500,000,000 worth will be bought in the current fiscal year alone...Congress has appropriated $4,762,000,000 for guided missiles since 1950.

Of that, $2,962,000,000 was for production, $1,600,000,000 for research, and $200,000,000 for miscellaneous facilities. About $1,800,000,000 unspent will be carried over into fiscal 1956."

On October 16, 1954, Bangkok, Siam, newspapers reported a flying saucer over Bangkok, saying that: "uninvited guests from outer space...are directing their attention here with a friendly attitude toward the people of Bangkok."

On the same day, a man in Perpignan, France, a retired customs officer named Damien Sigueres, said that he had seen a flying saucer, shaped like a large red sphere, land, while a tall man dressed in a "diver's suit," stepped out. The man, on seeing Mr. Sigueres and his two dogs, jumped back into his craft and the sphere took off, noiselessly.

On October 22, 1954, an English investigating commission, after sifting into the cause of the crash of two jet propelled Comet airplanes off the coast of Italy this year, gave its report. Its conclusions: the two craft exploded from air pressure within them — they had pressurized cabins — when they reached stratospheric heights. The commission's solemn evaluation: flying saucers had nothing to do with the explosions.

And now, we come to another eyebrow-raiser.

LIFE Magazine, in its November 1, 1954, issue, which appeared on the newsstand on October 30 — Halloween — had a two-page spread on pages 28 and 29. The article said that, all autumn long, out of the skies of France from Brittany to the Riviera, "dropped a covy of unearthly vehicles and unearthly men. they were seen by good, solid citizens who swore they had seen them. They even drew diagrams and pictures to prove it. The vehicles the Frenchmen described were of many shapes; whirling discs, flying cigars, crowns, comets, and winged mushrooms.

"Air Force officials imply that for a number of reason the cannot deprecate saucers too freely (though they wish they could). ...somebody, someday, is apt to come along with a jet airplane resembling a saucer, and then the flying saucer advocates will say 'we told you so.'

"...there is a comparatively small group — but the most troublesome — the writers on the subject. Some of them have been making a good thing of the flying saucer interest and a few have been challenging the Air Force to state categorically that flying saucers do not exist."

"'Flying saucers' have been intriguing some Europeans, and the Air Force has received a photograph of some Sicilians gazing at two discs in the sky over Taormina, Sicily. The Air Force did not comment directly on this photograph but noted that still pictures in general were 'worthless' as evidence.

The rest of the article then went on to say that, of all sightings, 90% could be explained on one scientific basis or another. The remaining 10% could not be evaluated because of insufficient data.

Probable explanation of the saucers: optical illusions caused by "temperature inversions" in the air — the same thing said by scientists of the Civil Aeronautics Administration two years ago, following the "blip" rat-race over Washington in July, 1952.

Perhaps the public pronouncements of USAF with regard to flying saucers may be summed by this bit from *The World Telegram & Sun* for January 6, 1955. Under the title "*Heard in Washington*," and reviewing some of Scripps-Howard's scoops for 1954, Ruth Finney wrote: "*Flying Saucer Report.* We said last February that the Air Force knew what flying saucers are (and their denials since haven't shaken us a bit.)"

On the same date, in *The New York Herald Tribune*, Art Buchwald wrote in this *Europe's Lighter Side* column, under the sub-head of Leftover Notes from Yugoslavia: "Flying saucers have never been much of a problem in Yugoslavia. As a matter of fact, according to a Zagreb editor, no one in the country believed in them until October 25 (1954). On that date, saucers were seen all over Yugoslavia, and people started believing. "The first day," the editor said, "we put our science editor on the story, but then on the following days it became so important we assigned to it our political editor.

"One theory advanced by a newspaper was that the saucers were American-made, but because of friendly relations with the United States, no one in official circles would admit it. Soon after the first flying saucers were sighted, translations of American books on the subject appeared in the bookstores and became best-sellers. "No saucers have been seen since then," the editor said, "but whereas the people were all united before against their existence, they are now divided. It isn't good for the country."

The whole year, 1955, was highly productive of interesting news items and magazine articles which may or may not have had bearing on the mystery of the flying saucers.

While very few reports of UFO's crept into the press, one appearing only occasionally as if in editorial defiance, there did appear numerous items that conceivably related to UFOS.

There is, of course, one other very interesting possibility. And that is that the Air Force has been telling the literal truth since the very beginning of the saucer mystery. Maybe the Air Force is almost — if not quite — as ignorant as the rest of us as to the real nature of the flying saucers. Perhaps it is quite true that no saucer has ever malfunctioned, no "little men" have ever been found dead or captured alive, no "hardware" has ever fallen from the skies or picked up on the ground.

Perhaps the only clues to the mystery that the Air Force has are the clues that the rest of the world has — hearsay evidence, no tangible proof; no good motion pictures, no good still photos. As for stories of landings and "little men," much of the evidence here can be regarded as highly dubious. Any such "little men" — and their craft — simply don't stay around to be weighed, measured, analyzed. They fade like flitting moonbeams, to leave only such questionable proof of their visits as a skid mark in the grass, a gash on a railroad tie.

It could be that the Air Force is up against something that it does not understand — and that its only cover-up is a cover-up of its own ignorance. In this case, everything that the Air Force has ever said would make complete sense — that there are some saucer sightings for which there is no explanation, that the possibility that saucers drift in from outer space has never been discounted completely, that no tangible proof exists to prove this, one way or the other. That USAF intends to continue its investigations because it feels an "obligation" to do so.

Perhaps this is too tenuous information to satisfy anyone interested in flying saucers — but it could be the one and only truth about flying saucers that makes sense.

In such case, the Air Force could suspect, like a great many other observers, that saucers are interplanetary. It could suspect, like others, that some of the stories of landings and "little men" emerging from sphere-shaped, disc-shaped, helmet-shaped craft are true. But how can the Air Force prove this, any more than you or I can?

One other factor may be a partial explanation of saucer sightings, as well as balloons, birds, mirages, etc., and that is a perfectly natural celestial phenomenon. In 1953, word came out that Clyde Tombaugh, discoverer of the planet Pluto, was put in charge of a project to locate some additional moons, or tiny satellites, attracted by the earth, and circling it at great speed out in space. This project, if other news is correct, was also engaged in by Dr. Lincoln La Paz.

In 1954, one of the satellites was discovered — -or, rather, rediscovered, since it was first discovered by a German astronomer in Heidelberg, Germany, fifty years ago. He named this little satellite, or asteroid, Athalia. According to The New York Herald Tribune, the asteroid showed up on photographic plates of the astronomy department of Indiana University.

The existence of such satellites had long been suspected. And the sighting of such miniature moons, traveling at great velocity, could certainly account for some sightings. But not for silver arrowheads flashing past a conventional lane flying at 10,000 feet, or for a giant disc, roaring like thunder, that buzzed an airfield, nor for many other sightings of helmets, spindles, and other odd-shaped craft.

CHAPTER 13
THE POSSIBILITIES OF HOAX

What are the possibilities that the whole affair of the flying saucers is a hoax? Let us change the word hoax to hallucination and see if the saucer "scare" can be traced to this.

There is, in a great many of us, *the will to believe.* The will to believe in natural mysteries yet unsolved. The will to believe that all the laws of physics are not yet known. The will to believe in an unseen world to which our physical senses cannot take us. The will to believe in upsets of the laws of nature as we know it.

It is this urge in many of us that accounts for a great number of science fiction magazines and for FATE Magazine. It is this same urge that accounts for the existence of well-known psychical societies — and for the existence of research into extra-sensory perception at Duke University. This same urge is also behind the pulling power of every sermon ever given in every temple, church and cathedral in the world.

But because of this will to believe, this eagerness to be persuaded of the existence of things hidden from us, or of the existence, in this instance, of beings or intelligences from other worlds, people have often fallen for the most colossal of hoaxes, for the most hysterical of hallucinations.

On Halloween Eve, 1938, Orson Welles broadcast his famous dramatization of H.G. Well's *War of the Worlds.* Mr. Welles thought the story was a little dated and dull for 1938, so he tried presenting it with a modern reportorial technique. He chose, as a site for the Martians' mythical landing, a spot called Grover's Mill, New Jersey.

So brilliant was this presentation technique — later to be widely copied in radio and television — that a great part of the audience, tuning in late, thought that the Martian "invasion" was real. According to *Current Biography*, 1941, "an appreciable part of the population of New Jersey took to the hills." Broadcasting switchboards were swamped by calls from alarmed listeners. So were the police. The "landing of the Martians" caused a serious panic, a panic so serious that it became the basis for a Princeton University thesis on mass psychology: *The Invasion From Mars* (1940) Hadley Cantril.

This was not a deliberate hoax. It was perpetrated in all innocence. But thanks to the realism put into the production by Mr. Welles' genius, thousands were hoaxed.

There have been other less innocent hoaxes.

Back in 1833, the noted astronomer John Herschel traveled to Africa's Cape of Good Hope to map the stars of the southern sky. Since communications were so slow in those days that little news of the expedition got to America, a reporter on *The New York Sun*, one Richard Locke, concocted some stories of his own. He reported that Herschel had invented the world's most powerful telescope and, with it, had discovered life on the moon.

The public — including leading scientists of the day — was completely duped. People clamored for more details. And Locke gave them those details — in spades. He told of hills of sapphire, flying unicorns, flying moon-men with bat-like wings, and of great, sphere-like things rolling across moon's "oceans."

Readers fell completely for this balderdash. *The New York Times* and *The New Yorker* of that day did, too.

When the news got to Herschel, that most reputable and eminent of scientists was apoplectic with rage.

It took over a year for the hoax to be unmasked.

But by that time, Locke and his publication cared not a fig. For circulation had risen by 300%.

People like to be fooled.

And then, there was the practical joke pulled by Hugh Troy, American artist and master practical joker, while a student at Cornell. Borrowing a wastebasket made from a rhinoceros foot from the home of Louis Agassiz Fuertes, famous bird-painter, Troy and a friend suspended the foot by cords on a long pole, weighted it heavily, and then walked across a couple of inches of snow on the campus, making rhinoceros tracks at proper intervals. They made the tracks to the edge of a lake — the source of Ithaca's water supply — and there ended them at a large hole in the ice on the lake.

The next morning, there was the usual furor over anything so strange. A professor confirmed the "fact" that a rhinoceros had crossed the campus, fallen into the lake and drowned. Local newspapers blazed the story. Local townspeople stopped drinking tap water, saying they could "taste" rhinoceros.

They didn't know they had been "taken" until several days went past and Troy let the news leak out.

People like to be fooled.

Here's another. In March 1952, the town of Mantoloking, New Jersey, was electrified by the finding of huge, bird-like tracks along the beach. They led from the water up to high-water mark. The prints were a foot long, a foot across, and web-shaped, as if they might be from the legendary Roc of Arabian fairy tales. Excitement about the tracks ran at high pitch in the town. Schools let out early, so children could see the tracks. Newspaper reporters put the story on the wires. People got up early to watch for the great bird that had made the tracks. One man, a hotel employee, reported that he had actually seen the "thing." A group of students from Stevens Institute of Technology made an overnight camping trip to catch the creature. They took plaster casts of the prints. But the "bird" did not show.

On December 9, Mantoloking got an explanation. James J. Turner, a retired insurance broker, of 888 East Avenue, Mantoloking, explained. It was all a hoax. "It gets awfully quiet and lonely around here in the winter," Mr. Turner explained to friends. "I thought I'd see if I could liven things up." Then he hauled from a closet the two giant "bird's feet" he had made from linoleum, cork, plywood, stones and brass, with some old shoes mounted on the top. The shoes fit Mr. Turner.

There is in people the will to believe.

People like to be fooled.

And then, there have been the religion zealots who, time after time, have persuaded the credulous that the world would come to an end on a certain day, and have persuaded these dupes to sell their property, end their businesses, desert their farms and gather on a hilltop — only to find that their prophet of doom was grievously mistaken.

The world has seen many of these individuals.

One cropped up in December 1954. His name won't be given here, because he suffered enough persecution already. But he was a college professor who was dismissed from his job for saying that the world was going to end on December 21, 1954. It was this man's belief that, when the world ended, on the date given, flying saucers from Mars would rescue some of the survivors. The professor was later examined by a sanity board, at the request of his sister, and found completely sane.

Then, there is another element which may enter into the flying saucer mystery — and that's the element of science fiction.

Now science fiction has been written — and read avidly — for a good many years. About the best that has ever been done was written by the old master himself, Jules Verne, the brilliant Frenchman, who started this school of literature back in 1873 with the publication of *his Twenty Thousand Leagues Under the Sea.* Verne wrote with a fabulously prophetic eye, foreseeing the submarines, modern aircraft, radio, telephone, television and other modern commonplaces long before there were a gleam in an inventor's eye.

Since Verne's time, science fiction has been published by the billions of words. There are dozens of science fiction magazines on the newsstand today. There are hundreds, thousands of science fiction books. There are even science fiction clubs, all across the country.

There is nothing wrong with science fiction. It is one of the great forms of literary entertainment, like "who done it's," like westerns, like love stories, like adventure stories. Even *The Saturday Evening Post* publishes science fiction, and very good science fiction, including stories centered around flying saucers, occasionally.

Well-known scientists read science fiction. And well-known scientists write science fiction, supplementing their university or governmental salaries with their creations.

It's all good, clean fun, except that you will note, if you will read science fiction magazines, carefully, that both writers and editors, in their zeal for realism, will sometime write of completely fantastic subjects as if they already existed.

It is not without the realm of possibility that some science fiction writers and, conceivably, science fiction editors, catering to readers' will to believe, have let some of their fantasy creep into the flying saucer picture, fanning the fires of sensational for the credulous.

And odd facts to consider here along this line are that Frank Scully's book before he wrote on flying saucers were on the humorous side. George Adamski wrote a book on esoteric Tibetan philosophy before he wrote his first book on space ships. His collaborator on his latest book — *Flying Saucers Have Landed* — Desmond Leslie, is a writer on mystic, occult and esoteric subjects.

Gerald Heard's writings, before his book on flying saucers, were chiefly on the side of the fantastic.

Donald E. Keyhoe, according to this own words, as described by Dr. Donald E. Menzel of Harvard, was a science fiction writer.

And Dr. Menzel, according to Mr. Keyhoe's angry rebuttal, once wrote science fiction himself.

Ray Palmer, co-owner and publisher of FATE Magazine, also owns and publishes a sister publication, *Other Worlds*, which is out-and-out science fiction.

In considering the possibilities of hoax, it is interesting to point out that TRUE Magazine hired J.P. Cahn to investigate the Scully book — and then labelled the whole thing hoax.

Major Donald Keyhoe , himself, a leading exponent of the extraterrestrial theory on flying saucers, labels the story told by George Adamski as a fake.

And — with regard to Adamski book, Arthur C. Clarke, reputable scientist, Chairman of the British Interplanetary Society, and author of the scientifically-accurate book, *The Exploration of Space*, has had a few things to say about it. A quote about the Adamski close-up pictures of flying saucers: "uncanny resemblance to electric light fittings with table-tennis balls fixed underneath." That's about what the editor of FATE said.

With regard to the Adamski pictures of "space ships near the moon," Mr. Clarke has said that the saucers must have been inside the telescope itself to obtain such images.

Other odd, and perhaps unrelated facts to consider also are that two of the "witnesses" of George Adamski's visit with the Venusian, George H. Williamson and Alfred E. Bailey, also wrote a book on flying saucers. Their book is about "saucer people" who contacted them by means of automatic writing and radio.

Two other books on flying saucers, published by British Book Center, publisher of the Adamski book, are in great part paens of praise of the Adamski revelations.

Harold T. Wilkins, another author of a book of flying saucers, has long been a writer on occult and esoteric subjects.

As for my own writing, aside from the writing of advertising copy, which is my profession, my few published efforts have been in the field of juvenile fiction. So, if the writing of flying saucer books puts one in the raised eyebrow category, I am in that category, too.

Now, is it possible that some writers on flying saucers have created a mystery out of no mystery, simply by using certain "atmosphere" words and techniques?

Let's take the word, mysterious. Or the word, mystery. It's amazing what one can do with those words in writing up something of an improbable or unknown nature. A "mysterious" light crosses a field. It could be a farmer with a lantern. But no matter. It's "mysterious." You hear a creak in your house at night. It's a "mysterious" sound. It could be caused by the settling of the house, or by expansion or contraction due to changing temperature in the weather. No matter, again. It's "mysterious." You hear a chair creak as you sit quietly reading a book at night. The creak isn't due to the fact that another member of the family has been sitting in it recently and that it is readjusting itself after those stresses have been removed. No. It's "mysterious." Someone from another world, perhaps, or one of your long-dead relatives, is sitting there, quite invisible. That's what made the chair creak.

And that's one school of writing you will find in books on flying saucers.

There is a similar school that asks coy questions, like: “Space ship looking us over, maybe? Or: “Man from Mars, perhaps.” This school also uses liberal punctuation with exclamation marks. If it were permissible to use three, instead of one, it would be natural to find three used. In most of these books, there is no verification whatsoever for any claims made.

In other books there is a kind of panting, breathy excitement, like that of a fat beagle chasing a rabbit, that comes lolloping at the reader. This is the suspense school, in which something of earth-shaking significance is going to be imparted — and backed up with official proof by the U.S. Air Force — but never quite is.

In still other books there is a cozy intimacy with people from outer space who fly the saucers. The authors of some of these books not only claim to have seen saucers, but to have entered them, to have flown in them, and to have talked on many occasions to their crews. None of these authors agree on the exact names for the saucers, where they come from, or the names of the people who fly them. Most of the names encountered sound suspiciously like those you will encounter in any pulp magazine devoted to science fiction. Each author claiming “contact” with the “saucer people” seems to have been contacted by a different race of extraterrestrial entities, with no linguistic connection whatever between names given by different authors.

If you read enough of these literary efforts, you'll think you are in the land of the pixies. Read a few more, and you'll start talking to yourself. A few more, and you'll be out on your front law, waiting for something to come down out of the sky and contact you, and wind up at the stage where you are cutting out paper dolls — or speaking before civic groups of your "experiences."

Reading a lot of these books, you get the impression that a lot of people would like to believe that space craft, with people from other planets, are keeping an eye on us. This old, sad world has been savage and brutal for millennia. And all of its science today, good and great though most of it is, can still lead to the ultimate horror in brutality and savagery.

How wonderful to suppose that there might be a much more intelligent — and benevolent — race with a less of the ape in it, that might lead us to a new heaven and a new earth. Poor, fragile vessels that we are, how much to be hoped for is this — one alternate solution to blowing ourselves up, and with ourselves — the earth.

Could this wishful thinking have led to the writing of much about flying saucers that is, shall we say, unauthenticated?

Captain E.J. Ruppelt, writing in TRUE Magazine, had this to say on some saucer books: "The cult is nourished by a small group of literary procurers who seize on every sighting and process it for consumption. They strip each report of any information that points to a natural explanation. They drop off all qualifying data. They omit the analysis, — except when the project frankly admits it is baffled. Then they present the residue as fact 'straight from the files of Bluebook.' A popular variant on this is 'from Air Force secret records.'

"In the scripture of the cultist, everything is a saucer. The actual report may describe the UFO as a light six inches in diameter, an orb twice the size of the moon, a black spot in the sky, a strange blip on a radarscope, a cone-shaped object, a vague glow in the sky, a cigar-shaped figure, or a splash of light like a comet's tail. These dissimilar objects are converted, with the flick of a typewriter, into saucers."

In considering all of the writing on saucers, it would be interesting to know how many of the writers — or, for that matter, how many of the sighters of so-called saucers — have read Charles Fort.

Is it conceivable that their writing — or their eyesight — might have been affected by their reading of him?

But such a question is obviously absurd. The idea of a hoax, started and continued by readers of Charles Fort, is by members of the Fortean Society, is untenable. Too many people, people who could only have heard of, or read the writings of Charles Fort by the wildest of coincidences, especially among the European peasantry, have reported seeing unknown objects, both in the skies, and landed on earth. And thousands of people have reportedly seen these objects — at least, the ones in the sky — at one time.

Such reasoning might lead to the asking of another question: Are Major Keyhoe, Ray Palmer, Kenneth Arnold, George Adamski, Harold T. Wilkinson, Donald E. Menzel, Frank Scully — and all other writers on the subject of saucers — counter espionage agents for the U.S. Government? Are all of them, by official directive, muddying-up the greatest cover-up job of modern times?

Such a question is equally absurd in the light of the record, in the light of the fact that saucers — or of things with the same attributes of saucers have been sighted for centuries, if not for millennia.

Furthermore, it is equally inconceivable, in trying to explore the possibility of hoax, that FATE Magazine, LIFE Magazine and TRUE Magazine, with their circulations and their reputations at stake, would deliberately involve themselves in a hoax. It is inconceivable that the *Readers' Digest*, with its millions in circulation, would reprint the LIFE article claiming that saucers are extraterrestrial, or publish

J.R. Aswell's article on saucer sightings for 150 years, if its editors thought saucers were a hoax. It is equally inconceivable that LOOK Magazine, with its millions in circulation, would first cling to the side of scientific explanation, then follow-up with an article on the seriousness of the Air Force's search, and later on, in October 1953, publish excerpts from Major Keyhoe's book, *Flying Saucers From Outer Space*, even though the editors said they did not commit themselves one way or the other. It is inconceivable that LIFE would publish an *article Flying Saucers Bounces Off Design Board*, a completely factual report on Canada's flying saucer and how it could work, and then follow, in its November 1, 1954 issue, with an equally factual report on what various Frenchmen claimed they had seen in the way of "little men" climbing out of flying saucers in the fall of 1954. It is inconceivable that *The New York World Telegram & Sun* should claim, early in 1955, that the U.S. Air Force knows what flying saucers are — if WT&S had any belief that they could be a hoax.

It is likewise equally inconceivable that men of the stature of Professor Herman Oberth, international rocket authority, Air Chief Marshall Lord Dowding, Commander in Chief of the British Air Force, Dr. Maurice A. Biot, leading American aerodynamicist, Dr. Walther Riedel, once chief designer and research director of the German rocket station on Peenemunde, and now doing work for the U.S., should have expressed the belief that saucers are real — and extraterrestrial — unless they had real reason for doing so.

It is inconceivable to think that hundreds, thousands of sober conscientious people, including Frenchmen, Italians and Portuguese who reported "little men" climbing from strange, unearthly vehicles, lied when they said they had seen these things.

It is similarly inconceivable that the camera lied when, photographing objects on at least two continents, it showed amazing similarity in what it caught on film.

It is inconceivable that Captain E.J. Ruppelt, once official head of "Project Bluebook," writing as a civilian following that duty — and disillusioned though he was — to write that saucers are either non-existent, or extraterrestrial space craft.

Inconceivable that USAF would buy and install diffraction-grid cameras, or that the U.S. and Britain would exchange flying saucer information, or that the U.S. would establish formalized procedures for interrogating Air Force crew sightings, or that the U.S. Air Force would request its air trainees to aid at solving the mystery of the saucers — if the whole thing was a hoax.

Inconceivable also the possibility of hoax when you read such items as this: In The New York Herald Tribune for December 3, 1954, there appeared an editorial about a meteorite that ripped through the roof of the house of Mrs. Hewlett Hodges of Sylacauga, Alabama, striking her on the hip and hand. USAF reportedly requested the meteorite for study. *The World Telegram & Sun,* in an article the same day, said that the rock was being studied at Wright-Patterson Air Force Base, Dayton, Ohio. That's headquarters for saucer investigations. Later, in the February 13, 1955, issue *of American Weekly,* Mrs. Hodges, writing as Ann Elizabeth Hodges, stated that one of the policeman who called at her house following Mrs. Hodges' call to them "explained that all police departments throughout the country were under orders to turn over to the Air Force any object that fell from the skies." It is hardly conceivable that USAF would issue such an order — unless it expected something could fall from the skies.

And here's another one: At least twice in 1954, Dorothy Kilgallen, in her column in *The New York Journal American*, had cryptic remarks. One: “Is it possible that new peeps through the telescope on Mt. Palomar indicate that many a scientist — and textbook — could have been wrong about the universe?” And again, in her column *Broadway Bulletin Board* on November 15, 1954, Miss Kilgallen stated that “a Harvard professor is telling his classes that he can prove that there are people on other planets.”

These things don't sound much like hoax.

Nor does this one:

On Monday night, December 6, 1954, on the television program “Big Town,” 10:30 P.M., E.S.T., sponsored by A.C. Sparkplugs, a division of General Motors Corporation, there was a broadcast a “true life” story of flying saucers. This story “in which only the names of the people and names of the city have been changed” was about a man who claimed to have seen a landed saucer, to have talked with the people from it — who were from Venus — to have visited the inside of the saucer, and who received an invitation to fly in a saucer to Venus. The man, according to the dramatized broadcast, was asked to take a lie detector test, which he did. The test showed that he lied. Later, it developed that the machine was faulty. So the newspaper editor who had printed the man's story, telephoned him to see if he would take the test over again. Payoff: the man had disappeared. He left his forwarding address: Venus.

During the showing of this program, there was shown about a ten-second sequence from a motion picture showing a saucer sweeping through the air. The movie looked authentic.

The program ended with the well-known quotation from Voltaire to the effect that “while I may did agree with you, I'll defend your right to say so,” etc.

One cannot imagine General Motors Corporation lending itself to a hoax, meant to fool the American people. The objective of the corporation is to maintain and build good will, not ill will, for the purpose of selling its many products. It is inconceivable that the corporation would sponsor such a broadcast, even in "dramatized form, of anything so questionable, unless it had pretty good reason to believe that there was something in back of the story — and to publicize it for some reason other than mere entertainment.

It is inconceivable — unless General Motors is one of the prime contractors in making the components for U.S. Government flying saucers — and used the medium of the television program to further the cover-up of the existence of man-made saucers.

One cannot conceive of a hoax — unless the U.S. Air Force itself, inventor of a fantastic new craft, or an absolutely unbelievable series of crafts — or knowing Russia to be the inventor — started the whole saucer furor, initiated the extraterrestrial theory, and then fed the fire constantly by getting various publications and authors to confuse the picture as much as possible. But a cover-up of this nature would take fantastic ingenuity, as well as unlimited funds.

It would take a madman to even dream it up — let alone attempt to carry it out.

Let alone to create the master creation of them all — "little men" in a variety of colors, mostly pleasing pastels. And one little man, tapping a Frenchman inquiringly on the shoulder, a solemn little man with, in the center of his forehead, one single, solitary, unearthly and unwinking eye.

Hoax?

It doesn't read like that.

Although, if you will read the record carefully, you will see that the great mass of protagonists for the extraterrestrial theory for saucers are oculists, not scientists. And among the scientists who have espoused this theory, most of them are in the aircraft industry, or are government consultants, with every reason in the work to cover-up on man-made craft that fit into the saucer category.

And a couple of other facts that add a nice note of skepticism to the theory of extraterrestrial space visitors is the fact that Ohio Northern University, that initiated a saucer-study project, dropped it because of lack of data to study. And the Canadians, who set up a saucer observation station with a great many electronic devices, discontinued the station's operation. If saucers were popping in from Mars or other planets regularly, and if the authorities knew this to be absolute fact, then one would expect the establishment of hundreds of new special projects, not the abandonment of them.

Hoax? Not probable.

And neither is what the occultists have written about saucers.

CHAPTER 14
THE OTHER SIDE OF THE COIN

Now, let's turn the coin over and take a good, long look at its other side.

We have seen that there is considerable evidence to indicate that flying saucers are from outer space. Although no one to date, so far as is known, has publicly exhibited a saucer, fragments of a saucer, or a "little man from Mars," the evidence still exists. It cannot be frowned down by a long stare. And, although no one has yet collected the $100,000.00 reward offered by *The Saturday Review of Literature*, or the 10 million francs ($28,000) offered by an inhabitant of Locronan, France, or the equally inviting offer by the French newspaper "Express" for a "man from Mars," this does not disprove the theory of space visitors.

In addition to evidence that saucers are extraterrestrial, there is also a great deal of evidence to show that they are perfectly natural aerial phenomena, explainable by astronomers, meteorologists and physicists in terms of known objects, reflections, air lenses, etc.

There is also plenty of evidence to indicate that saucers are Air Force balloons, night photography flares, canopy reflections and other well-known objects or mirages.

Furthermore, there is evidence to show that there might be a certain amount of literary charlatanism, if not downright fraud, in the saucer picture, although the possibility that the whole saucer "scare" is a hoax seems the most remote possibility of all.

Now, what evidence is there to show that, incredible though it may be, that saucers are actually none of these things — but new, secret, and utterly fantastic guided or piloted missiles or craft that are made right here on earth?

There is considerable evidence to support this belief.

And perhaps this is really the one and the only correct explanation of flying saucers. Perhaps Henry J. Taylor, Billy Rose, and some other commentators were right when they said, quite early in the game, that flying saucers are secret weapons. The only trouble was, they said they were U.S. weapons. Such may not have been the case at all. But certainly, the Taylor "expose" was the one thing that drew instant, emphatic and universal denial by every branch of the armed services, with even a spokesman for the President considering it important enough to issue a White House denial. There has been no such overwhelming denial of the extraterrestrial theory — there has even been no such overwhelming denial of the extraterrestrial theory — there has even been semi-encouragement of this theory all along by the Air Force — although on one occasion, a press conference was held following Major Keyhoe's article in TRUE that claimed saucers were from outer space, and there was another denial when President Eisenhower said, in late 1954, that he had been told that saucers were not from outer space.

But, when it was said that saucers were U.S. secret war craft, there was instant, overwhelming denial.

Yet there is evidence that saucers may be a new and different type of earth craft.

This evidence is not secret. It has been published to millions of people in newspapers and magazines. This writer has had no access to classified information of any kind. There is absolutely nothing here that does not come from a public record. There is nothing here that the Intelligence Headquarters of Russia, England, Italy, Spain, Sweden, Yugoslavia and every other country of any consequence of the face of the globe does not know — or could easily acquire by the most amateurish of efforts.

There are no secrets here in this phase of the questioning of the nature of saucers. If there were secrets, they have long since been revealed and given away.

But no writer, to this author's knowledge, has ever brought together the bits of this part of the jig-saw puzzle. Yet they are very significant bits and merit the consideration of anyone trying to understand the mystery of the saucers.

Let's try to put some of the bits together:

Practically all writers on the subject of saucers have discounted the possibility that the saucers have their home nest right here on earth for three for four reasons — and, at first sight, these are very good reasons indeed. Among these are:

1. The extremely high speed.
2. The seemingly impossible maneuvering and the matter of G-pull — the pull of the earth's gravity — on any occupant or occupants.
3. The lack of sound in objects flying faster than sound. The motors of conventional planes roar, or their jets sound like giant blowtorches in the sky. And when a plane of conventional design passes through the sound barrier, it causes a noise like a clap of thunder. Many saucers observed were noiseless, even when going from a stationary position or a slow speed into speeds that would take them through the sonic barrier.
4. Glow. Many reporters of saucers described them as flowing, either with a greenish-blue glare on the inside, or with completely glowing exterior — reddish, orange, yellow, or other shades of the spectrum.

Now, how about these points? Do they absolutely eliminate the possibility that saucers may be earth craft, after all? Most writers, citing these points, have dismissed the possibilities. But let's take the points, one by one, and analyze them.

1. Speed. Conventional craft, using a principle of "boring through" air, or being forced through air, can get red hot, have metals creep, can fall apart or burn to a crisp from friction. However, by utilizing the principle of "Coanda's Effect," with the object flying in a partial vacuum of its own making, this problem could be overcome. In the opinion of Professor Henri Coanda, discoverer of the effect, as given to Art Buchwald, it would be overcome. In many observations of extremely high speeds in saucers, the most extreme speeds were not observed in the dense, lower layers of our atmosphere, but at higher altitudes, far, far above the earth. And a great many observations of saucers have indicated that they rise in a series of "stairsteps," and achieve greatest velocity only after gaining the upper reaches of the atmosphere where density, air resistance and friction would be much less.

And on this subject of speed, it is well to remember that speeds seemingly impossible to earth craft in 1947, when the first saucers were widely reported, seem terribly old-fashioned today. In 1947, men were trying to break the speed of sound — and secretly had succeeded. But this speed of something over 700 mph became old hat in just six years, when Maj. Charles E. Yeager, in December 1953, flew a plane of conventional "boring through the air" design at more than 1,600 mph, or something more than two and one-half times the speed of sound.

And by May, 1953, scientists at Langley Field, Virginia, were reporting that they were doing research on guided missiles that might reach the speed of 15,000 mph. The scientists pointed out that then (1953) they were flying missiles at speeds of 3,000 mph from Wallops Island, Virginia. By August 1956, we were supposed to launch man-made moons which would attain a speed of 18,000 miles per hour.

Speed, and speed alone — even the fantastic higher speeds reported in saucers — would not seem to rule out completely the possibility that saucers are earth-made.

2. Maneuverability and G-pull on occupant. A great deal has been written about the impossibility of having anything human survive the mad maneuvers observed in saucers; acute-angled turns with no slackening in speed; high-speed circling of two discs in the air, as if they were "charging their batteries;" tremendous acceleration from practically zero to thousands of miles an hour; abrupt reverses in direction.

But do all these things rule out the possibility that saucers might be man-made?

Not at all. First, they might be unmanned missiles — especially the tiny saucers that have been reported. Next, new things are coming to light about G-pull and the amount a human can survive, about "weightlessness," about other factors that may enter into the picture.

For instance, in the magazines *Flying*, March 1951, p. 34, First Lieutenant Hugh F. McLaurin, USAF, answered the following questions: "What would happen if you were shoved into a rocket plane and suddenly catapulted into the sky at 13,000 mph? Would you explode? Would you sweat blood? Would you be killed by acceleration or by pressure change? The answers are all no. Lt. McLaurin knew. He went through such a speed in a simulated test and survived.

Again, on G-pull, Major Donald E. Keyhoe, writing in TRUE, December 1952, wrote: "By applying thrust in an opposite direction, abruptly reversing thrusts, an object can be halted in seconds. Tests made with G-sled by the Air Force has shown that, for a fraction of a second, human beings can take a force of 45 G's and survive."

Maybe Major Keyhoe was a little premature in his announcement of this fact, but as proof of it, USAF, on December 27, 1954, announced that one of its officers, Lt. Col. John P. Stapp, had gone from a record land speed of 623 mph to a dead stop in 1.5 seconds without ill effects.

This quick stop was made at Holloman Air Development Center at Alamogordo, New Mexico. In the test, Col. Stapp was strapped to a 2,000-pound rocket sled. The only ill effects he suffered were a few blood blisters from dust particles in the air and two black eyes, caused by his eyeballs being thrown forward against his eyelids during the deceleration period.

In stopping, Col Stapp withstood a pressure equal to 33 G's. His "weight" was more than three tons.

On the evening of December 28, 1954, there appeared in *The New York World Telegram & Sun* a write up of an interview with Col. Stapp, made on the 27th, in which the colonel said that he expected to travel at 1,200 mph on the sled. This would be nearly twice as fast, with proportionate step-up in G-pressure with a violent stop.

Can man withstand the violent maneuvers and sudden decelerations observed in flying saucers?

What do you think?

Another factor sometimes overlooked by writers on flying saucers is the phenomenon of *weightlessness*. If you don't weigh anything, i.e., if you have a condition of zero gravity, you can't very well be slammed around by violent maneuvers in the air. Some writers have, however, pointed out that extraterrestrial craft, using some form of magnetic propulsion, might create their own gravitational fields and thus be free of gravitational pull from the earth. Maybe it is not as complicated as all that. In TRUE for July 1954, writer Don

Dwiggins described weightlessness as experienced in a two-seater plane flown by Maj. Edward J. Rackham, USAF acceptance pilot at Lockheed's Van Nuys, California plant. They went up to 20,000 feet and then went into a ballistic curve. the result was weightlessness. Mr. Dwiggins photographed a pack of cigarettes floating fee in the cabin of the plane.

If weightlessness can be achieved with a ballistic curve, perhaps it can be achieved in some other, but fairly easy way. And such weightlessness might permit violent maneuvering, such as has been noted in flying saucers.

But, if you will read further on the subject of weightlessness, you will find that this phenomenon presents grave hazards to the airman. LIFE Magazine, in an article in its December 6, 1954 issue, pointed out that weightlessness is a highly pleasant sensation. No airman has been able to stand it for more than 45 seconds. It produces severe disorientation. It dislocates all sense of direction. It produces nausea, nervous distress, loss of ability to co-ordinate, inability to guide the complex machinery of today's flying craft.

So one argument negates the other here.

3. The *lack of sound* in objects traveling faster than sound. Here, again, let us refer to the new principle of flight, the "Coanda Effect." If a craft is flying in a partial vacuum, not pushing and compressing the air in front of us, or "boring through" it, conceivably it might be possible to glide through the atmosphere and pass through the sound barrier without the "clap of thunder" made by conventional planes. As for the lack of sound issuing from the vehicle itself — motor, engine, turbine, jet — if there exists some new and little publicized principle of flight, plus some news and unpublicized method of propulsion — magnetic, anti-gravitational, atomic — it might be possible to achieve soundlessness or near soundlessness.

4. Glow. This is one to really stump the experts, in trying to explain saucers as completely terrestrial craft. But certain atomic, radioactive materials glow with the same kind of blue-green glare noted in some saucer interiors. But how a crew could be protected from gamma rays emanating from such materials poses an unanswerable question. As to glowing exteriors — Major Keyhoe has written at some length, theorizing that the glow of extraterrestrial space craft could come from varying degrees of heat caused by friction — from practically white-hot, to red-hot, to orange-hot, to yellow-hot, going from highest speeds to the lowest, and of colors caused by corona effect. Perhaps this same principle would hold true of earth-made craft, as well as extraterrestrial vehicles. As to the question of materials which could withstand these heats — present rocket speeds, as published in newspapers — are above 4,000 mph. Such speeds must cause temperatures that make rockets glow — like saucers.

All this may be very thin evidence that saucers would be earth craft. But it is certainly no thinner than a lot of evidence used in support of the extraterrestrial school of thought. And there is a great deal of other evidence that is factual, not based upon pure supposition and theory.

For instance, Professor Coanda discovered his new principle of flight back in 1937. This principle, described previously, in essence is that if you curve a jet of air, or many jets of air, you can create an artificial cyclone, with the tremendous lift of a cyclone, and can lift and maneuver a many-ton object because you create a vacuum above the whirling blasts of the jets.

Here is a note that may fit:

In The Washington Daily News for May 14, 1949, was a copyrighted story that the flying discs were of Spanish-Nazi origin. The author held the view that the discs were very real, and that they were of a new "gyroscopic" design.

Here is another note that also fits somewhere into the picture: On May 22, 1952, there died in Rome, Italy, Giuseppe Belluzzo, seventy-six, Italian scientist and former cabinet member. To quote from an article about him in The New York Herald Tribune:

"Mr. Belluzzo, who was Minister of National Economy and Minister of Public Instruction during the Fascist regime of Benito Mussolini, was also an authority on cannon and projectiles and a firm believer in flying discs.

"In a newspaper article in 1950, he said that models for flying discs had been drawn in Germany and Italy at about the same time in 1942, and were shown to both Mussolini and Hitler.

"'There is nothing supernatural or Martian about flying discs,' Mr. Belluzzo wrote. 'But they are simply rational application of recent technique. He expressed the opinion that 'some great power is launching discs to study them.'

"Though he had never seen one, he described it as a jet-propelled guided missile which gained its flying speed by a whirling action. 'The principle of the flying disc is simple,' he said, 'and construction with light metal is very easy.'"

Another thing to be remembered: The secret of the Foo Fighters, or Kraut Balls that appeared over Germany in World War II, and that followed or chased aircraft, has never been disclosed. These colored lights, often winking in and out, may or may not have something to do with the balls of colored fire flying over the Gulf of Finland in the past few years, ostensibly from Russia.

Another thing: When the Americans, the English and the Russians slugged their way into the heart of Germany, each government sent emissaries rushing ahead of armies to make contact with German scientists, and to capture the secrets of the Nazi's wartime laboratories. These secrets, supposedly, were shared equally between the three powers. Writing in *Collier's*, in January 1955, Dr. Walter Dornberger, once in charge of the German Rocket Station at Peenemunde, said that, while the Russians got more actual materials of projects in progress from the Germans, the Americans succeeded in getting more technicians. But who got the best plans — and the best technicians — for making the flying discs?

Another factor to consider: On December 29, 1948, a new project was initiated by the U.S. government. It was a project for the conquest of space. Spearheaded by the Air Force, it was named the *Earth Satellite Vehicle Program.* It was a project calling for research and development of a man-made satellite to circle the earth some 200 to 250 miles out in space.

This was not a crazy pipe-dream, but a serious, completely official program. Well-defined areas of research were allocated to all three branches of the military.

Estimated speed needed for the satellite to escape earth's gravity — 23,000 mph.

Another note: On September 10, 1952, Senator Mahoney of Wyoming told the U.S. Senate that "the U.S. is *acquiring* highly secret weapons that can conquer the atmosphere." (The italics here are mine, not the Senator's.)

This speech of the Senator's closely followed an announcement by the British — on August 29, 1952 — that their scientists had developed a guided missile that could take off automatically and chase an enemy plane, no matter where it might go. It was at this time that Sir Frank Spriggs, director of a group of companies making missiles, was reported to have said that the new weapons were so fantastic that it took a madman to order them.

It was only five months later — on February 11, 1953, that news came down from Canada that a company was building a real, honest-to-goodness, live flying saucer. This news had been trickling down from Canada orally for months before. The saucer was to fly by "Coanda's Effect."

In a report dated August 8, 1953, according to FATE Magazine, a Norwegian newspaper reported the finding of a crashed saucer near Spitzbergen. The disc, made of an unknown metal, had a crushed cockpit, and was empty. There was a transmission panel, powered with a nucleus of plutonium. "The object, probably from Russia, has been brought by ship to Narvik, Norway," the article is reported to have said.

On September 17, 1953, *The New York Times* reported that top defense scientists from the United States conferred with Canadian officials in Toronto on details of the new flying saucer to be made by Canada, on September 16, 1953.

In December 1953, the Swedish Air Force ordered an official investigation of a speeding object seen over the southern Swedish town of Hassleholm on December 17. A round, spherical missile or craft, was seen on that date, in sight for six or seven minutes. The Swedish press speculated that it might have been of Russian origin.

On December 28, as reported in London, the Russians came out with a scathing denial, accusing the "aggressive forces" in the U.S. and other western countries of inventing imaginary flying saucers to fan war hysteria and so obtain larger military appropriations.

If the saucers are, or were originally, Russian, this could account for the Soviet diatribe against them.

And despite this blast by the Russians, despite the fact that practically every writer about saucers and every governmental spokesman speaking about saucers has discounted the possibility that they might be developments of the U.S.S.R., there have still been hints that they appear from behind the Iron Curtain.

One indication that they could quite possibly be Russian is that no sightings of saucers, no landings of saucers, were reported from either Russia or China until Inez Robb, in her column in the New York World Telegram and Sun on (date) wrote that the Russians were in a flap about them. While practically every other country on earth has reported sightings — from points as far apart as Hong Kong and American Antarctica, no mention has been made among the Reds or their satellites. Andrei Vishinski said that saucers were shipped to America in Scotch whisky. The official Russian press said that they were imaginary inventions of the western warmongers.

All of these things could add to the fact that saucers are never flown where there is a possibility that they might fall into Russian hands.

Or — that they might actually originate from Russia.

Yet time and time again, authors and USAF spokesmen have dismissed the possibility that the saucers are Russian.

This low-rating of Russian technology could be as deceiving to the people of the U.S. as the low-rating the Japanese got in some quarters before World War II. "A tin can fleet. They'll turn turtle at the first salvo. No air force. Cheap imitations of the real thing," were some of the jibes or wiseacres made about the Japanese before they sank most of our fleet at Pearl Harbor on the morning of December 7, 1941, and then proceeded to take over vast areas of the Pacific. What actually happened wasn't at all like the prophesies of the wise boys. The Japanese fleet was a very tough fleet indeed. The Japanese air men was anything but a pushover. Japanese jungle warfare was something entirely new to the sitting ducks at Singapore, with their guns pointed in the wrong direction. The Japanese took a lot of stopping by a lot of very brave men.

As for the Russians, they should not be low-rated with the same smug, self-satisfied assumption that any American can lick any ten men of any other nationality. Their technology is not backward. It is highly advanced. The Russian civilization at present, despite the fact that its citizens do not have automobiles, good clothes, an abundance of food, enough homes, and slick appliances, despite the fact that they are slaves of the state, is *not* a horse-and-buggy civilization. It is greatly because of the fact that its citizens are denied everything but a bare subsistence level that the Russians have been able to pour unlimited funds and manpower into technological advances...and graduate far more physicists from their universities than we do.

Their advances have been many.

This author, be it said here, is an ardent anti-Communist. He even happens to vote Republican. But he doesn't low-rate the Russians. Let it be remembered that the Russians, not the Americans, perfected the technique of the blood transfusion. The Russians, not the Germans or the British or the Americans, developed the first mechanism for the mass firing of rockets in infantry warfare. In addition, the Russians have always played an interested role in aviation, even in Czarist days, and some of our very best aircraft designers — de Seversky, Sikorsky, and others — have been Russian in origin.

Time and time again, year after year, we have been told by authoritative writers in our press that our Intelligence, accused in many quarters of *overestimating* Soviet capabilities, have generally sadly *underestimated* them.

They were underestimated in their timetable on their first jet fighter. While experts tried to console themselves that the first Russian jet, appearing in the late 1940s, was a propaganda model, they watched in dismay in Korea as the Soviets gave the Chinese enough MIG-15s to maintain a 7-to-1 superiority over our own jet fighter force — while still having enough planes left to dominate the European skies.

Then, the Russians exploded an atom bomb, far in advance of the "timetable" set down by our global planning experts. Many of these experts lulled themselves into a cocoon of false security by believing that had it not been for the espionage of the Goldbergs, the defaulting of such men as Fuchs and Pontecorvo, the Russians could have never had achieved so great a technical achievement.

But on August 12, 1953, came news that the Russians had been woefully underestimated again. For on that date, people of the U.S. — and the world — were told that the Russians had exploded a hydrogen bomb — and evidently a super hydrogen bomb, judging by the hysterical note underlying the newspaper reports. There were even guarded hints that it might be the ultimate in destructive weapons — not a hydrogen bomb — but a cobalt bomb, or some other technical advance so brilliant that it shattered forever any idea that Russian technology is backward. In fact, it established the sobering possibility that their technology might be considerably in advance of ours.

Again, in 1954, our master planner's faces were red again. This time, the Reds had developed jets with twice the horsepower of our own, according to reliable Washington correspondents.

For other indications that the Russians may enter the flying saucer picture somewhere: In February 1953, reporting on Canada's flying saucer, *The Toronto Star* was quoted as saying: "reports have been so persistent and apparently consistent concerning the Canadian craft that western scientists consider the possibility that Soviet Russia has carried similar developments to a more advanced stage."

On July 13, 1954, in Art Buchwald's column in *The New York Herald Tribune*, Mr. Buchwald reported that it was the opinion of Professor Henri Coanda, discoverer of "Coanda's Effect," that the saucers were Russian in origin.

Again, it was the opinion of Dr. Anthony O. Mirarchi, one of the experts investigating flying saucers, that they might be photographic missiles of some foreign power.

To get some further idea of Russian progress in guided missiles, read Dr. Walter R. Dornberger's article, "Can Russian Missiles Strike the United States?" in *Collier's*, January 7, 1955.

Dr. Dornberger was at one time the major general in charge of the German Army Missile Experimentation Station at Peenemunde. "Many of the missiles Russia now has are advancements of projects I started," write Dr. Dornberger. "Many of my former subordinates went to Russia after the war and worked on these projects."

Dr. Dornberger, now missile consultant for Bell Aircraft Corporation, and who has applied for American citizenship, states that the Russians picked up development of the V-2 rocket where German technicians left off. "They have increased the range to at least 300 miles, and claim accuracy within 1,500 feet."

It was Dr. Dornberger's expressed opinion that the U.S. and U.S.S.R. at present are on a par with regard to missile development, but that in three years, the U.S. would be ahead of the Soviets. Neither Russia nor the U.S., in Dr. Dornberger's opinion, have an intercontinental guided missile now — but will have soon.

Other facts brought out by Dr. Dornberger: U.S. probably has edge, because this country got the top 200 German scientists, many of whom were the key brains in Germany's missile technology. Among them: Dr. Wernher von Braun, now chief of the guided-missile division of the Army's Redstone Arsenal; Dr. Ernst Steinhoff, specialist at the Air Force's Holloman Air Development Center; Dr. Walther Riedel, senior project engineer for North American Aviation's propulsion facility; Dr. Rudolph Herman, professor of aerodynamics at the University of Minnesota; and Professor Theodore Buckhold, now with General Electric.

For another evaluation of Russian progress: In *The New York Herald Tribune* for November 3, 1954, in the syndicated column, *Matter of Fact*, written by Joseph and Stewart Alsop, it was reported that top planners in Washington were debating a "crash" program to build the artificial earth satellite because of a boast in one of the Soviet military publications that a Soviet satellite would take the air in ten years. To quote: "As in the case of the H-bomb debate, the American fate and future is quite probably bound up in the satellite debate. But far from being carried on before the American people, this debate that may so deeply influence the people's future has been closely restricted to the most secret circles."

This article highlighted what a number of people already know or suspect: that the race to build the earth satellite is the key struggle of our time. On its outcome probably depends whether we — or any other democratic power — will survive.

And in this race the Russians have been neither idle — nor backward.

Is it possible that the flying saucer mystery is part of this race to hang a satellite in outer space — and that the Russians, working with captured plans and eagerly cooperating German technicians, perfected the first flying saucers, and that the Canadians, the English and the Americans are just now catching up with them?

Maybe. And maybe it was two Russians who were seen, in heavy fur coats, emerging from a wingless craft landed near Caerphilly, Wales, in the year of 1906.

Or maybe the English developed flying saucers first and sent the U.S. Air Force into a tizzy until it learned that the development was British. Has it been a case of the U.S. guarding the security of British and Canadian weapons or missiles and exchanging atom bomb information for working plans?

This explanation of the mystery also make very good sense. Quite early in the confusing picture of flying saucers that has been painted over the years, there appeared the explanation that they were of English origin. Major Keyhoe, in his first book, explored this possibility a little. He wrote that it has been reported to him that they *were* English — that the English had been sending them out, like doves from the Ark, without U.S. technicians knowing about them. That then, when saucers, getting out of control, appeared over the U.S. and Mexico in 1947, the English told the U.S. about them, and enlisted the support of USAF in tracking them.

Major Keyhoe discounted this possibility.

But there is some little evidence to support this explanation.

The English, early in the game, transferred their rocket testing grounds to Woomera, in Australia. Concurrent with news of this move, the English were clamoring for a sharing of atomic secrets with the U.S.A.

Then, every time the English released a press notice about their wonderful guided missile, the Americans came out with a counter release, claiming equal "bird-dog" genius for their weapons.

U.S Senator Mahoney told the Senate that the U.S. was acquiring highly secret weapons that "can conquer the atmosphere."

On February 11, 1953, news broke that the Canadians were building a saucer, designed by English-born John C.M. Frost, being built by A.V. Roe Canada Ltd., and planned to fly by a use of "Coanda's Effect."

Now — could either the Russians or the English have stolen a march on the U.S.A. by developing practicable flying saucers" Could such a thing have happened?

Either one, or both of them, could have happened. Giuseppe Belluzzo said that drawings of the flying discs had been shown to both Hitler and Mussolini. Quite a number of technicians must have known how they were constructed and what made them work.

Is it impossible to suppose that our top military planners, completely engrossed in a fascination with global bombers, conventional jets,   jets or what have you, could have brushed aside a new form of flight, to keep on building flying mechanisms that make progress by "boring through" the air?

Is it impossible to suppose that there are men in high places so mule-headed that they could pooh-pooh an entirely new principle of flight — one in which the object flies in a vacuum of its own making?

It is not at all impossible, but it is highly implausible. Yet this, if it happened, could cause a suppression of facts on flying saucers. Even if the Russians did not first send them aloft, and if it was the clever Swiss, or the Italians, or the Yugoslavs who did it — there would still be an extremely red-faced U.S. Air Force — until it had manufactured such devices.

Or, supposing another factor is involved, a simple thing, but an important one in this world of ours. Supposing it was a case of merely acquiring patent rights, the right to manufacture, from a friendly country.

No matter what happened, you may be sure of one thing: Actual man-made flying saucers either exist now — and have existed for some years — or they will exist before very long. The principle of the circular air foil is completely sound dynamically. The flying principle behind such an air foil is well-known. The power needed to drive such a circular flying disc could be kerosene, gasoline, crude oil, plutonium, magnetism, or something else equally prosaic or fantastic. And if spies and defectionists could get away from both us and England the deepest secrets of the atom bomb, you can bet a hat that there are no secrets on man-made flying saucers in any of the chancelleries of the world any more. By now, every power of any consequence must be building them.

And there is something else you can bet a hat on: If saucers were originally a Russian development, there have been enough defections from the Russian side among high-placed intelligence officers, security policy and the military for us to have obtained any secret long ago.

Now, where does this shuffling of papers, this assembly of dates and data leave us?

Probably not much nearer a solution to the mystery than we were in the beginning.

We know that the Canadians have, or will have soon, a flying saucer. We know who designated it, who is making it, and how it flies. From this we know that the English have, or will have, flying saucers. We know, from published reports, that the U.S. has conferred with the Canadians on the flying saucer. We can suspect that the Italians, the French, the Swedes, the Yugoslavs, the Russians, and indirectly, the Chinese, have or will have real, honest-to-goodness flying saucers, manned by men, capable of flying at speeds of from 1,500 to 2,000 mph — or faster.

But does that mean that we have leaped, practically overnight into the Age of the Future, and that our airmen are skimming along upstairs at speeds of from 9,000 to 18,000 mph? Does it mean that the truly mysterious things that have been reported — glowing, changing shape, splitting up into three or four different segments that fly echelon — are part of the air forces of different earth governments?

Not at all.

If you will refer to LIFE, December 6, 1954, and read the article, *Jet Age Man*, you will see how far man still is from whizzing around in the stratosphere at speeds of 9,000 mph in flying saucers.

Quote:

"The jet age has made flying so difficult that fliers like the air commander (above) who guides his B-47 bomber through the sky at nearly 500 mph are driven by the strain close to the limits of human capability."

Facts brought out by LIFE article: At high speeds, the G effect will practically black out flyers at the slightest swerve of high-speed planes. A pierced pressure cockpit above 63,000 feet will let his blood boil. Flight in a curving arc will result in weightlessness, a confusing experience that can throw the pilot into a complete state of disorientation.

In addition to these problems, there are problems of heat and cold, heat so intense it can turn a plane into a red-hot projectile, and cold so intense it can freeze you to death if you are subjected to it long.

To get a further grasp of the incredibly complex problems involved in space flight, read *Flight Into Space* by J.N. Leonard, Science Editor, *Time*, copyright 1953, published as a 35¢ Signet Book, November 1954. Or read *Exploration of Space*, by

Arthur C. Clarke, Chairman British Interplanetary Society. This book was first published in June 1952, and was brought out in a Cardinal 35¢ edition in June 1954.

When you finish reading these books, you will come to the conclusion that, despite fantastic progress in rockets and guided missiles, neither this country nor any other has solved many of the problems involved in flight into outer space, and that "saucers," if they actually exist, are not earth craft at all.

This same pessimistic view of man's traveling in space at the moment will also be reached if you will read the trade press only casually. One would suppose that any far-reaching advancements in aviation or guided missiles could be read between the lines in editorials or advertisements here, but the tenor of a great deal of trade press editorial mention has been that the U.S. has lagged behind in aviation.

Thus, we read in *Aviation Week*, March 2, 1953: "Red Air Reserves for Korea Worry U.S.," A quote: "If the Reds used their potential air strength, they could drive Fifth Air Force out of Korea in less than a week," one high-ranking Fifth Air Force officer said.

In this same issue of the magazine was another article, "*Missile Program Still Lags Dangerously.*" Quote: "After eight years of research and development which have cost the better part of $3 billion, we have succeeded in catching up to the point the Germans reached about a decade ago. In spite of more optimistic statements by military and civilian leaders, we are at least two years away from the tactical use of missiles. We have no volume production of any missile. We have no missile worth standardization as a weapon. We can only dream of intercontinental weapons." This article, reviewing the U.S. missile program, called missiles by their names, gave their performance. Result of that performance: Nothing sensational to date. Another quote: "Our potential enemy has a long record of rocket work, going back to 30 years or more. He has used rockets in the field longer than any other nation on either side. He received free—as did we — the fundamental work done by the Germans at Peenemunde. He has welded that collective experience into new weapons along the same general lines of our developments."

In this same issue, another article: "Research Pinpoints Our Ignorance." Quote: "But the research picture in the United States is not a bright one."

In the August 17, 1953 issue of *Aviation Week* are more articles on guided missile testing and performance — at Holloman, at Alamagordo, at Edwards, at Cape Canaveral and other launching sites. There is still nothing of a sensational nature.

In among the editorials in this and other aviation publications you will find such statements as: "this company has manufactured over 300,000 rocket powerplants for service use;" "Bolts to withstand a swirling inferno;" "Martin Aircraft Forms Solid Ingots of Scrap Sheet Titanium with Sciaky Spotwelder;" "After 5G Turn Is the Data Valid?"; "100,000 horsepower 50,000 feet high 2,000 miles an hour;" "Pittsburgh Glass Used in Douglas X-3...Pittsburgh technical representatives will be glad to work with you, to help you work out proper glazing for your aircraft."

But no matter how much you may read in the technical publications, although you might pick up a few scraps of information with regard to plastics, or metals, or insulated cable, you will not find much to indicate sensational advances in U.S. aircraft. Rather, you will find that U.S. technicians are fighting hard to overcome problems connected with aircraft that are still "boring through" air.

Yes, you will read about Douglas Honest John, the U.S. Army's ground-to-ground missile, a free flight rocket without a complicated guidance system that strikes ground targets without warning. In a Grumman advertisement you will read that "Grumman's new fighter slips through the sonic barrier as if air at the speed of sound were smooth instead of strange. Supersonic, she can make the fastest bomber prey for her missiles."

Yes, you will read in another manufacturer's advertisement of "an entirely new principle of flight." It could be the "Coanda Effect."

You will read hints of speeds and heights not yet given to the public at large, of temperatures encountered and surpassed, of materials now being put to use in missiles and aircraft.

But read how you will and where you will, you'll not read anything that can explain speeds of from 9,000 to 18,000 mph, the ability to make acute turns at such speeds, the ability to fade, or disappear. And while you will find hundreds of advertisements for skilled engineers, experts in design, metallurgists, and similar trained technicians in jets, ram-jets, missiles and ordinary prop-driven aircraft, you will not, you positively will not, find a find a single advertisement for "LITTLE MAN. Not over 30 inches tall. Wanted for flying secret U.S. aircraft."

Let us add one more note to this: In the Italian magazine Epoca, November 14, 1954, was a brief squib which said that the French had developed a new kind of aircraft, a "flying tube." The pilot's cabin was described as situated towards the after part of the tube. The difference in pressure between the upper and lower part of the tube furnishes the force to sustain it. Speed of the craft described: 2,500 kilometers an hour.

CHAPTER 15
CONCLUSIONS

Well, there you are.

Now you have some of the story of the flying saucers — at least, some part of it that is in the public record. And the whole story simply bring us to full circle again, looking baffled and saying, "But what are flying saucers?"

Are they earth craft? Are the extraterrestrial?

This author does not know, does not pretend to know.

There is evidence to show irrefutably that they are from outer space. There is evidence just as irrefutable — and far more believable — that they are experimental aircraft or missiles, or the very ultimate in aircraft or missiles, that are being flown by one or more powers on this earth. There is also irrefutable evidence to indicate that a great deal that has been written on the subject of saucers is pure baloney.

One possible guess is that the mystery of the flying saucers is a cover-up — and a most successful one — of the development of a new kind of man-made missile or craft — of things which perform in a way in which no aircraft have ever performed before. It can also be guessed that the Air Force, by its policy of non-interference, has let the mystery be compounded to the point of utter incomprehensibility by the occultists, the mystics, and the boys and girls out to make a fast buck.

Flying saucers, so far as this writer is concerned, still fall under the classification of Security — and security with a great big capital S.

As to the tightness of this security — or the need for it — this writer will hazard no opinion. The subject was covered quite fully by the Also brothers in their article in *The Saturday Evening Post* for February, 1955, pleading that the government take grim matters of the moment to the people and not conceal facts from them, following the philosophy that "Daddy knows best."

The day after the article appeared, the first comprehensive information on hydrogen bomb fall-out and far reaching lethal effects appeared in the nation's newspapers. Immediately following this release, there appeared an article that the government's over-zealous security regulations were going to be re-examined.

Perhaps the time will come, before long, when the secret story of the flying saucers will be told.

Until that time, anyone is entitled to a guess.

This author's guess is that flying saucers are very much connected with a world armament's race — with a race to see who will first hang an artificial satellite in the sky — the race to see whether to endure as a nation of free people — if we are permitted to exists at all. It is a race to develop new kinds of flight, new kinds of power, and, among other things, intercontinental missiles that will fly at speeds between 5,000 and 15,000 miles per hour, fly unerringly accurate, fly without any defense against them, and strike without warning. Quite conceivably, the story of the flying saucers is one of the grimmest — or one of the happiest stories ever told.

I think that they are ours — or will be. And I shall hazard a guess that when their story is told, it will be quite as fantastic, quite as exciting, and as full of promise to the future as the arrival of an enlightened race from another world. For, if extraterrestrials are not arriving, we will still be able to go to them — and find out for ourselves if other worlds are habitable.

When the story is told, this author feels quite sure, it will be a part of a continuing story of great minds, great research, great know-how, and a very great many courageous men — men who risk their lives daily so that the rest of us may feel secure — at least as secure as high courage and intricate machinery can ever let us feel. Men up aloft, into the wild blue yonder, that stretches wider and wider as their wings spread and soar.

As to the little men who keep stepping out of odd craft here and there throughout the world — maybe they're part of the picture, too. Maybe it's all true.

But this author will believe it when the first little man lands his craft in our backyard and asks for a bucket of water for atomic fuel.

As for you, if you see one, don't shoot at him.

You might hit one of Singer's midgets, flying for the U.S. Air Force.

THE END

UFO-RELATED AUTHENTICITY OBSERVATIONS

Robert Wood and Ryan Wood

A scan of the original pages shows many added notations to the originally-typed manuscript, including ball-point and felt pen inks, pencil, security classification stamps, and a special blue stamp that has appeared on other questioned documents. Much of the writing is that of Vernon Bowen, making corrections to his original typed text in pen.

There is extensive underlining, thought to be done by one of the reviewers to call attention to various phrases or ideas. In addition, there are short, crisp comments, focused on specific items in the text. These follow here.

p. 190 "New Mexico 1947 cases"

p. 193 "1950 Texas/Mexican border?"

p. 221 "Blue Book files written in 1954. Maybe should never be used. If so, should be brought up to date"

p. 224 "Twining's 9-23-47 secret report to COSUSAF"

p. 227 "Project Moon Dust"

p. 229 "Twining? (Lt. Gen.)"

p. 272 Deletion opposite "No hardware has ever fallen from the skies or picked up on the ground."

p. 285. "I hope DM keeps his big mouth shut"

p. 285 underline on "muddying up the greatest..."

p. 288 "Highly dubious source of information" (Dorothy Kilgallen)

p. 288 "What is DM doing?"

p. 292 "This was written in 1954. Today, it reads like ancient history." (CVB initials)

p. 296. "This should not get out" (But do all these things..."

p. 315 "Project Silver Bug"

It is presumed from comments by Vernon Bowen that this manuscript was voluntarily delivered to the Air Force for their review and approval before possible publication. Clearly, they elected to keep it for longer than he had planned, since he died at 78 never having published the book, and it was returned to Tim Cooper in June 1999. Before interpreting the intent of the various reviewers, it is valuable to have some information on when the comments might have been made. For this, we turn to the accepted methods of forensic testing of questioned documents.

The typewriter was determined to be an Underwood Portable manufactured in 1939 by comparison with reference samples by James Black, forensic document examiner. The paper was either unwatermarked, or watermarked with a script "Royal Writing." One of the watermarks is listed in Reference 1 as being manufactured by the S.E.&M. Vernon Company, New York City. Pat Bowen states that he knows that the typewriter his father used still exists but has not been able to locate it. Pat took the typewriter with him to law school and typed several pages every day for class preparation. He hopes to locate it in early 2003. The typewriter and the paper are all consistent with having been typed by Vernon Bowen in the 1950s.

The determination of the age of the inks is done by a process called thin layer chromatography, whereby a small specimen of the writing is punched out of the paper (about the size of a small paperclip diameter, dissolved in a solvent, and then allowed to migrate under the force of gravity to provide a "spectrum" that is then compared with a library of known inks to determine the best match. When a match is found, it is possible to state something like, "This handwriting was made after this pen was introduced to the market, which was in 1977." Before further discussion, therefore, we will now summarize the findings of the earliest ink production dates for the questioned chirography.

Title page: "Submitted to Project Blue Book in 1960. Unclassified and Unevaluated.")(ball point 1977 ink)

Page 187: "Wrong. 001 has prints" (felt tip 1962 ink)

Page 187 Marker in deleting security caveat (after 1962)

Page 187: "Fakes? Real? Make up your own mind." (ball point 1961 ink)

Page 188: (Extensive remarks by "Ben")(ball point 1977 ink)

Page 189: "Submitted to Project Blue Book 1954. Unclassified and Unevaluated") (ball point 1977 ink)

Page 190: "New Mexico 1947 cases" (ball point 1977 ink)

Page 221: "Written in 1954. Maybe should never be used. If so, should be brought up to date." (felt tip 1962 ink)

Page 222: "As a semi-official recognition of the extra-terrestrial theory," (felt tip 1962 ink) (ball point 1961 ink)

Page 227: ("Project Moon Dust?) (felt tip 1962 ink)

Page 285: (underline on "Charles Fort"))(ball point 1977 ink)

Page 285. "I hope DM keeps his big mouth shut" (after mid 1950s)

Page 285: "reportedly" (ball point 1961 ink)

Page 287 underline of "extraterrestrial space craft" (1977 or later)

Page 288: (underline on "fell from the skies" and "fall from the skies") (ball point 1977 ink)

Page 288 "Highly dubious source of information" (Dorothy Kilgallen) (1977 or later)

Page 288: "reportedly" (ballpoint 1977 ink?)

Page 288: (underline on "studied at Wright Patterson...")(ball point 1977 ink)

It would appear that at least one of the 1961 or later notations were actually those of Vernon Bowen, which suggests that he may not have actually delivered before 1961, not 1960. In particular, the addition of the word "reportedly" and "As a semi-official recognition of the extra-terrestrial theory," and "Fakes? Real? Make up your own mind." Are all three the kind of corrections that Vernon would have made editorially. Therefore, if the dating of the 1961 pen is accurate, he did not turn the manuscript over to the Air Force until 1961 not 1960.

In addition to these marginalia comments in several different handwritings, it appears that the author was the one making hundreds of extensive editorial corrections of a proofreader's nature: improving grammar, correcting spelling errors. Also, occasionally deleting or adding phrases to subtract or add a thought. As a senior employee of an advertising agency in New York City, Mr. Bowen was a skilled writer.

Significant Marginalia on Pages of Bowen Manuscript

Streamline Table 2 of the 2001 MUFON paper.

- Association of the significance of the notations with UFO events and personnel
- Speculation on the objectives of the Air Force review and evaluation

The above ideas are yet to be added to this introductory material.

Printed in Dunstable, United Kingdom

64222729R00167